C0-AUT-898

DISCARDED

Privatization
and Economic Reform
in Central Europe

Privatization and Economic Reform in Central Europe

The Changing Business Climate

Edited by
Dennis A. Rondinelli

Q

Quorum Books
Westport, Connecticut • London

Library of Congress Cataloging-in-Publication Data

Privatization and economic reform in Central Europe : the changing
  business climate / edited by Dennis A. Rondinelli.
      p.   cm.
    Includes bibliographical references and index.
    ISBN 0-89930-851-1 (alk. paper)
    1. Privatization—Europe, Eastern—Case studies. 2. Post-
communism—Europe, Eastern—Case studies. 3. Europe, Eastern—
Economic conditions—1989- —Regional disparities. 4. Europe,
Eastern—Economic policy—1989- I. Rondinelli, Dennis A.
HD4140.7.P748 1994
338.947—dc20   93-27714

British Library Cataloguing in Publication Data is available.

Copyright © 1994 by Dennis A. Rondinelli

All rights reserved. No portion of this book may be
reproduced, by any process or technique, without the
express written consent of the publisher.

Library of Congress Catalog Card Number: 93-27714
ISBN: 0-89930-851-1

First published in 1994

Quorum Books, 88 Post Road West, Westport, CT 06881
An imprint of Greenwood Publishing Group, Inc.

Printed in the United States of America

The paper used in this book complies with the
Permanent Paper Standard issued by the National
Information Standards Organization (Z39.48-1984).

10 9 8 7 6 5 4 3 2 1

ECC/USF LEARNING RESOURCES
8099 College Parkway, S.W.
      P.O. Box 06210
Fort Myers, FL 33906-6210

Contents

Preface

A fundamental characteristic of the global economy during the 1990s is the reinvigoration of the private sector as the driving force for economic growth and social progress. The limits of the state's ability to plan, direct, and control national economies have been clearly exposed. Yet private enterprise cannot flourish where public policies do not provide an environment conducive to the efficient operation of markets. The 1990s is a period during which an appropriate division of decision making must be sought between the state and the market, and new cooperative arrangements must emerge between government and private enterprise.

The process of economic restructuring is especially important and particularly complex in Central Europe, where Poland, Hungary, the Czech and Slovak republics, Slovenia, and other independent states of former Yugoslavia are struggling to transform themselves from socialist to market economies. These countries differ in their experiences with market competition and in the degree to which their private sectors have been allowed to function over the past 40 years. Each country faces equally complex challenges, however, in creating a new business climate that will nourish domestic enterprise and attract investments by multinational corporations. These challenges include (1) privatizing state-owned enterprises that have dominated the economies of socialist countries; (2) developing public policies and programs that support the private sector, especially small- and medium-scale enterprises; (3) decentralizing the state administrative structure to allow regional and local governments to play a more active role in providing public services and supporting private enterprise; and (4) restructuring industry, agriculture, and services in order to diversify and reinvigorate the economic base (including infrastructure) of regions surrounding cities that are still dominated by heavy- (and now largely obsolescent) manufacturing industries.

With financial support from the Johnson & Johnson Corporation, the Kenan Institute of Private Enterprise at the University of North Carolina at Chapel Hill collaborated with universities and research institutes in Central Europe to examine and analyze each of these issues. The objectives of the research were threefold. First, we sought to determine the scope and direction of public policies that Central European governments are pursuing to transform their socialist economies into competitive markets. Second, we assessed the magnitude and dimensions of the problems facing Central European countries in privatizing socially owned or state-owned enterprises, in stimulating private sector expansion, and in decentralizing the administrative and political structures to promote regional economic development. Third, we evaluated the policies for privatization and economic reform as well as their impacts on specific companies within a comparative framework.

This book surveys the situation in Central Europe during the early period of transition from late 1989 to early 1993 when governments in Poland, Hungary, the Czech and Slovak republics, and Slovenia were experimenting with privatization and economic reform. The authors assessed how privatization and economic reform policies have changed the business climate in this important region of the world. Chapter 1 provides an overview of economic reforms in Central European countries, offers a framework by which to compare them, describes the approaches to privatization their governments adopted, and identifies the problems and challenges that each country faces in attempting to create a market-oriented economy. In chapter 2, Kálmán Mizsei, Maria Móra, and Gyorgy Csaki examine in greater detail the experiences with privatization and economic reform in Hungary while focusing on the crucial role of foreign investment. Joze Mencinger analyzes the debate over centralized versus decentralized approaches to privatization in Slovenia in chapter 5. Michal Mejstrik and James Burger describe in chapter 8 experiments with a combination of approaches to privatization that were carried out in the Czech and Slovak republics. In chapter 11, Marek Mazur, Tomasz Dolegowski, Jerzy Suchnicki, and Igor Mitroczuk assess both the political environment in which privatization policies were shaped in Poland and the progress toward implementation during the early 1990s. Each of the authors describes the public policies and programs for private enterprise development enacted by national governments after the collapse of the Communist regimes in Central Europe: policies for creating capital markets and financial institutions; programs for industrial and agricultural sector restructuring; the legal framework for private enterprise expansion; policies for providing infrastructure and public services; changes in labor practices, employment, and training and education programs; revisions of foreign trade and export regulations; and tax and incentive programs affecting company growth and domestic savings and investment. Moreover, the authors analyze the economic and political conditions under which private enterprise development policies were formulated and will have to be implemented as well as the roles of foreign and domestic investors in privatization.

In all of the countries in this region, central control of the economy during the Communist era spawned large and inefficient bureaucracies that remain as obstacles to private enterprise expansion and local economic development. Experience in developing countries in other regions of the world indicates that given a conducive set of macroeconomic policies, private enterprise development and economic growth will, to a large extent, be stimulated from the "bottom up." Entrepreneurship arises in small- and medium-scale enterprises in localities that provide adequate infrastructure and services and appropriate incentives and conditions for profitable investment and efficient business operations. In market economies, the political system and government structure must be sufficiently decentralized to allow for multiple channels of political representation, rapid and responsive provision of public services and infrastructure, locally tailored incentives, efficient provision of licenses and approvals, and fair and efficient enforcement of regulations. Local resources for investment and growth will be forthcoming only when citizens have a strong stake in their economic and political systems and believe that they have some influence over how local and national decisions are made and carried out. Thus, political and administrative decentralization are essential to effective operation of market economies and to regional and local economic development.

Therefore, we examined carefully how economic reform and privatization policies in Poland and Slovenia are affecting subnational regions. In chapter 6, Pavel Gantar describes the impact of Communist policies on the Slovenian economy prior to 1990 and how reforms of the Slovenian government after independence changed the business climate in the Ljubljana region. In chapter 12, Maria Ciechocinska compares the transformation of enterprises in various regions of Poland after the reforms of 1989 and 1990; and in chapter 13, Malgorzata Bednarczyk, Janusz Jaworski, Janusz Kot, and Kazimierz Zielinski look at the implications of economic reform for the city and region of Cracow. These authors describe the existing economic conditions in Cracow and Ljubljana as well as characteristics of their economic base, major sources of production and employment, prospects for growth and expansion, and conditions needed to create an environment conducive to local and regional development, which include the legal apparatus, social services and physical infrastructure, employment, training and education, and incentives for private enterprise expansion. They conclude that the economic structure of subnational regions like Cracow and Ljubljana will have to be diversified in order to establish a viable base for private enterprise expansion and sustainable economic growth.

Finally, the success of policies for creating competitive markets in Central European countries will depend on the ability of thousands of private enterprises to increase their production, market their goods, create jobs, and engage in international trade. Experience in other regions of the world suggests that macroeconomic reform is necessary but not sufficient for stimulating economic growth in a market-oriented system; private companies must assume risks and take initiatives to expand their investments and improve their operations. No serious study of privatization and economic reform in Central Europe, therefore, would be complete without probing the effects of the traumatic economic reforms that were enacted from 1989 to 1992 on individual enterprises. Thus, along with assessments of the national and regional policies for economic restructuring are case studies of companies that underwent privatization in Central Europe during the early transition period. In chapters 3 and 4, Erzsébet Poszmik examines the experiences of an electronics company and an automotive parts firm in Hungary. In chapter 7, Uroš Korže and Marko Simoneti describe the negotiations and transactions that led to the sale of a tobacco company in Slovenia. John Hannula and Kit Jackson trace the transformation of a Czech electronics company in chapter 9; and in chapter 10, Jonathan Gafni and Mark Niles explore the challenges facing a Czech tool-manufacturing firm. In chapter 14, Dolegowski and Suchnicki describe the restructuring of a clothing company; and in chapter 15, Suchnicki appraises the transformation of a major furniture manufacturer in Poland.

The Kenan Institute of Private Enterprise is grateful to the Johnson & Johnson Corporation for financial support for the project, to all of the authors for their contributions to this book, and to Dr. Marjan Svetlicic for coordinating the cooperative research in Slovenia. Several people at the Kenan Institute helped to make this book possible. I appreciate the support of my colleagues Jack N. Behrman, who helped to initiate the project, and John D. Kasarda, who encouraged it. Patricia Harrison and Jay Yurkiewicz assisted with editing and proofreading; Kelly Russell and Frieda Martin helped with typing; Jean Elia provided administrative support; and Patricia Zigas offered timely information and research services. None of this would have been possible, of course, without the financial support of the William Rand Kenan, Jr. Charitable Trust and the William R. Kenan, Jr. Fund and without the continuing generosity of Frank Hawkins Kenan for whom the Institute is named. The opinions and interpretations reflected in this book, however, remain the responsibility of the editor and the authors and should not be attributed to the organizations with which they are affiliated.

Dennis A. Rondinelli
Chapel Hill, North Carolina

Privatization
and Economic Reform
in Central Europe

Privatization and Economic Reform in Central Europe: Experience of the Early Transition Period

Dennis A. Rondinelli

The Central European countries of Poland, Hungary, Czechoslovakia (later the Czech and Slovak republics), and Slovenia were among the first of the former Soviet satellites to attempt to transform themselves from socialist command economies to market-oriented systems. In 1989, when the citizens of these countries quickly and unexpectedly wrested political control from the Communist parties that had dominated their societies for nearly 40 years, they anxiously pursued the exhilarating task of creating new political and economic systems. Soon after independence, however, the initial euphoria of political freedom began to wane as the devastating results of four decades of economic decline under Communist regimes became more apparent. The new political leaders in Central Europe quickly realized that the success of their macroeconomic reforms depended on two fundamental achievements. The first challenge would be to privatize the large, inefficient, and unproductive state-owned manufacturing firms that had dominated these regions' economies and that had become serious obstacles to future growth. The second task was to create a critical mass of small- and medium-sized businesses that could generate jobs and income for the millions of workers who would inevitably be displaced by industrial restructuring.

When these four countries began the process of privatizing state enterprises and reestablishing their private sectors in 1990, they had no successful models to follow. No country had yet transformed itself from a centrally planned to a market economy in the manner being attempted in Central Europe. Although Britain, France, the United States, and many developing countries had experimented with privatization of public enterprises during the 1980s, and although China was moving gradually toward the creation of a socialist "planned commodity economy" in which market forces would coexist with government control, none had undergone a transformation of the scope and magnitude envisioned in Central Europe.

Nor did the early attempts at transformation in Central Europe proceed smoothly. Economic and political reform in Yugoslavia came at the cost of ethnic violence and military conflict, which resulted in the splitting of that nation into several querulous republics. In the face of unresolved differences over political autonomy and economic reform, Czechoslovakia (CSFR) also disintegrated, albeit under more peaceful circumstances. And in Poland and Hungary, conflict among competing political factions marked the evolution of their privatization policies and economic reforms.

Although by early 1993 the process of privatization and private enterprise development was only in its initial stages in Central Europe, these same four countries had each put in place the fundamental processes that would be needed to restructure their economic and political systems. During this early transition period, reformers set the foundation for privatization, private enterprise development, and economic transformation; but it became increasingly apparent that it would take at least a generation to build a fully functioning market economy on that foundation. The experiences of the early transformation period from late 1989 to early 1993, however, offer important insights into the processes and challenges of economic reform and privatization as well as potential lessons for governments in (1) the Eastern European, Balkan, and Baltic states; (2) the former Soviet republics; and (3) other countries that have been set on the path to economic restructuring by the collapse of the Soviet empire. A review of these experiences can provide information that is useful to both government and business leaders for modifying and adjusting their strategies in the future. Moreover, as executives in multinational companies become interested in the possibilities of investing in or trading with the former socialist countries, an analysis of this early transformation experience can help them understand the background and dimensions of Central Europe's struggle to reshape its economic systems. Finally, for students of private enterprise development, economic development, and social change, the early period of economic reform in Central Europe offers a glimpse at the political and social dynamics through which public sector and business leaders in these four countries attempted to transform their societies.

THE DIMENSIONS OF ECONOMIC AND POLITICAL REFORM

When the Communist regimes in Central Europe collapsed in 1989 and 1990, the role of the private sector in the economy was extremely limited. The contribution of private enterprises to gross domestic product was only 3 percent in the CSFR and 15 percent each in Poland and Hungary.[1] Old, large, state-owned companies produced more than 90 percent of national output in the CSFR. Nearly 89 percent of employment was in the state-owned industrial and service sectors, with an additional 10 percent in state-dominated agricultural cooperatives; less than 1 percent of the population was self-employed.[2] The state sector in Poland accounted for more than 80 percent of national output and 88 percent of employment in the nonagricultural sectors. Only 300 of the state-owned enterprises (SOEs) accounted for 59 percent of the net income of Poland's 3,177 state industrial enterprises. Although both Hungary's and Yugoslavia's production structures were somewhat more decentralized, much of the manufacturing in all four countries took place in huge, inefficient, and unproductive SOEs that rapidly lost their markets in the former Soviet Union and other socialist countries after the "domino effect" of political independence swept Central and Eastern Europe. Most of the giant SOEs were overstaffed and had obsolete technology and deteriorating facilities that made it difficult for them to compete effectively with Western multinational firms in new markets. The situation that reformers faced was one of completely restructuring state enterprises whose characteristics were adverse to sustainable economic growth. The report of the Organization for Economic Cooperation and Development (OECD) on the need for economic reform in Central Europe concisely summarized the nature of the socialist enterprises:

Large enterprises were in some respects more like government departments than business enterprises. . . . They faced no financial objectives or meaningful budget constraints and aimed, rather, to meet production targets, usually defined crudely in quantitative terms with only limited specifications in terms of quality. Costs did not enter into the definition of targets, so there was a strong incentive to hoard labor, to accumulate inventories of inputs, or to integrate vertically as protection against chronic supply shortages. Since there was no need to monitor and control costs, there was little incentive to develop the requisite accounting and management skills. Furthermore, because the planning agencies performed so many functions carried out by markets in OECD countries, skills which Western businesses routinely required in areas such as marketing, quality control, product development, and finance were not deemed necessary. On the other hand, enterprises often carried out activities that are normally the responsibility of governments, particularly in the area of social services.[3]

Most economic reformers in Central Europe understood from the outset that developing the private sector and privatizing state enterprises were essential for creating a market economy. Theories of privatization had been well developed by international assistance organizations by the end of the 1980s. The staffs of the International Monetary Fund (IMF), the World Bank, the International Finance Corporation, and others argued that privatization was essential (1) to free the public resources that had been used to subsidize money-losing SOEs for investment in infrastructure and social programs; (2) to increase the size and dynamism of the small, existing private sector; (3) to distribute ownership more widely; and (4) to promote both foreign and domestic private investment.[4]

Moreover, privatization would generate revenues needed by the state to create new jobs for workers displaced by industrial restructuring, would reduce the state's administrative responsibilities and the burdens of government intervention in enterprise management, and would provide consumers with more efficiently produced goods. At the same time, enterprises would benefit from private ownership through increased productivity, expansion of productive capacity, and increased profits.

Economic reformers in Central Europe soon discovered, however, as did the former undersecretary of state in the Ministry of Privatization in Poland, that the "post-Communist privatization process is not merely a divestment of state assets—that is, a selling of state companies. It is a process of reconstructing economies and societies damaged by many years of Communism."[5] Government officials in all four countries quickly discovered that the process of privatization could not be divorced or separated from massive and rapid economic restructuring.

After 40 years of economically debilitating socialist rule, the success of privatization and private enterprise development depended initially on restoring efficiently operating markets. Market development and privatization required structural adjustment and stabilization policies that would curb inflation, liberalize trade, deregulate the economy, and recreate a complex network of institutions through which market transactions could take place (see figure 1.1). These included financial and legal institutions, an education system that could prepare graduates to work effectively in a market economy, efficiently operating labor markets, a system of property rights, and effective distribution systems. Market development also required the expansion of foreign trade and investment, the development of small- and medium-sized enterprises, the restructuring of large companies, and the attraction of investments in domestic industries by multinational corporations. The success of the economic and political reforms as well as the survival and expansion of privatized enterprises depended ultimately on human development, that is, on the expansion of the pool of entrepreneurs, market-oriented business managers, and skilled technical and support workers. All of these changes had to be initiated quickly in order to create a momentum that would allow a market economy to come into being as well as to survive the dislocations and hardships inevitably accompanying traumatic political, economic, and social changes.

When they began their economic reforms in 1990, each of the Central European countries started from a different base of experience. The socialist regimes in Hungary and Yugoslavia had experimented with various forms of "marketization," decentralization, and self-management within state-owned enterprises in the 1970s and 1980s. Although the Communist party in Poland held tighter control over the economy and had more slowly and grudgingly diverged from socialist planning, it had been under political pressures from the Solidarity labor union and other groups to make reforms for nearly a decade be-

Figure 1.1
Framework for Assessing Privatization Policy

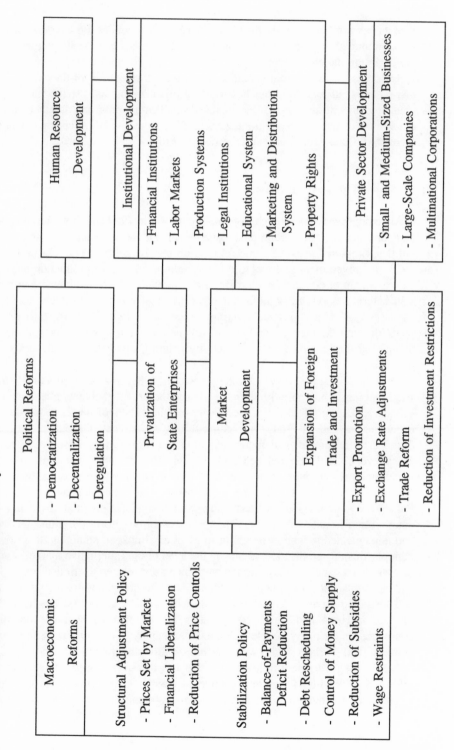

fore its downfall in 1989. In the Czech and Slovak republics, on the other hand, the Communist regime had wiped out nearly all vestiges of private enterprise by nationalizing the entire economy.

Regardless of their initial conditions, however, after the fall of their Communist regimes, all four countries had to begin privatization and private enterprise development with structural adjustment and stabilization programs and then move quickly to create the legal framework and economic institutions that would facilitate business formation and the restructuring of state enterprises.

"Shock Therapy" in Poland

Although Poland's approach to economic reform in 1989 and 1990 was drastic and far-reaching, the Communist government had been under economic and political pressures to make some reforms during the early 1980s. As early as 1983, the government had replaced the system of obligatory production targets with a system of contracts and orders. In 1986 the laws were amended to allow state enterprises to issue bonds and to enter into joint ventures (JVs) with foreign capital. By 1988 a two-tiered banking system had been authorized; restrictions were lifted on the creation and size of private enterprises; and the government had passed the Law on Economic Activity granting equal status to all forms of ownership.[6]

After the Solidarity government took power in 1989, it announced a rapid and wide-ranging stabilization program to address the urgent problems plaguing the economy. During 1990 the economy showed the results of nearly a decade of economic stagnation: National income fell by 13 percent; investment growth dropped by 8 percent; and industrial production declined by 23 percent from 1989 levels. Inflation reached 584 percent; and unemployment, previously nonexistent, rose to more than 6 percent.[7] Prime Minister Leszek Balcerowicz's plan sought to reduce the high levels of inflation and rapid depreciation of the Polish zloty, to reverse the deepening state budget deficit, and to stem the deterioration in national output. The macroeconomic reform program, devised and implemented in a short period of time, freed almost all administrative price controls, devaluated the zloty almost to the level of the "alternative market" rate, increased taxes substantially, limited wage increases, relaxed restrictions on trade and payments, cut government spending, limited monetary and fiscal expansion, and restricted credit.[8] The drastic and swift reforms advocated by the IMF lowered inflation and stabilized the zloty but brought wrenching economic consequences for many people in Poland—especially SOE employees, farmers, and unskilled workers—who were not prepared for the transition.

The Polish government followed up its "shock therapy" approach to economic reform in 1990 with a program to change the country's legal framework in order to promote privatization. Along with macroeconomic reforms, it amended the

Law of Economics of State-Owned Enterprises to allow SOEs to suppress the management system directed by the employees' council as a prelude to privatization, to define more clearly the responsibilities and powers of the Treasury and the SOEs, and to permit SOEs with severe financial problems to be turned over to a recovery commission. The government also expanded the Law on Financial Management of State Enterprises to allow periodic revaluation of enterprise assets, changed the Civil Code governing property ownership rights, and modified the Commercial Code regulating the organization of commercial companies. Parliament later enacted a bankruptcy law, created laws allowing the public trading of securities and mutual funds, and established rules for foreign investment in Poland. In addition, Parliament enacted antimonopoly legislation and a land law regulating real estate transactions.[9]

Rapid Reform in the CSFR

Although many political leaders in the CSFR wanted to resist the "shock therapy" applied in Poland, Federal Finance Minister Vaclav Klaus pushed for rapid, comprehensive, and transparent reforms that could be adjusted as they were implemented. In response to political critics who feared that the CSFR would suffer the harsh economic consequences of radical reforms like those adopted in Poland and who, therefore, argued for a more gradual program based on more detailed planning, Klaus insisted that the CSFR could not wait. In order to overcome the inertia of 40 years of bureaucratic control, the government had to implement reforms quickly based on what economists already knew about the requirements for creating a market system. "When we stress a comprehensive reform, it doesn't mean that we must wait for an all-embracing reform blueprint," Klaus insisted. "In my opinion, waiting for an ambitious, intellectually perfect, all-details-elaborated reform project is a suggestion to start the reform in the year 2057. It means postponing the reform process to eternity; there will never be a reform." He argued that waiting for a blueprint for reform "leads very quickly to a chaotic disintegration of the economy."[10]

At Klaus's urging and at the insistence of the IMF, the National Assembly began passing a number of laws in April 1990 that would stimulate the growth of a market economy. These included laws (1) giving all citizens the right to establish their own businesses without restrictions on the number of their employees or the amount of property they could own; (2) granting equal status to the owners of private, cooperative, and state property; (3) breaking up huge state-owned monopolies and, thereby, giving state enterprises more flexibility in management and operations; (4) removing price controls on most goods; and (5) initiating measures to make the koruna (crown) internally convertible. The government moved quickly in allowing foreign nationals to set up businesses and to obtain both the credit and property needed to conduct their business activities.

It also created a social safety net to protect Czech and Slovakian citizens from the most serious adverse effects of changes consequent in the transformation from a command to a market-oriented economy.

These changes were supplemented by others that were aimed at creating the institutional structure needed for privatizing state enterprises and for creating a small- and medium-sized business sector. Foreign banks were allowed to operate in the CSFR in 1992 without creating subsidiaries. Branch banks that were not previously restricted by their licenses could accept deposits, extend credits, invest in securities, issue credit cards and travelers checks, and grant guarantees and letters of credit. The banking reform law also allowed branch banks to engage in brokerage and financial service activities as well as trade in and purchase foreign currencies.[11] The law made the central bank Statni Banka independent of both the federal and republic governments.

In order to promote foreign investment and international trade, the government also adopted a new set of accounting laws that made procedures compatible with those of the European Community; and it issued regulations standardizing the annual financial statements of companies doing business in the CSFR.[12] Import surcharges were reduced from 20 percent to 10 percent. All of these changes took place within a framework of macroeconomic austerity required by the IMF. These measures included tight monetary policies, budget restraints, and anti-inflationary fiscal policies.[13]

Gradual Transformation in Hungary

Although the Communist government in Hungary had been experimenting with economic changes and had allowed state enterprises to reorganize themselves in the late 1980s, the new government that came to power in 1989 began the process of privatization with extensive legal changes that created a more market-oriented economic system. The industrial reform program that had been enacted in the mid-1980s sought microeconomic stabilization as well as increases in competitiveness and efficiency of Hungarian industry by imposing stronger financial discipline on SOEs, by restructuring industries, and by increasing the mobility of labor and capital. These reforms had only limited impacts, however; and with assistance from the World Bank, the government modified the program in 1988 by cutting producer and consumer subsidies, by encouraging convertible-currency exports, and by reforming the tax system. Again, the program faltered because of the government's inability to enforce financial discipline on SOEs and because enterprises participating in restructuring merely increased their exports to other socialist countries.[14]

After the fall of the Communist regime in 1989, however, the new government undertook more comprehensive economic restructuring with assistance from the IMF and the World Bank. In 1989, it enacted the Law of Transformation and other legislation that restored ownership rights and allowed for privatization of state enterprises. The pressures to expand the reforms were fueled in 1990 by the economy's fall into serious recession. National income declined by 5.5 percent; investments dropped by 7 percent; and industrial production fell by 4.5 percent. Inflation remained a relatively modest 29 percent, so the government's economic reforms were aimed at maintaining stability and restructuring production. Policies enacted in 1990 sought to liberalize trade and reform prices, reduce subsidies, and limit public investment to the most critical areas of physical and social infrastructure. At the same time, the government sought to reform basic social policies, including health, social security, unemployment compensation, and housing.

Parliament enacted amendments to foreign investment laws, thus making it easier for multinational companies to participate in privatization and private enterprise development; abolished special license requirements for establishing joint ventures; and removed restrictions on the use of convertible currency. The banking system was restructured, and the National Bank of Hungary was given a largely independent status. The government encouraged the creation of a capital market, and the Budapest Stock Exchange began operations in 1991. Although trade volumes and margins initially were low and investors were cautious, in 1991 the Hungarian government was able to finance part of its deficit through the Budapest Stock Exchange. Work began on a new tax administration system. An Office of Economic Competition was established as an independent state agency to oversee compliance with the antitrust law and to prevent unfair business practices. In 1991, Parliament passed the Bankruptcy Bill that allowed companies that were unable to pay their debts within 12 months to declare bankruptcy beginning in 1992 when a new accountancy law conforming to European Community guidelines took effect. State-controlled companies, however, were barred from filing for bankruptcy. Parliament also enacted a national welfare system and initiated programs that dealt with rising unemployment as well as the support of those unemployed.

By 1992 the Hungarian Parliament had also passed laws allowing cooperatives to become private enterprises. Industrial, farming, commercial, banking, service, and construction cooperatives could choose to divide cooperative property among members, to transform the cooperative into a shareholding enterprise, or to remain a self-governing cooperative organization.[15]

Uncertain Changes in Slovenia

The economic reforms that preceded attempts to privatize state enterprises in the Republic of Slovenia before its independence in 1991 were largely directed by the federal government of Yugoslavia. Initial attempts at economic reform were made in 1983 when the government obtained support from the World Bank and the IMF for its Long-Term Program of Economic Stabilization. This program sought to improve pricing policy, liberalize foreign trade policies and the allocation of foreign exchange, and adjust interest rates. These early reforms failed, however, because the government could not maintain financial discipline or implement the stabilization policies effectively.[16] After seven years of negotiation, the World Bank and IMF supported another series of stabilization reforms in 1989. These followed after Yugoslavia had experienced five years of near-stagnant growth in gross domestic product as well as inflation that had averaged 106 percent a year and peaked at 1,240 percent in 1989.

With assistance from IMF, the federal government (1) enacted new enterprise and banking laws to stimulate investment; (2) liberalized prices, foreign exchange, and trade policies; (3) tightened enterprise bankruptcy procedures; and (4) sought a wider base for financing social benefits. The stabilization program pegged the exchange rate for the dinar to the deutsche mark, froze prices of energy and public services, imposed tight controls on personal incomes and credit, reduced public consumption through fiscal austerity, and limited the growth of the money supply. Although the immediate effects of the program were to reduce inflation rates dramatically, both the inability of the federal government to control personal incomes and prevent price increases as well as the growing rebellion against federal authority in the republics undermined its overall success.[17]

In 1990 the Yugoslav government also began to pursue an economic restructuring program in which privatization of state property was the key element. In order to limit increases in personal incomes and stimulate restructuring and foreign investment in social enterprises, the government enacted a new Law on Social Capital that allowed workers to purchase "internal shares" in their enterprises at deep discounts and required employers to make payments of increases in nominal wages in these shares or in other securities. Ownership of social property would be transferred first by nationalizing and then by privatizing state assets. Nationalization was essential because, under the old Law of Social Property, there was no identifiable owner to collect the proceeds of privatization. Nationalization allowed the government to sell off some segments of state enterprises and to develop an efficient system of management for others.[18]

After the breakup of Yugoslavia, economic reforms and privatization processes were taken over by the newly independent republics. This initiated a strong debate in Slovenia over the merits of centralized versus decentralized privatization. The Slovene Parliament suspended the provisions of the Law on Social Capital soon after independence because of the opposition to what was widely considered a giveaway of social property. Although spontaneous privatization and decentralized privatization were allowed to continue, by mid-1992 the Parliament of the Republic of Slovenia was still debating the most effective approach and was moving toward a compromise.

THE EXPERIMENTS WITH PRIVATIZATION
IN CENTRAL EUROPE

Governments in all four Central European countries began to privatize their massive state enterprise sector in an atmosphere of uncertainty: The reformers were unsure of how to proceed and of the expected results of alternative approaches. In the absence of appropriate and reliable models, they experimented with several different approaches, including restitution and reprivatization; spontaneous privatization; self-privatization; auctioning of small companies; corporatization and the transformation of large SOEs into joint-stock or holding companies as a precondition for mass privatization; management and employee buyouts; trade sales; and asset privatization and liquidation.

Restitution and Reprivatization

One of the first tasks that the governments in all four countries had to accomplish before privatization could proceed was the clarification of property ownership rights and the settlement of ownership claims of people whose property had been confiscated or nationalized under the Communist regimes. The question of who owned the property had to be settled before it could be sold.[19]

All four governments, therefore, enacted laws of restitution, reprivatization, or compensation. These laws were aimed not only at meeting public demands for equity and justice but also at quickly returning to private ownership a large number of small service and retail units that could create the base of a small-business sector. Social and political pressures in the CSFR, for example, led the government to privatize some of the property confiscated by the state under the Communist regime by reinstating the ownership rights of the original owners or their descendants of the 70,000 properties expropriated between 1955 and 1961. The restitution law allowed property owners or their descendants to claim property that had been forcibly confiscated by the state during this period. Another law was passed to cover claims of former owners of nonagricultural land expropriated between 1948 and 1989. The laws allowed former owners or their heirs to take over property after paying for improvements or to accept monetary compensation limited to the equivalent of U.S. $1,000 in cash and the remainder in shares of companies that would later be privatized. By the end of 1991, more than 50,000 requests were filed for the return of property or the settlement of entrepreneurial titles under the restitution and extrajudicial rehabilitation laws.[20]

The post-Communist government in Poland allowed claims for restitution of property confiscated by the Communist government in 1944. By 1991, more than 70,000 claims had been filed for confirmation of property ownership. However, the outcome of the restitution plan remained in doubt during the early

1990s because it did not envision the huge burdens that would be placed on the state budget. If all claims were paid, compensation would cost the Polish government at least $1 billion in 1991 and eventually would require payments of more than $23 billion, a cost that was clearly beyond the government's resources.[21]

Under Hungary's 1991 Compensation Law, former landowners were eligible to reclaim property expropriated between 1949 and 1990 only if they were willing to keep it in agricultural use for five years. Compensation to those not reclaiming property would be paid in vouchers or bonds that could be used to buy land or shares in companies offered for privatization. The government agreed to return land confiscated from religious groups. Factories and other large companies would not, however, be returned to original owners.

Auctioning of Small Companies

Another means of privatizing those small businesses that could not be reclaimed through restitution was to auction them to the public. The arguments used in all Central European countries for small-scale privatization were (1) that it could be accomplished rapidly, (2) that it would involve large groups of people lacking substantial amounts of savings or capital, and (3) that it would generate revenues for local and national governments. Small-scale privatization would demonstrate quickly the benefits of involving large numbers of small shopkeepers in the process and would also improve the efficiency of service enterprises by removing them from state control. The auction process would be open and transparent and would allow market prices rather than political privilege to guide the allocation of state assets.[22]

The government of the CSFR, for example, authorized under its Small Privatization Law the auctioning of 100,000 small state-owned businesses such as hotels, restaurants, barber shops, shoe-repair shops, and retail stores to private individuals. The two-round auction limited bids in the first phase to those who held Czech or Slovakian citizenship after 1948; the second round accepted bids from any potential investors. More than 13,000 of the 21,500 available small businesses in the CSFR had been auctioned by September 1991. In most cases, however, only a lease was auctioned; for only about 25 percent of the sales involved actual real estate or property. In Hungary the privatization of small retail outlets through auctions was authorized in 1990, but implementation had to be postponed until April 1991 because the government did not know how many businesses would be eligible for auctioning. After it was determined that more than 10,000 units would be available, many companies petitioned for exemption; and although most exemptions were denied, the review process caused delays. When the auctions did commence, the initial results were disappointing. Access to credit was limited; interest rates were high; many of the companies were overpriced; buyers could only purchase leasing rights in most cases; and the condition of many of the shops was poor. By the end of 1991, less than 15 percent of the businesses had been sold.[23]

Spontaneous Privatization

The reform governments in all four Central European countries initially allowed spontaneous privatization, that is, the sale of state enterprises by the managers of the SOEs without direct control by the government. During the brief period after the fall of the Communist regimes when governments allowed unsupervised spontaneous privatization, many SOE managers moved quickly to transform their companies in ways that would protect their own positions or allow them to gain financially. The Republic of Slovenia had to rely on spontaneous privatization in 1990 and 1991 because the government did not yet have a legally approved process for privatizing socially owned enterprises. Trade sales, management buyouts, and employee share purchases were used by Slovene state enterprises to transform their ownership without direct intervention by the government. Following the passage of the 1988 Company Act in Hungary, the terms for privatizing a business were at the discretion of the enterprise councils. Both the Company Act and the Law of Transformation encouraged a form of spontaneous privatization by allowing state enterprises to reorganize themselves into market-style company structures. The process decentralized these companies but did not initially transfer ownership to private investors. Later, the laws allowed units to form JVs or transfer assets to affiliated companies.

In both Slovenia and Hungary, public criticism of spontaneous privatization grew quickly after the practice became known. The typical abuses, which Uroš Korže called "wild privatization," occurred when managers of SOEs (1) established a new company controlled by themselves or their cronies and then transferred the most valuable assets of the SOE to their new private company; (2) contributed the most profitable assets of the state company to a private JV in return for a block of shares in the JV; (3) helped foreign investors buy the SOE at very low prices in return for job security or other considerations; (4) contracted out the most profitable part of the state enterprise's operations to a private company that either they owned or in which they had interests and then allowed it to charge above-market prices for its services; or (5) leased or sold the assets of the state enterprise at below-market prices.[24]

Although spontaneous privatization succeeded in transferring assets rapidly from the public to the private sector, the *nomenklatura* (holdover officials from the Communist regime) were usually the major beneficiaries. The managers of many SOEs in Poland, Hungary, and Slovenia stripped the assets of their enterprises, thereby leaving "empty shell" companies. Because of these abuses, spontaneous privatization was limited; and a program of self-privatization was adopted in which SOE managers proposed a privatization plan that had to be approved by a government organization such as the State Property Agency in

Hungary, the Ministry of Privatization in the Czech and Slovak republics, or the State Privatization Agency in Slovenia.

State-Supervised Self-Privatization

After the abuses of spontaneous privatization became apparent, the governments in all four countries moved quickly to create state-supervised programs of self-privatization in which the managers of the SOEs—usually with external assistance from consulting firms or financial institutions—proposed a plan for privatizing themselves through a variety of legally approved methods.

In Hungary, the Law of Transformation was adopted in 1989 to address many of the problems of spontaneous privatization. The State Property Agency (SPA) was established in March 1990 to oversee all further privatization and to prevent SOE managers from undervaluing state-owned assets in order to transform them quickly. The SPA could initiate the privatization of SOEs under ministerial control but had to obtain the cooperation of those controlled by enterprise councils. The SPA could privatize state-owned companies by offering shares on the stock exchange after the company was incorporated as a joint-stock company (JSC), by seeking competitive bids from preselected prospective buyers, or by accepting offers from foreign or domestic investors.

In the CSFR the federal government required the management of SOEs to submit plans for their privatization, which would be approved by both the Ministry of Industry and the Ministry of Privatization in the Czech and Slovak republics. Each SOE had to describe the financial and strategic situation of the company, identify the parts of the enterprise that could be privatized, suggest the most suitable form of privatization, and recommend an appropriate level of foreign investment. Companies designated as part of the voucher privatization process had to submit completed project plans to their founding ministries and to the privatization ministries. After projects were approved, the enterprise became the property of the National Assets Funds in the appropriate republic; and it was then responsible for supervising the implementation and the signing of contracts.[25] At the same time, outside investors or units within an enterprise could submit alternative privatization projects that would compete for approval with the one offered by the SOE management. After the deadline for submission of alternative projects in December 1991, foreign investors could buy enterprises directly.[26]

Mass Privatization

In Poland, the CSFR, and Hungary, each government sought to overcome a number of problems, such as the public's lack of money to purchase shares of

SOEs and its inexperience in participating in capital markets by nationalizing state enterprises and converting them into JSCs owned entirely by the state. The creation of Treasury-owned enterprises would allow the government to distribute shares free of charge, as proposed in Poland; to sell shares to the public by providing low-cost vouchers, as was done in the CSFR; or to allow companies to be taken over by financial intermediaries, holding companies, investment trusts, and other organizations, as was done in Hungary. In addition, by "corporatizing" the SOEs and cutting state subsidies to them, the governments attempted to make them more efficient until they could be privatized. Reformers thought that nationalization prior to privatization would mobilize political support by allowing mass participation and, thus, would overcome the criticism that SOEs were only being sold to foreign investors or to the management or employees of the companies.

The mass privatization plan adopted in Poland in December 1991 designated about 400 state enterprises to be transformed into Treasury-owned JSCs (see figure 1.2). These companies would be prepared for privatization through a plan that allowed the government to retain 30 percent of the shares of all companies it offered for sale. Employees could be sold 10 percent; and the remaining portion would be sold to National Wealth Management Funds, in which every adult Pole would be given an equal value of shares.[27] One of the 20 or more closed-end funds that were expected to bid on the companies would become a major owner with 33 percent of the shares, while the remaining 27 percent would be split among the other funds. The major fund owner would play a significant role in guiding the management of the company, thereby overcoming the problems of governance that more fragmented ownership would create.[28]

Under the Large Privatization Law, the CSFR federal government authorized a three-stage process of privatizing large state-owned monopolies: first, by breaking them up into smaller companies; then, by transforming them into JSCs owned entirely by the state; and finally, by offering shares in these smaller companies to private individuals and foreign investors. Under this law, the government also began restructuring the huge state-owned companies (e.g., Skoda, a diversified heavy-manufacturing conglomerate) into smaller JSCs. Shares in these restructured companies were offered to private individuals and foreign investors through a variety of privatization procedures, including a voucher scheme. Skoda's automobile division, for example, was purchased by Volkswagen; and other divisions were purchased by, or became JVs with, other companies.

In early 1992 the government of the CSFR initiated a voucher scheme allowing all citizens over 18 years of age to obtain coupons at a nominal cost (about U.S. $37). These coupons could be used to bid on shares in JSCs that would be privatized by the voucher method. The voucher booklets containing 1,000 points would be tradable on a stock market that was expected to begin operating in early 1993. In the first round, the government would offer shares in about 1,466

Figure 1.2
Poland's Mass Privatization Plan

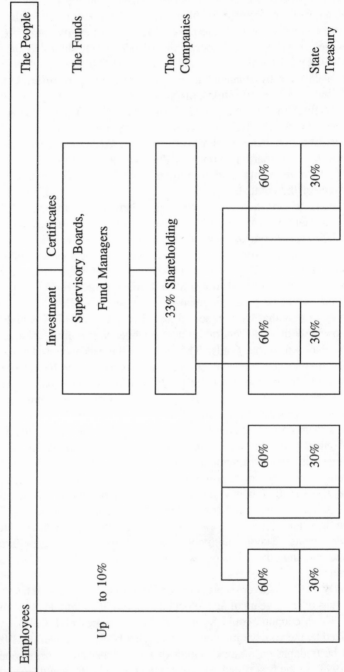

state enterprises at a uniform price of three shares per 100 points. Bids would be matched with the stocks available. If a company had more bidders than its available stocks, its shares would be offered in a later round at a higher price. If a company had more stocks than bidders, the shares would be distributed to those making offers; unsold stocks would be offered in a later round at a lower price (see figure 1.3). The average stake to be sold in all firms would be 50 percent, but it ranged from as little as 10 percent of some companies to 97 percent of others. At least 3 percent of the shares in every firm would be reserved for restitution claims.

Although the voucher sales had been slow during the early offerings, a strong government advertising campaign and aggressive marketing by private investment funds spurred sales. By March 1992 more than 8.5 million citizens (about 80 percent of the adult population) had purchased vouchers—far more than had been expected to participate.[29] The strongest stimulus to sales came from the vigorous campaign by private investment (mutual) funds to attract subscribers who exchanged their coupons for shares in these mutual funds, some of which promised payments of up to ten times their face value within a year.[30] Using the pooled vouchers, the investment funds would bid on shares of companies and manage the portfolio much like mutual funds in the United States.

Many reformers saw mass privatization as a better alternative than decentralized approaches because it was guided by the state in the "public interest," but in all four countries there were problems and drawbacks.[31] Government-directed privatization was often complicated, uncertain, and slow—in both Poland and Hungary the responsible government agencies had insufficient numbers of trained people to review and approve privatization plans; thus, the process was seriously delayed. The standardized processes of privatization adopted in both countries often failed to differentiate between the conditions and needs of SOEs and the interests of potential investors in their assets. Privatization by free distribution of shares or voucher sale did not generate much revenue for financially strapped governments or capital-starved companies. And widespread distribution of shares in the CSFR threatened to create problems of corporate governance and direction after privatization was completed.

Management and Employee Buyouts

All four Central European countries also experimented with management and employee buyouts of SOEs. Reformers saw the major advantages of this approach as its potential for increasing managers' or employees' motivation to make the company more profitable and for mobilizing support within the company for privatization. In Hungary, the Company Act and the Transformation Law either required or allowed state enterprises that transformed themselves to issue shares to employees. Limited companies had to provide employee

Figure 1.3
Czechoslovakia's Voucher Scheme

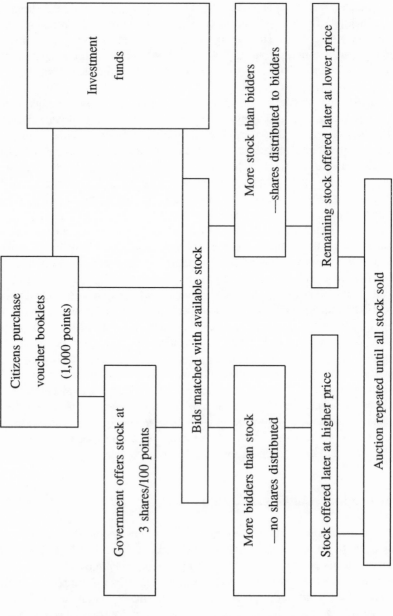

Citizens purchase voucher booklets (1,000 points)

Investment funds

Government offers stock at 3 shares/100 points

Bids matched with available stock

More stock than bidders —shares distributed to bidders

Remaining stock offered later at lower price

More bidders than stock —no shares distributed

Stock offered later at higher price

Auction repeated until all stock sold

shares at discounts of up to 50 percent for an amount not to exceed 10 percent of the founding capital. Employees could acquire up to 10 percent of the company's total assets. Managers and employees or a consortium of both could buy up to 15 percent of SOEs being offered for privatization.[32] The Polish law on privatization passed in July 1990 required that up to 20 percent of the shares of privatized companies be reserved for workers of the enterprise at a 50 percent discount of the issue price. Workers could not, however, obtain discounts for an amount that was more than that of the employee's salary for the previous six months. The law sought to create 4 million small investors among SOE employees.[33]

Critics argued that these buyouts were socially undesirable. They did not increase a company's managerial or employment skills —an essential condition for improving productivity and competitiveness. The assets of the company were usually undervalued; and because the companies were operated by essentially the same management and labor force, it was difficult to obtain external capital investment and credit from commercial lenders. In both Hungary and Slovenia, the public believed that management and employee buyouts gave inside groups unfair advantages in obtaining state assets. Other critics noted (1) that the interests of workers, that is, employment and remuneration, were in conflict with the public's interest in promoting efficiency, quality, and the lowest possible prices for goods; (2) that employees could not provide effective supervision or direction for management; and (3) that employee or management control of a company would lead to long-run inefficiencies in a market economy.[34]

Even when employee or management buyouts were not the principal instrument for privatization, governments in all four countries made provisions for employee shareholding in their negotiations with many private investors in SOEs. The governments in all four countries encouraged foreign investors to give employees and managers preferential treatment or protection. In Poland, for example, the government negotiated special treatment for employees and suppliers in the American Gerber Products Company's bid to purchase the Polish Alima Baby Food and Juice Company. The approval of Gerber's bid hinged on guarantees to maintain existing employment levels in the company for at least 18 months after the acquisition was completed. The 1,000 employees and 4,500 agricultural suppliers of Alima were also allowed to buy up to 40 percent of the shares in the company at a 50 percent discount on the issue price.[35]

Trade Sales

The governments in all four countries also permitted trade sales as a means of privatizing state companies; that is, they promoted the sale of all or part of a state enterprise to a single private investor or a group of investors through direct acquisition. Advocates of trade sales argued that there were few other alternatives that would be as rapid until Central European countries developed strong equity markets. Other means were far slower and less promising ways of selling financially ailing companies. Even in Hungary where an equities market was created quickly, trade sales were used to privatize companies that were too weak to be sold on the stock exchange or that had unfavorable competitive positions or ineffective managements. From October 1990 the State Property Agency in Hungary accepted direct bids for all enterprises it owned. Prospective buyers could place an offer for a specific company with the SPA, which had to respond to the offer within 30 days. After that, the prospective buyer had up to three months to make a final bid. During this time, the company was evaluated by the SPA and had to transform itself into a JSC. The SPA searched for other bidders; and if none were found and the bid was in line with the audit evaluation, the offer was accepted. In 1991 about 90 percent of the privatizations in Hungary were trade sales to foreign multinationals.[36]

But critics of this approach pointed out that trade sales often got bogged down in difficult and complex valuation problems and resulted primarily in the sale of the most profitable companies to foreign interests. Limited wealth and savings in all four countries constrained the number of companies that could be sold to domestic investors. Moreover, the proceeds of the sale often went to the state Treasury rather than to capitalizing the companies.[37]

Asset Privatization and Liquidation

Finally, governments in Central Europe pursued privatization through the sale of company assets and liquidation. Using this approach, the state sold physical assets belonging to SOEs that were beyond restructuring and for which ownership shares in the company were not attractive. Governments or SOEs usually turned to asset sale when a state company could not be sold in its entirety or when some assets had value, but the company as a whole did not. Asset privatization was, in many cases, a prelude to liquidation.

The most successful aspect of privatization in Poland during 1990 and 1991 was liquidation. From 1990 until early 1992, about 540 state enterprises with a work force of more than 175,000 were liquidated so that management, employees, and investors could buy them. Most of the liquidated companies, however, were small units with low capital-investment requirements.[38] Liquidation allowed state enterprise property in Poland to be sold, transferred to a newly created company, or rented more quickly than any other form of privatization. Most of the liquidated companies were involved in construction, communications, transport, agriculture, or manufacturing.[39]

In its second privatization program in early 1992, Hungary attempted to liquidate and privatize the assets of the "empty shell" companies left from the process of transferring assets of machinery and equipment to small units during previous organizational reforms. This phase of privatization sought to liquidate 14 parent or holding companies whose units had previously become manufacturing affiliates. These parent companies had retained some of their buildings, machinery, and other assets. Under the second privatization program, the affiliated companies were separated from the parent companies and were allowed to buy whatever assets they desired from the parent enterprise.[40]

As the foregoing descriptions clearly illustrate, all four countries in Central Europe experimented with various forms of privatization, all of which had both advantages and weaknesses. No single form of privatization was suitable for all state enterprises, and each had potential drawbacks that could create problems later. Through trial and error, governments amended their laws and regulations and initiated new economic reforms to anticipate or resolve problems as they arose.

CHALLENGES TO PRIVATIZATION AND ECONOMIC REFORM IN THE EARLY TRANSITION PERIOD

Not all of the reforms enacted during the early transition period from 1989 to 1992 were implemented effectively, however; nor did they progress without opposition and delay. In all four countries, reformers initially envisioned rapid privatization of massive numbers of state enterprises in a short period of time. But they quickly discovered that the process would be far slower and much more complicated than they expected. In the CSFR the process of privatization and small-business development was especially slow for a government with ambitions to privatize 70 percent of its state enterprises by the end of 1991. Of the more than 100,000 nationalized small businesses and shops that the government wanted to sell, only about 800 had been sold by April 1991.[41] Political conflicts and bureaucratic delays slowed the process in Poland as well. The Ministry of Ownership Transformation reported that less than 9 percent of the 8,443 companies that had been targeted for privatization had been transformed into Treasury-owned companies or had been liquidated by mid-1991.[42] The privatization law still had not been finalized in Slovenia by early 1992. The year after the first round of privatizations in Hungary, few completed sales had been accomplished. By mid-1992 economist Jeffrey Sachs, an adviser on privatization to Poland and Russia, began to call the programs undertaken in the region a debacle. "Every Eastern European country has failed, and failed significantly," he concluded, "to find new owners for state-owned enterprises."[43]

Although other observers were less pessimistic, many agreed that privatization in Central Europe had progressed more slowly than they had expected. The delays in implementing economic reforms, privatizing state enterprises, and developing the private sector were attributable to a mix of macroeconomic, political, bureaucratic, and structural problems. They included (1) the difficulties of implementing changes rapidly in an environment of economic uncertainty, (2) the initial political ambivalence over the pace and scope of economic reform that emerged in all four countries, (3) early opposition by many managers and workers in SOEs to restructuring and privatization, and (4) bureaucratic complexities and delays in formulating and carrying out privatization procedures. Privatization and private enterprise development were adversely affected as well by the weak market economy management skills found among SOE managers and new business owners; by the incomplete restoration of property rights; by inadequate supplies of capital and credit to purchase SOEs or to start new enterprises; by weak business infrastructure to support enterprise expansion; by burdensome business taxes and regulations remaining from the Communist period; and by initial social hostility toward business owners as the economies of Central European countries were transformed from socialist to market-oriented systems.

The Environment of Economic Uncertainty

Privatization and private enterprise development were hampered by the environment of economic uncertainty that accompanied the demise of the Communist regimes in Central Europe in 1989 and 1990. Despite deteriorating economic conditions, 40 years of socialist control brought with it some sense of job security for workers. But the reforms enacted in 1990 raised fears among many Central Europeans—especially among middle-aged and older people —about their economic security in the future. Although opinion polls taken in 1990 found that most of the Czech and Slovakian people, for example, supported the conversion to a market economy, and many groups advocated rapid and radical transformation, an underlying fear of unemployment and decline in production and living standards made most Czechs and Slovaks anxious about the pace and direction of change. About one-third of the respondents—fearing widespread unemployment, increases in rents, and high levels of inflation—expressed strong opposition to drastic changes.[44] These fears plus caution toward implementing rapid economic changes were reinforced when the koruna was devalued in early 1991, after already having been devalued the year before. Limits on wage increases intensified the opposition to reform of those concerned about unemployment and declining income.[45] During 1991 nearly all macroeconomic data reflected the seriousness of the recession that had begun in 1990. Gross national product declined by 16 percent; personal consumption dropped by 28 percent; gross industrial output decreased by 22 percent; and gross investment fell by 30 percent.[46] Real average monthly wages fell by 28 percent at the same time that the consumer price index increased by nearly 58 percent. Exports fell by 7.5 percent, and unemployment increased to 6.6 percent.[47] Not only did prices of consumer goods increase rapidly; but there also remained considerable uncertainty over the supply and price of energy, which directly affected the cost of production for both privatizing SOEs and small businesses. Coal production decreased substantially as did oil supplies from the former Soviet Union.[48] Economic uncertainties made it difficult to privatize businesses rapidly in the other Central European countries as well. Recession created adverse conditions for the privatization of financially weak SOEs and for entrepreneurs trying to start new businesses. In 1990 when private enterprise development was beginning in Poland, national income was declining by 13 percent; investments were down by 8 percent; and industrial production was declining by 23 percent. Inflation had reached 584 percent.[49] In Hungary, recession and declining traditional markets for exports in former socialist countries in Eastern Europe made SOEs less attractive to domestic and foreign investors. Gross domestic product fell by 4 percent in 1990, and unemployment had risen by 10 percent for the whole country and by more than 25 percent in some of the eastern provinces of Hungary in 1991. Consumer price inflation increased by more than 35 percent at a time when real incomes were declining by 9 percent. At the same time, the country was struggling to reduce foreign debts of more than $21 billion.[50]

In all four countries, small-scale entrepreneurs as well as managers of privatizing SOEs were trying to establish their businesses in a period of economic recession and instability. Because of low wages, rising prices, threats of continuing inflation, and decreasing exports, demand for the products of SOEs was declining; and the market for many consumer goods was limited throughout Central Europe during a period when all four countries had to make drastic changes in the structure of their industries and the characteristics of their economies.

Problems of weak consumer demand and stagflation prevented many SOEs from reversing their losses and paying their debts, thus making it difficult to find buyers or investors. The problems associated with weak domestic economies were exacerbated by collapsing markets for goods in the former Soviet Union and other former socialist economies on which SOEs depended for substantial amounts of their exports. Potential foreign investors in SOEs were more cautious in their purchasing and investment plans because of declining export markets. The Italian firm Ansaldo, for example, postponed substantial restructuring and investment in the Hungarian Ganz Electricity Works during 1991 because Ganz's leading customers—the Hungarian State Railways, the Hungarian Electricity Trust, and Budapest Transport—were all financially ailing from rapidly declining Soviet sales.[51]

For many SOEs, privatized companies, and new businesses, the most important challenge was simply to survive during their first few years in the face of high inflation, lower purchasing power, continued low wages, and depressed economic conditions.

Political Ambivalence over the Pace of Economic Reform

The traumas of political and economic change also created political ambivalence toward, and some resistance to, rapid reform and privatization. On the whole, the public in Central Europe initially evaluated economic reform policies very critically.[52]   Opinion polls taken in 1991 in Hungary, the CSFR, and Poland showed that 63 percent of the Hungarian people interviewed believed that changes in the country were going in the wrong direction; only 53 percent in Poland and 58 percent in the CSFR believed that they were going in the right direction.   Only 4 percent of the Hungarians, 6 percent of the Czechs and Slovaks, and 12 percent of the Poles said that their personal economic situations were better one year after the collapse of the Communist regime; and most believed that their situations would not improve in the immediate future. More than two-thirds of those surveyed in all three countries believed that their family's standard of living would drop markedly in the future; and more than a majority feared that the economic reforms would fail. Only about 17 percent of the respondents in Hungary, 30 percent in Poland, and 23 percent in the CSFR stated that they would prefer to work for a state-owned company; but when asked if all or most SOEs should be privatized, only 60 percent of the Hungarians and 61 percent of the Czechs and Slovaks responded positively. About one-quarter of the respondents in all three countries said that only small businesses should be privatized.

This ambivalence toward reform and privatization was clearly rooted in fears of unemployment and inflation and translated into some resistance and outright opposition to rapid economic changes in all three countries. In the CSFR the rapid and comprehensive reforms advocated by Finance Minister Klaus did not always win strong political commitment and support from the Federal Assembly or in the National Council of the Czech and Slovak republics. After the initial euphoria of independence waned, political attention was refocused on issues of power and control between the republics and on the political impacts of economic reforms on workers.   When the short-term impacts of economic changes were more directly felt by individuals, political support for the two major political organizations—Civic Forum in the Czech Lands and the Public against Violence in Slovakia—seemed to weaken. Inflation increased by 14 percent by the end of 1990, and production fell by nearly 4 percent. Rumors of the harsh consequences of the rapid and radical economic reforms in Poland made many people and some political leaders in the CSFR wary of Polish-style adjustments. Progress on economic reform was slowed by the opposition arising from the Slovaks' fear that their poorer economy would suffer harsher effects than the Czechs'.[53]   Later, these political differences over the pace and scope of economic reform contributed to the Slovaks' decision to leave the federation.

The process of privatization in Poland was delayed by contention among the numerous political factions within Parliament and the government.   In the

October 1991 elections, 29 political parties won seats in Parliament, thus making it difficult for President Lech Walesa to form a new government. The Democratic Union party, which won the most seats in the *Sejm*, the lower house, received only a little more than 12 percent of the vote and held only 62 of the 260 seats. "From the very beginning, privatization was under strong political and social pressure," inside observers noted. "The majority of liberally oriented economists and politicians demanded that it be done immediately, while Workers' Council activists demanded that it be arranged in such a way that it did not manage their influence in the industrial system."[54] In March 1992 the *Sejm* rejected Prime Minister Jan Olszewski's economic reform program that focused on expanding the money supply to promote more investment. The opposition in Parliament and by President Lech Walesa arose from fears that the policy would allow a return to hyperinflation. In addition to the difficulties of obtaining consensus on economic reforms and privatization proposals, several changes in Polish cabinet positions during the early transition period disrupted continuity in leadership in the Ministry of Ownership Transformation and other agencies dealing with privatization. "During a two-year period, three different leaders supervised the privatization policy program," Gregory Jedrzejczak and Henryk Sterniczuk pointed out; and they had to spend more time "fighting for a budget and defending its subsequent versions than actually implementing it."

Opposition by Some Managers and Workers in SOEs

In addition, the implementation of privatization and private enterprise development was slowed by the initial opposition of many managers and workers in SOEs. Having found a secure place in a known system, many managers feared the unknown challenges of a market economy and of working in a private company. Most were used to operating under socialist principles and with assured markets in the Soviet Union and CMEA (Council for Mutual Economic Assistance) countries; they feared the removal of state subsidies and the uncertainties of the market. Many managers and workers were ill-prepared psychologically to deal with real competition. In all four Central European countries, socialist leaders pushed state enterprises to create jobs for everyone who was willing to work and made it difficult for SOEs to terminate employment. As a result, managers had no incentive to use workers efficiently or effectively. At the same time, workers were not motivated to be productive: Their jobs were secure; their pay was low; and a large portion of their consumption came from state subsidies for housing, transportation, medical care, housing, and education.[55] The prevailing attitude of workers toward management was reflected in the aphorism "I'll pretend to work and you pretend to pay me."

The elimination of state subsidies in 1990 and 1991 forced some unprofitable companies out of business; others went bankrupt with the collapse of Soviet and

CMEA export markets.[56] Many of the companies whose traditional markets were cut off could survive only by reducing production costs, by eliminating the large number of excess employees that state enterprises were required to hire, and by limiting wage increases. Under these conditions, many workers raised objections to the economic changes. In the CSFR, the Trade Union Federation lobbied against the rapid pace and broad scope of reforms, especially those affecting employment and wages.

Thus, despite their commitment to eliminating subsidies for SOEs, the governments of Poland and the CSFR had to bail out some inefficient companies in order to limit unemployment and prevent the demise of large producers.[57] In Poland, for example, the government decided to prevent the bankruptcy or liquidation of the giant Ursus tractor plant in Warsaw despite the fact that the company had accumulated more than $30 million in debt by 1991 and had monthly operating losses of $3.5 million. The company's demise would have adversely affected the company's 24,000 employees as well as 10,000 employees in cooperating plants and 80,000 workers in the 300 companies that were supplying tractor parts to Ursus.   Because of the serious unemployment implications and the likely protests and demonstrations by the Solidarity labor union, the government chose to try to restructure the company gradually—despite its continuing losses—rather than allow it to be liquidated.[58] Many managers of state-owned companies in all four countries were reluctant to release excess labor and to cut wages for fear of antagonizing trade unions, and the trade unions and workers were reluctant to see changes in ownership that might jeopardize their jobs.

Bureaucratic Complexity and Delays

Privatization and private enterprise development were initially slowed as well in Central European countries by bureaucratic complexities arising from unclear and complicated procedures; by inadequate numbers of skilled people within government ministries and agencies to review and approve privatization plans; and in some cases, by deliberate delays in approving applications for privatization or small-business creation by unsympathetic or rent-seeking bureaucrats. Many of the initial problems in Poland, the CSFR, and Slovenia were due to complex and unclear regulations and procedures for privatization.

The lack of guidelines for approving privatization in the early years of transformation in the CSFR, for example, led to differences in interpretation and standards of approval in various ministries and agencies in the federal and republic governments.   Private business development was also slowed by bureaucratic red tape.   In the CSFR it was relatively easy for very small businesses to obtain licenses by applying to the municipal government office; but larger businesses had to register through the courts, a procedure that became more complex. In 1990 and early 1991, the complexity of the regulations seriously slowed the process of private business creation because at least 14 different licenses were needed from as many different ministries in order to start a new business.[59] The delaying tactics of the large number of *nomenklatura* still in the government made it difficult for some potential entrepreneurs to receive permits to establish new businesses.[60]

Both foreign investors and domestic companies in the CSFR and Poland found that requests for permission, permits, licenses, or reviews were often slowed deliberately by government officials until they received a "thick envelope" to help expedite bureaucratic procedures. In mid-1992, business analysts were still warning that in the CSFR "the country's forbidding bureaucracy can significantly obstruct the simplest tasks, such as registration of the company or changing the location of the office. Despite many claims that the people and country have changed since the 1989 Velvet Revolution, the situation is now not much different from what it was in the past."[61]

Weak Market Economy Management Skills

Although managers of privatizing companies were often technically skilled, most lacked the capacity to operate in a market economy. Surveys taken between June 1991 and March 1992 in the CSFR, Poland, and Hungary identified a number of weaknesses common to Central European managers and executives from the perspective of Western businesses that were potentially interested in investing in SOEs. Among the most serious problems were the lack of flexibility, accuracy, and timeliness in their business practices and behavior. The most serious problem, however, was their seeming unwillingness to take on responsibilities and to take risks.[62] This should not have been surprising, of course, because Central European managers had worked during the Communist era in an environment that rewarded obedience, conformity, and meeting planned targets. Many were unused to taking responsibility for decisions. They did not know how to assess competitive opportunities, how to deal with risk, how to mobilize and invest capital to create market advantages, how to use information systems for business operations, or how to value the assets and liabilities of their companies. Managers of the state companies for which they worked were also unfamiliar with cash-flow management and standard systems of accounting. Many adopted Soviet accounting principles that were complicated and confusing; these systems became useless in dealing with international companies.

Nearly all state-owned companies that were scheduled for privatization as well as owners of newly created small companies faced serious marketing problems. Most of the heavy-manufacturing companies lost their protected markets in former COMECON (CMEA) countries and the Soviet Union. These markets accounted for up to 60 percent of the production of many state companies in the

CSFR, for example. At the same time, they saw declining markets at home because of secondary insolvency—their customers were also facing export losses. The manufacturers were not paid for deliveries; and they, in turn, could not pay their suppliers. In highly integrated manufacturing companies, the loss of markets for primary goods sent a ripple of production cutbacks through the whole system of producers and suppliers of intermediate goods.

Under the Communist regimes, few companies in any of the four countries had to worry about marketing; for they operated under a command system in which they merely had to fulfill quotas. Many state companies eliminated their sales departments or kept on only a few personnel who performed clerical and administrative duties. Few companies were experienced in domestic or international marketing; and many had not developed sales staffs, had never had to engage in advertising, and were not experienced in dealing with overseas agents. Those companies that did find potential overseas partners discovered quickly that the markets for their goods were limited because of poor packaging and because Central European production standards were lower than those demanded by foreign markets.

Incomplete Restoration of Property Rights

Another obstacle to more rapid privatization and private enterprise development during the early transitional period was uncertainty over property rights. Foreign companies interested in acquiring all or parts of companies in Central European countries initially had difficulty purchasing property. Although the government in Hungary opened property ownership to foreign investors without the need for formal government approval in 1991, foreign companies often experienced serious problems in determining from whom to purchase the land that was nationalized by the Communist regime. Property rights were unclear, and title to land was clouded by potential restitution claims by former owners. Although Parliament passed the Compensation Act in 1991 to make property rights more transparent and to allow transfer of SOE property to the SPA, land acquisition was initially slowed by the cautious approach of all foreign investors.[63]

For many people in the CSFR, property restitution was extremely slow. Many who made claims for family property had to wait in long lines at municipal buildings to get access to real estate books documenting that they or immediate relatives had purchased the property. Moreover, they had to go through several months of collecting other documents proving family ownership. Even after they obtained the property, many had to pay previous occupants for improvements and inventory as well as raise the capital for reconstruction to make it suitable for business operations.[64] Difficulties in evicting tenants with legally protected leases also slowed the restoration of business properties to the original owners.

Inadequate Supplies of Capital and Credit

Both small-business development and the privatization of SOEs were slowed because of limited access to credit. In Poland, Hungary, and the Czech and Slovak republics, the government's ability to privatize through public share offerings was limited by inadequate domestic savings and wealth. Domestic savings were inadequate to absorb more than a small fraction of the companies that would be available for privatization, and many of those who did have savings either retained them as a hedge against an uncertain economic future or used them to start small businesses. Foreign companies entering JVs with Hungarian enterprises found that the lack of access to credit was creating serious payment problems for many Hungarian companies and that the banking system was unable to provide timely credit assessments of Hungarian businesses. Privatized companies were reluctant to take on new customers because of the payment risks associated with the tight credit market as well as the inability of banks to provide credit ratings.[65]

Neither entrepreneurs wishing to start small businesses nor managers of privatized SOEs were able to get easy access to domestic capital or credit during the early years of transition in the Czech and Slovak republics and in Hungary. In the CSFR, the State Investment Bank would only make short-term loans to small businesses for operating expenses; it would not make loans for capital investment unless the entrepreneur could provide substantial collateral. Because property rights were not completely restored, it was difficult for most people starting a business to find adequate capital. Most commercial banks would not make capital investment loans to small-scale entrepreneurs except in special circumstances.

No special programs had been established for small businesses until mid-1992 except provision of loans at about 1 percent below the standard rate for those that provided 100 percent collateral. The State Investment Bank rates in mid-1991 ranged from 19 percent for one-year loans to 24 percent for four-year loans. Neither state nor commercial banks were qualified to assess proposals from small-business owners who, in any case, did not generally have the capacity to prepare the types of business plans that the banks could evaluate. The CSFR did not have a guarantee program to secure the loans of small businesses, and the banks were reluctant to change their lending policies in the absence of guarantees.[66]

Although many new small businesses did not need large amounts of start-up capital, they did need loans to expand and to cover accounts receivable. Privatizing state enterprises needed capital to repair and maintain deteriorating physical plants, to replace obsolete equipment, and to obtain new technology. Because only limited amounts of capital were available from state or commercial banks in Central European countries, managers of privatizing SOEs were relying heavily on foreign investment or loans from foreign banks.

Inadequate Business Infrastructure

The large backlog of housing demand, slow construction, and the lack of building maintenance during the Communist regime left little business space for those wishing to start up or expand their operations in Poland, Hungary, and the Czech and Slovak republics. In Czech and Slovakian cities, for example, Soviet-style large-scale apartment buildings had insufficient space for living and virtually no space for commercial activities, thereby inhibiting the start-up of home-based, small-scale production activities as well as small trade and service businesses. Some successful private vending operations appeared on the streets in 1990, and office and production space was beginning to be made available as leasing of excess space became more common in 1991. But in cities like Prague, the rents for commercial and production space rose rapidly due to scarcity; and most small businesses simply could not afford them. Office rents were reported to start at about $80 per square meter in the central areas of Prague, compared with $55 in Warsaw and $45 in Budapest.[67] Foreign investors could acquire apartments only as a JV with an exemption from the Ministry of Finance and if they were willing to accept the risks arising from the vagueness of ownership rights. Housing shortages severely limited the ability of owners to demolish housing units in order to convert them into offices or business establishments.

Even when entrepreneurs could find adequate space, they were often unable to acquire the equipment and services necessary to allow them to operate efficiently. Operations in General Motors' (GM) joint venture with the Hungarian truck and engine producer Raba was initially hindered by the lack of local infrastructure needed to do business efficiently. The inability to get sufficient numbers of telephone lines required GM to use mobile telephones connected to the network in Austria. Months of negotiation were required among GM, its JV partners, local government authorities, the Hungarian Electricity Trust, and the Hungarian Gas and Oil enterprise in order to obtain adequate supplies of gas and electricity. Lack of housing in the area around the JV's plant in Hungary required GM managers to live in nearby towns in Austria and commute every day to the plant in Hungary.[68]

In 1991 it still took at least two months to obtain a telephone in Prague even if a business owner could afford to pay up to $800 in bribes, on top of the official cost of about $66.[69] Foreign investors attempting to get around the constraints imposed by the slowness and incapacity of the state telecommunications company to respond to demand by using equipment supplied by private firms still had to pay more than $1,000 in hookup fees. After the equipment was installed, managers had to cope with an extremely inefficient domestic telephone system plagued by busy lines and long delays in completing calls. Ironically, foreign calls could often be placed faster than domestic ones.

Burdensome Business Taxes and Regulations

Privatization and private enterprise development were seriously affected during the early transition period by taxes and regulations that were held over from the Communist regimes and were only slowly changed. Both privatizing SOE managers and small-business owners in all four countries had to continue paying substantial taxes and social benefits for employees as well as adhere to both old regulations and new restrictions that raised the cost of doing business after state enterprises were privatized. In the CSFR, for example, the Federal Assembly imposed a 22 percent turnover tax on all businesses that sold goods as well as a profit tax ranging from 15 percent for profits of more than 65,000 crowns (about U.S. $25,000) to 55 percent for profits of more than 500,000 crowns (U.S. $173,000). The 1991 federal budget sought 54 percent of its revenues from the turnover tax and another 25 percent from enterprise duties.[70] The government also levied a 30 percent tax on many export goods. In both Hungary and Poland, privatized companies also had to pay heavy social security and benefit costs for employees in order to support the "safety net" of social programs established under the socialist regime and kept in place to reduce social tensions during the transition period. In the CSFR, owners of small companies found it particularly difficult to pay social security and benefits taxes on employee wages up to 50 percent. As a result, managers of privatizing SOEs and small-business owners were generally reluctant to take on employees.

Social Hostility toward Business Owners

Finally, private enterprise expansion was slowed in the early 1990s by the deep suspicion that existed in Poland, Hungary, Slovenia, and the CSFR of those who could afford to purchase or create businesses. In the CSFR and Hungary many shop workers who could not afford to bid in auctions for small businesses complained that the only people who had the capital to buy them were black marketeers, corrupt *nomenklatura*, and people illegally backed by foreign investors. The strong sense of egalitarianism inculcated by the Communist regime still shaped people's attitudes and caused resentment of the possibility that some people would become far richer than others through individual enterprise.

Many of the spontaneous privatizations that took place in Central Europe before the passage of laws controlling or supervising the process led to public outcries against the *nomenklatura* who managed the SOEs. In the privatization of the HungarHotels, for example, the management of Hungary's premier hotel and restaurant chain used foreign investments for the creation of a dummy corporation in Sweden that arranged to buy the state enterprise at a small fraction of its real value. The deal would have yielded substantial profits for the *nomenklatura* who served as directors and managers of HungarHotels and would have protected their positions while excluding other potential buyers from bidding on the company. After public opinion turned against the deal, the Hungarian Supreme Court blocked the sale on a technicality; but the adverse publicity reinforced public hostility toward all of the spontaneous privatization schemes.[71]

CREATING AN INSTITUTIONAL BASE FOR PRIVATE ENTERPRISE DEVELOPMENT

Although reformers in Hungary, Poland, Slovenia, and the CSFR faced serious challenges in implementing privatization and private enterprise development policies during the early transition period between 1989 and 1992, all four countries had also achieved some progress in transforming their economies from socialist command systems to market-oriented systems. All four had adopted comprehensive macroeconomic reforms that helped stabilize and restructure their economies in a relatively short period of time. They had also adopted the basic legislative and policy changes needed to create market-oriented institutions, and all had experimented with and begun to implement their privatization programs by 1992.

Before the disintegration of the federation, the federal government in the CSFR had been successful in implementing a complex voucher scheme for privatization of a large number of companies that might not have been transformed through other means. In 1991, foreign investors brought in about $900 million through JVs and acquisitions of Czech and Slovakian companies.[72] By early 1992 the government expected up to $3.5 billion in foreign capital investment in the 859 companies that were scheduled to be privatized under the first wave of voucher privatization.

Despite political conflicts and false starts on privatization in Poland, by 1992 some progress was being made in privatizing that country's economy. After more than a year of disappointing results, privatization began to accelerate in 1991; and by the end of February 1992, about 258 state-owned companies had been converted or liquidated, while more than 400 had been transformed into Treasury-owned companies as a prelude to mass privatization.[73] More than 300,000 new private enterprises had been created in Poland by the end of 1991. Private firms employed about 38 percent of all nonagricultural labor in Poland and accounted for more than 24 percent of the total industrial production. Private companies were responsible for 80 percent of domestic turnover, and the number of JVs had tripled between 1990 and the end of 1991. Moreover, small-scale private businesses were employing more than 2.6 million people.[74] By mid-1992 about 80 percent of Poland's retail stores had been privatized, and 40 percent of all registered imports were managed by the private sector.[75]

In Slovenia it was estimated that more than 450 socially owned enterprises had been restructured by the end of 1991—even before the republic had a legally approved procedure for privatization—and that many were partially privatized through management and employee buyouts and the creation of JVs.[76] Conflicts and setbacks slowed but did not totally immobilize the process of privatization in Hungary. By the beginning of 1992, Hungary's Privatization Research Institute estimated that the government owned less than 50 percent of all companies in the country. The value of the private sector expanded to 500 billion forints ($6.6 billion).[77]

By the beginning of 1992, the number of JVs and wholly owned affiliates in Central Europe had also grown: In Poland, there were 5,100 JVs representing more than $670 million in foreign equity; in the CSFR, 4,000 JVs attracted $480 million in foreign equity; and in Hungary, about 11,000 JVs brought in a little more than $2 billion in foreign equity.[78]

Despite this relative progress, all four countries remained far from creating private sector economies and sustainable market systems at the end of 1992. The early transition period had achieved some impressive results in macroeconomic policy reform, some modest successes with privatization, and steady advancement toward private enterprise development. But economic recovery was sluggish in all four countries: All faced serious problems of rising unemployment; all were still in serious recession; and all were trying to cope with wrenching social and environmental problems. Privatization had proceeded far more slowly than economic reformers and political leaders had originally anticipated. The successes were largely with enterprises requiring small amounts of capital investment, with JVs, and with acquisitions of the more profitable and promising state enterprises by foreign investors. The weaker and more problematic SOEs were far more difficult to liquidate or privatize, especially if they employed large numbers of people who would have difficulty finding new jobs.

In the closing months of 1992, all four countries still faced serious challenges in transforming their economies and strengthening the institutions that would be essential to support privatization and private enterprise development.

First, an urgent need that had been given relatively little attention by governments in all four countries during the early transition period was to provide management, technical, and financial assistance to individual entrepreneurs and managers of small- and medium-sized businesses. Some of the problems that small-scale entrepreneurs and managers of privatizing SOEs faced in establishing and expanding their businesses would eventually be addressed by reforms in the tax law, the development of new accounting standards, and changes in laws affecting business operations that were being prepared in 1992. Others, however, would require external assistance from international development organizations, such as the World Bank and the European Bank for Reconstruction and Development, as well as considerable self-help by entrepreneurs and business managers themselves. Unless top-down macroeconomic reforms were supplemented by programs to encourage bottom-up private enterprise development, however, the benefits of reform would not quickly spread. The attention given to macroeconomic policy reform during the early transition period often masked recognition of the fact that it would be the small- and medium-sized enterprises that would have to create sufficient numbers of jobs or absorb enough people in gainful employment to offset the large amount of surplus labor that would be released from SOEs during restructuring and privatization.[79]

Among the most urgent needs of enterprise managers and small-business owners were the following: (1) access to information about the business-formation process, business systems, business practices and procedures, and markets; (2) practical counseling and consulting services on the legal environment, business planning, financing, and marketing; (3) broad-scale business ownership and management training offered particularly in short, practical workshops and seminar formats; and (4) development of carefully planned business-development facilities to help overcome current scarcities of commercial and production space for new businesses and provide training and management assistance programs.[80]

A second basic requirement for effective reform that was only beginning to be addressed during the early transition period was to find ways of creating new institutions to support private enterprise development. Once macroeconomic policy reforms were in place, much more attention had to be given to develop financial institutions that could extend credit and facilitate financial transactions; to rationalize and reorient labor markets; to create the system of legal institutions through which business transactions could be legitimized and conflicts could be settled; to strengthen the system of property rights; and to develop reliable and efficient marketing and distribution systems.

A third challenge remaining by the end of 1992 was to develop the human resources needed in Central Europe to participate in domestic and international commerce by expanding knowledge of how market economies work and how businesses operate within them. Although all four countries had a long tradition of manufacturing and trade before Communist regimes adopted socialist planning, they entered the reform period of the early 1990s lacking experience with private enterprise and the institutional infrastructure needed to support business development. As the former deputy minister of foreign affairs in the CSFR pointed out in 1991, "The four-decades-long isolation and enforced predominance of Marxist doctrines entirely prevented the country from accumulating the critical mass of management and business know-how. There are no domestic centers that are ready to disseminate [principles of] market-economy–based business management."[81]

Few managers or business owners in Central Europe were formally trained in corporate or small-business management or in the basics of market economics during the Communist regimes. Intensive programs were needed to change the curricula of elementary and secondary schools that focused on Marxist social and economic theory and political indoctrination during 40 years of Communist rule. Training was needed for elementary and secondary schoolteachers to expose them to the principles and operation of market economies and democratic systems. Special attention had to be given to secondary vocational schools that could offer apprenticeship training and where the introduction of courses on small-enterprise development could have a strong impact in providing opportunities for many of the graduates of these technical and vocational schools—who were unlikely to find good opportunities for employment in privatizing SOEs—to start their own businesses.

All four countries faced the challenge of creating nationwide programs of training for management development and business education in colleges and universities. Completing the transition to a market economy would depend, in part, on creating a more vigorous business sector, which, in turn, would depend on establishing broad-scale, comprehensive, and sustained programs of business management and market economics training throughout the educational system. Among the areas in which training and education were most urgently needed were (1) privatization and market economy operations; (2) management functions; (3) management tools, including total quality management, project management, information technology management, and management information systems; and (4) human resources management and development.[82]

In sum, the willingness and ability of foreign and domestic investors to participate in privatization and private enterprise development in Central Europe will depend, in the future, not only on the success of macroeconomic policy reforms but also on the ability of each of the Central European countries to establish effective market institutions and to develop their human resources. The success of their macroeconomic reforms depends, in turn, on privatizing the large SOEs that now dominate the manufacturing sectors; on attracting investment by multinational corporations that have the technology, managerial know-how, and market networks that will be essential to making privatized companies more productive and efficient; on improving the efficiency of SOEs that cannot be quickly privatized; and on developing a critical mass of small- and medium-scale enterprises that can generate employment and income. Institutions will be needed for providing small-scale enterprises and privatizing SOEs with management and technical assistance; the educational systems will have to be reoriented to provide a better and more pervasive understanding of how market economies and democratic systems operate; and the capacity will have to be developed within institutions of higher education to produce the next generation of entrepreneurs, democratic political leaders, and managers of market-oriented enterprises.

NOTES

1. Organization for Economic Cooperation and Development, *Reforming the Economies of Central and Eastern Europe* (Paris: OECD, 1992).

2. Gerald A. McDermott and Michal Mejstrik, "The Role of Small Firms in Industrial Development and Transformation in Czechoslovakia" (Prague: Charles University Center for Economic Research and Graduate Education, Working Paper, 1991).

3. OECD, *Reforming the Economies*, p. 20.

4. The most concise statement of the case is found in International Finance Corporation, *Small Scale Privatization in Russia: The Nizhny Novgorod Model— Guiding Principles* (Washington, D.C.: IFC, 1992).

5. Gregory T. Jedrzejczak and Henryk Sterniczuk, "Privatization in Poland —1991," in Marko Simoneti and Andreja Bohm, eds., *Privatization in Central and Eastern Europe 1991* (Ljubljana, Slovenia: Central and Eastern European Privatization Network, 1992), pp. 45–60; quote at p. 45.

6. Center for International Private Enterprise and the Futures Group, "Poland Case Study," *Economic Reform Today* 1, no. 1 (1991), pp. 9–15.

7. Reported in Slovoj Czesany, "Stabilizing Aspects of the Economic Reforms and the Macroeconomic Developments in Hungary, Poland, the USSR and Czechoslovakia," in S. P. Prasad and R. B. Peterson, eds., *Advances in International Comparative Management* vol. 7 (Greenwich, CT: JAI Press Inc., 1992), pp. 157–168.

8. Jedrzejczak and Sterniczuk, "Privatization in Poland—1991," pp. 45–60.

9. Ibid.

10. See Vaclav Klaus, "A Perspective on Economic Transition in Czechoslovakia and Eastern Europe," in S. Fischer, D. deTray, and S. Shah, eds., *Proceedings of the World Bank Annual Conference on Development Economics 1990* (Washington, D.C.: World Bank, 1990), pp. 13–18; quote at p. 13.

11. "New Law Allows Foreign Branches, Sets Rules for New Banks, Subsidiaries," *BNA's Eastern Europe Reporter* 2, no. 5 (March 2, 1992), pp. 164–166.

12. "Accounting: New Law Adopts EC Standards," *BNA's Eastern Europe Reporter* 2, no. 1 (January 6, 1992), p. 10.

13. Klaus, "A Perspective on Economic Transition," pp. 13–18.

14. See Ullrich R. W. Thumm, "World Bank Adjustment Lending in Central and Eastern Europe," in V. Corbo, F. Coricelli, and J. Bossak, eds., *Reforming Central and Eastern European Economies* (Washington, D.C.: World Bank, 1991), pp. 43–58.

15. See "New Law Will Allow Cooperatives to Become Private Enterprises," *BNA's Eastern Europe Reporter* 2, no. 2 (January 20, 1992), p. 46.

16. See Thumm, "World Bank Adjustment Lending," pp. 53–54.

17. Ljubomir Madzar, "Privatization in Yugoslavia 1991: Programs, Obstacles and Results," in Simoneti and Bohm, *Privatization in Central and Eastern Europe 1991*, pp. 105–119.

18. Uroš Korže and Marko Simoneti, "Privatization in Yugoslavia" (Ljubljana, Yugoslavia: World Bank and United Nations Development Programme, paper prepared for delivery at the Conference on Privatization in Eastern Europe, November 1990).

19. For a summary of restitution laws, see Michael S. Fischer, "New Laws in Eastern Europe Set Terms for Restitution," *Business International* 38, no. 31 (August 5, 1991), pp. 261–262, 268.

20. Eva Klacova and Charles Jelinek-Francis, "Privatization in Czechoslovakia—1991: Legislative Requirements and Their Results," in Simoneti and Bohm, *Privatization in Central and Eastern Europe 1991*, p. 65.

21. See "Bids to Reclaim Property Increasing: Total Bill Could Reach $23 Billion," *BNA's Eastern Europe Reporter* 1, no. 3 (November 25, 1991), p. 113.

22. IFC, *The Nizhny Novgorod Model*, pp. 5–6.

23. Lajos Csepi, Gustav Bager, and Erzsebet Lukacs, "Privatization in Hungary—1991," in Simoneti and Bohm, *Privatization in Central and Eastern Europe 1991*, pp. 70–84.

24. Uroš Korže, "Decentralized Privatization Strategy: Pitfalls and Benefits—Slovenia," in Simoneti and Bohm, *Privatization in Central and Eastern Europe 1991*, pp. 140–153.

25. Deli Math-Cohn, "First Wave of Large Scale Czechoslovak Privatization," *Business Eastern Europe* 20, nos. 30–91 (July 29, 1991), pp. 233–234.

26. Jari Kobylka, "Privatization Process Slows in Czechoslovakia," *Business Eastern Europe* 20, nos. 47–91 (November 25, 1991), pp. 421–422.

27. See Jari Kobylka, "Polish Mass Privatization Could Be Disappointing," *Business Eastern Europe* 20, nos. 33–91 (August 19, 1991), p. 259.

28. "Officials Look to Private Sector to Pull Country Out of Recession," *BNA's Eastern Europe Reporter* 2, no.1 (January 6, 1992), pp. 29–30.

29. Michal Mejstrik and James Burger, "Privatization in Practice: Czechoslovakia's Experience" (Prague: Charles University Center for Economic Research and Graduate Education, 1991), especially pp. 18–20.

30. Jiri Havel and Eugen Kukla, "Privatization and Investment Funds in Czechoslovakia," *RFE/RL Research Report* 1, no. 17 (April 1992), pp. 37–41.

31. See Djorjija Petkoski, "Conference Report," in Simoneti and Bohm, *Privatization in Central and Eastern Europe 1991*, pp. 23–42.

32. See Csepi, Bager, and Lukacs, "Privatization in Hungary—1991," pp. 70–84.

33. Mario Muti, "Privatization of Socialist Economies: General Issues and the Polish Case," in Hans Blommestein and Michael Marrese, eds., *Transformation of Planned Economies* (Paris: OECD, 1991), pp. 51–63.

34. Roman Frydman and Adrzej Rapaczynski, "Markets and Institutions in Large Scale Privatization: An Approach to Economic and Social Transformation in Eastern Europe," in Corbo, Coricelli, and Bossak, *Reforming Central and Eastern European Economies*, pp. 253–274.

35. "Poland," *BNA's Eastern Europe Reporter* 1, no. 1 (October 28, 1991), pp. 37–38.

36. Nicholas Denton, "From Infancy to Mid-Life Crisis," *Financial Times* (July 3, 1992, Special Supplement), p. 4.

37. See Frydman and Rapaczynski, "Markets and Institutions in Large-Scale Privatization," p. 258.

38. Christopher Bobinski, "Poland: Much Lost Time Has to Be Made Up," *Financial Times* (July 3, 1992, Special Supplement), p. 4.

39. "Government Reports Accelerated Privatization Process in 1992," *BNA's Eastern Europe Reporter* 2, no. 7 (March 30, 1992), p. 243.

40. "New Privatization Program Launched to Break Up 'Hollow' Parent Companies," *BNA's Eastern Europe Reporter* 2, no. 8 (April 13, 1992), pp. 286–287.

41. Gail E. Schares, "Czechoslovakia: Reluctant Reform," *Business Week* (April 15, 1991, Special Report), p. 55.

42. "Sell-Off of State Companies Proceeding Slowly, Data Show," *BNA's Eastern Europe Reporter* 1, no. 1 (October 28, 1991), p. 13.

43. Quoted in Sharon Nuskey, "Eastern Europe's Private Affair," *Across the Board* (October 1992), p. 58.

44. Reported by Sharon L. Wolchik, "Czechoslovakia's Velvet Revolution," *Current History* 89, no. 551 (December 1990), pp. 413–416, and 435–436.

45. George Essaides, "Prospects for Profits: Czechoslovakia through 1993," *Business International* (February 25, 1991), pp. 68–69.

46. See Jan Vanous, "Recent Czechoslovak Economic Performance," *PlanEcon Report* 7, nos. 40–41 (November 8, 1991), pp. 1–44.

47. Kamil Janacek, "Survey of Major Trends in 1991," *RFE/RL Research Report* 1, no. 12 (March 20, 1992), pp. 31–32.

48. Milan Ruzicka, "Czechoslovakia Hopes to Be Energy Crossroads," *Journal of Commerce* (March 26, 1991), p. 8B.

49. Czesany, "Stabilizing Aspects."

50. Ben Slay, "Roundtable on the Hungarian Economy," *RFE/RL Research Report* 1, no. 29 (July 17, 1992), pp. 44–52.

51. Bela Papp and Joseph Hollos, "Hungary: Ansaldo Salvages Bankrupt Ganz Electric," *Business Eastern Europe* 20, nos. 33–91 (August 19, 1991), p. 260.

52. Penn and Shoen Associates Inc., *Democracy, Economic Reform and Western Assistance in Czechoslovakia, Hungary and Poland: A Comparative Public Opinion Survey* (New York: Freedom House and the American Jewish Committee, 1991).

53. Leslie Colitt, "Czech Parliament Told of Gloomy Economic Picture," *Financial Times* (March 28, 1991), p. 4.

54. Jedrzejczak and Sterniczuk, "Privatization in Poland—1991," p. 47.

55. Byron Brown, "Transforming Postcommunist Labor Markets: The Polish Case," *RFE/RL Research Report* 1, no. 32 (August 14, 1992), pp. 50–56.

56. Jiri Pehe, "Czechoslovakia: The Agenda for 1991," *Report on Eastern Europe* 2, no. 3 (January 18, 1991), pp. 11–16.

57. Leslie Colitt and Anthony Robinson, "Heavy Going Slows the Pace of Race to Reform Czechoslovakia's Economy," *Financial Times* (March 26, 1991), p. 2.

58. "Government Trying to Save Troubled Ursus Tractor Plant," *BNA's Eastern Europe Reporter* 1, no. 1 (October 28, 1991), pp. 13–14.

59. John D. Sullivan, "Barriers to Private Sector Growth: Prospects for Enterprise Development," *Economic Reform Today* (Fall 1991), pp. 23–24.

60. Jiri Pehe, "Building a State Based on the Rule of Law," *Report on Eastern Europe* 2, no. 9 (March 1, 1991), pp. 7–11.

61. Jari Kobylka, "The Hard Realities of Doing Business in the CSFR," *Business Eastern Europe* 21, nos. 32–92 (August 10, 1992), pp. 385–386.

62. Juliane Langenecker and Bela Papp, "EE Human Resources: East-West Perspectives," *Business Eastern Europe* 21, nos. 32–92 (August 10, 1992), pp. 387–388.

63. Russell Johnson, "Hungary: New Investment Frontier," *Business America* 112, no. 2 (October 7, 1991), pp. 2–7.

64. Lucy Ward, "The Long Road to Restitution," *Prognosis* (April 1991), p. 12.

65. See, for example, the problems of Addidas, "Addidas in Hungary: A Long-Term Commitment Beats Fancy Footwork," *Business International* 38, no. 32 (August 12, 1991), p. 271.

66. Dennis A. Rondinelli, "Developing Private Enterprise in the Czech and Slovak Federal Republic: The Challenge of Economic Reform," *Columbia Journal of World Business* 26, no. 3 (1991), pp. 27–36.

67. See "East European Statistics: Looking for Clues," *Economist* (August 10, 1991), pp. 58–59.

68. F. Angela Flaes, "GM in Hungary: Expanding the EE Production Base," *Business Eastern Europe* 20, nos. 27–91 (July 8, 1991), pp. 211–212.

69. "East European Statistics: Looking for Clues," p. 59.

70. Peter Martin, "The 1991 Budget: Hard Times Ahead," *Report on Eastern Europe* 2, no. 9 (March 1, 1991), pp. 12–16.

71. Keith Crane, "Property Rights Reform: Hungarian Country Study," in Blommestein and Marrese, *Transformation of Planned Economies*, pp. 69–94.

72. See "$3.5 Billion of Foreign Capital Seen in First Phase of Czech Privatization," *BNA's Eastern Europe Reporter* 2, no. 8 (April 13, 1992), pp. 280–281.

73. See "Government Reports Accelerated Privatization Process in 1992."

74. "Private Sector Grew Sharply in 1991 Despite Recession Government Says," *BNA's Eastern Europe Reporter* 2, no. 7 (March 30, 1992), p. 243.

75. Bobinski, "Poland: Much Lost Time."

76. See the Introduction in Simoneti and Bohm, *Privatization in Central and Eastern Europe 1991*, pp. 15–22.

77. "Nation Seen Facing More Hurdles, Making Additional Progress in 1992," *BNA's Eastern Europe Reporter* 2, no. 2 (January 20, 1992), pp. 46–48.

78. United Nations, *World Investment Report 1992*, ST/CTC/130 (New York: United Nations, 1992).

79. See Dennis A. Rondinelli, Jerry VanSant, and Scott Daugherty, "Management and Technical Assistance Needs of Small Businesses in Czechoslovakia" (Washington, D.C.: Central European Small Business Enterprise Development Commission, 1991), especially pp. 15–18.

80. Ibid., pp. 37–40.

81. Zdenko Pirek, "Czechoslovakia's Needs in Training in Market Economics and in Business Management" (Washington, D.C.: White House Conference on "Economics in Transition: Management Training and Market Economics Education in Central and Eastern Europe," paper prepared for delivery, February 26–27, 1991).

82. Ibid., pp. 3–4.

2

Experiences with Privatization in Hungary: The Early Transition Period

Kálmán Mizsei, Maria Móra, and Gyorgy Csaki

The decline and fall of the Communist regime in 1989 changed the economic philosophy of Hungary. Privatization became the centerpiece for the economic thinking of the new political elite. However, Hungary's experience with privatization had already begun nearly a decade before when economic reform policies diluted the socialist principles of state ownership of property and transformed the economy from a centrally planned socialist system to a quasi-market system. Therefore, Hungary's privatization differs in many ways from that of other Central European countries.

This study examines Hungarian economic reforms during the socialist period, assesses the privatization policies adopted after the fall of the Communist regime in 1989 by exploring Hungarian privatization during the early period of transition to a market-oriented economy from 1989 to mid-1992, and identifies the lessons of that experience for Hungary and other former socialist societies that are presently in transition to a market system.

ECONOMIC REFORMS DURING THE SOCIALIST PERIOD

In order to understand the economic reforms that took place in Hungary after the demise of the Communist regime, it is vital to distinguish between the two issues that influenced socialist thinking: nationalization and monopoly. The Stalinist economic order emphasized state ownership of property (i.e., the nationalization of productive assets) and the simultaneous formation of monopolies. But *monopoly* meant something different in Central European socialist countries than it does in Western market economies. Socialist doctrine emphasized the absolute concentration of economic activities and their control by government agents. This was the case not only in foreign trade and banking but also in production. For example, there was one State Brewery Company in which 15 breweries were horizontally centralized into one legal entity as well as a single State Tobacco Company where the different plants (which produced different brands of cigarettes) were centralized into one state-owned enterprise (SOE). This organizational structure reflected a Marxist dogma that the stronger the monopolistic structure of industry, the higher the level of socialization.

Nationalization took place in Hungary in the first few years after World War II, but the evolution of the monopolistic socialist structures took longer. The largest industrial reorganization campaign occurred in the early 1960s when Hungarian industries were organized through the merging of several factories into large enterprises. The damaging effects were numerous. As enterprises were concentrated, they absorbed smaller units; and these huge state monopolies became less flexible in their market reactions. The most serious problem, however, was that they exerted damaging political influence on macroeconomic policy and grew more politically powerful than enterprises in other European market economies.

Although the "real" privatization began only in 1988 and 1989, the move from total state ownership to private ownership had already begun in the mid-1960s with the adoption of reform-minded and pragmatic economic policies that allowed some forms of private enterprise. These reforms included market activities that created a relatively strong entrepreneurial climate in Hungary during the 1970s and 1980s. After 1968, for example, workers on state farms and in agricultural cooperatives were allowed to use their household plots for private economic activities. During the 1970s tenants were allowed to buy their state-owned apartments at 15 to 30 percent of their market value; employees on large collective farms bid at auction for subcontracts on work; and in the cities, auctions were used to distribute leases for restaurants and retail shops during the 1970s and 1980s. Furthermore, as a result of reforms in the 1980s, foreign investors could participate as minority partners in joint ventures (JVs). In 1982, Hungary became the first Communist country to start issuing securities as a result of joining the International Monetary Fund (IMF) and the World Bank. At that time, the pragmatic Hungarian political and economic leadership issued corporate bonds as the first step toward establishing capital markets.

But Hungary's 1968 reforms and subsequent economic policies sought to create market mechanisms without changing the underlying structure of property ownership. The primary aim of these reforms was to establish and strengthen "socialist commodity production": that is, to introduce a relatively flexible price system, to give some independence to companies, to create a more motivating wage system, and to introduce elements of a market-based banking system. However, all of these changes were introduced without changing the property structure and therefore had only limited effects. Also, the system of socialist commodity production only controlled manufacturing and trade, but capital goods. In effect, decentralization reforms strengthened the power of enterprise managers by dividing all property rights between state authorities and the enterprises.

However, sustained economic difficulties and the lack of structural flexibility (which would have been so helpful after the oil price shock of 1973 and the world economic crisis from 1974 to 1976) convinced the government that a change in the structure of ownership was necessary. During the early 1980s, economic work teams (EWTs) in SOEs allowed entrepreneurs to establish small profit centers. These teams, freed from many bureaucratic restrictions normally applied to enterprises, were able to engage in after-hours work for competitively determined wages. In 1985 an amendment to the Act on State Enterprises transferred the ownership rights of about 75 percent of the SOEs to enterprise councils.[1]

But this 1984 legislation (*vállalati gazdasági munkaközösség*, or *VGMK* to Hungarians), which had established EWTs, complicated the legal underpinnings of the economy even though the original aim had been to decentralize decision making and to strengthen company operations. In order to secure these aims, boards of directors and supervisory boards were established in large SOEs to provide the enterprises with greater independence. These boards consisted of representatives of the state (the supervising ministry) and management, trade union employees, banking agents, and some independent experts. It was hoped that direct control and interference of the ministries in the routine operations of companies would end.

It would be an oversimplification to condemn, as some analysts have, these partial decentralization reforms. Comparative analyses of Hungary and other Eastern European nations show that the partial Hungarian reforms brought significant improvements in microeconomic performance and laid the groundwork for current privatization policies. Despite these changes, however, the economic crisis deepened during the late 1980s. Structural rigidities remained; economic growth slowed down; and the economy entered a period of serious stagflation. The budgetary deficit worsened; foreign indebtedness increased; and as a result, the role of the Central and Eastern European socialist countries in the world economy declined. This economic decline pushed the Communist political hierarchy from power and opened the way for all-out reform in 1989.

EVOLUTION OF HUNGARIAN PRIVATIZATION POLICY

Despite different ideological roots and convictions, all economic reformers supported some kind of privatization after the fall of the Communist regime in 1989. They differed, however, on how to manage the transition. The alternatives considered in Hungary were similar to those considered in Czechoslovakia, Poland, and Yugoslavia. During the early transitional period between 1989 and mid-1992, Hungarians debated the following options for privatization:

1.   Expansion of small private businesses to the extent that they would dominate the economy and thus limit foreign acquisition of Hungarian assets;

2.   Auctioning productive assets to buyers who offered the highest price—the so-called "British way";

3.   Allotting shares to employees of the enterprise through employee share option plans (ESOPs);

4.   Allotting shares to the general population through a voucher system;

5.   Management buyouts in which those with some entrepreneurial skill could become owners of the same firms that they had managed under state ownership; and

6.   The creation of state holding companies, insurance companies, and nonprofit organizations as institutional purchasers of company shares.

To understand the reform policies adopted in Hungary, however, it is necessary to understand the antecedents to full-scale privatization that had evolved from the economic policies of the 1980s and how they had fundamentally changed the concept of state ownership of property.

Antecedents to Privatization

The Hungarian privatization that started in 1988 and accelerated in 1989 was called (somewhat misleadingly) "spontaneous privatization" because it was proposed, promoted, and carried out by the managers of SOEs. However, the primary aim of these managers was to save their own jobs. In several cases they invited former foreign trade partners to establish a JV. A typical case was the one established by a major foreign supplier and the Hungarian distributor or retailer to satisfy domestic demand. From this point of view, spontaneous privatization simply meant privatization that was not proposed by the state or by government authorities.

The privatization process was an outgrowth of 20 years of reform experience. Inefficient investments, accumulated state budget deficits, and ill-advised monetary policy produced weak macroeconomic conditions that were reflected in the weak financial position of the enterprises. Even before appropriate legislation was adopted, some large firms had tried to solve their financial problems by separating their "healthy" assets from their liabilities and by forming multilevel corporate structures. Some reformers supported this approach. They also went one step further than in 1968 and tried to divide the state and the business sectors. This was the focus of the reformers during the 1980s, and the 1988 Act on Business Organization (popularly known as the Company Law) became their instrument.

In addition to these internal structural changes, the economic reforms of the 1980s emphasized foreign participation. Direct foreign investment of more than $300 million in 1989 totaled more than that of all the previous years. Capital inflow remained below government expectations, although it exceeded direct foreign investment in other East European economies. But it was difficult to refine regulations without further experience with the behavior of foreign investors in the Hungarian market.

The structure of Hungarian ownership was changed not only through foreign participation but also through corporate transformation of state enterprises and small entrepreneurial units. The growth of small handicrafts and retail trade was robust, as was the increase in employment in those enterprises. From 1987 to 1989, the number of limited-liability companies (LLCs) increased from 137 to 4,500; and there were more than 300 shareholder companies by the end of 1989. No major change occurred in the number of state enterprises. The majority of the new companies were established outside the authority of the Transformation Act. This bill regulated the transformation of SOEs into joint-stock companies (JSCs) owned entirely by the State Property Agency (SPA)—the agency charged with selling the assets of SOEs. In 1989 only 6 state firms were transformed in accordance with this bill. The process speeded up in early 1990; and by May 1992, there were more than 60,000 economic units and almost 12,000 JVs operating in Hungary.

However, the extent of the transformation during the socialist period was exaggerated. Rough estimates indicate that less than 1.5 percent of industry moved into foreign hands. As of 1989 about 11 percent of state assets were transformed into corporate structures. There was no comprehensive analysis of the behavior of firms after denationalization, but sporadic data suggested that the bureaucracy in former SOEs was reduced quite sharply.

Changes in the Structure and Ownership of SOEs

Reforms during the late 1980s allowed enterprises to transform themselves into business associations, business organizations, or autonomously managed enterprises.

Transformation of SOEs into Business Associations. At the time of organizational changes in 1987 and 1988, the need to reduce state ownership was not even mentioned. Only the form of state ownership was changed by creating shares. From 1987, legislation permitted the formation of JSCs and LLCs as domestic legal entities, whereas, previously, Hungarian enterprises had only been allowed to form unlimited partnerships and subsidiaries. As a result, large enterprises (generally those operating several plants) made substantial organizational changes. The first reorganization, which served as a model for similar subsequent efforts, was undertaken by MEDICOR, a medical instruments manufacturer that had been a respected enterprise in Hungary but had accumulated enormous debts by 1987. Many other large enterprises followed suit in 1988; and under reorganization initiated from company headquarters, enterprises mostly transformed their factories and plants into JSCs while they organized such central functions as computer services and trade into LLCs.

In these new business associations, the trading companies that distributed their products and even the bank that kept their accounts were often included as partners. The majority of stock in the newly formed associations was held by the company headquarters, which retained the traditional SOE form. The changes were typically accompanied by staff reductions and changes in central functions, and the headquarters primarily served as holding companies. There were cases when the new associations formed from the same original enterprise held shares in one another (cross-shareholding).

This model was justified on the grounds that separating management and ownership functions would lead to more efficient forms of state control. In practice, however, enterprise managers were guided by more tangible self-interests. The MEDICOR model offered a good compromise in which the efforts of productive units to become independent were neutralized, and the headquarters also retained partial control. The changes allowed the enterprise's assets to be revalued in favorable terms and its debt to be reduced through debt-equity swaps. As the associations developed their own business relations, their borrowing increased and so did the possibility of attracting capital investments. This model was often used to avert the threat of bankruptcy. Reorganization was also motivated by the profits that tax preferences made available to new associations for a three-year period in 1988 (although abolished in 1989) and by the fear of expected stricter conditions. Enterprise managers were familiar with the draft of the Company and Transformation Laws, and those managers who thought they could not comply with the proposals therein advanced their efforts to reorganize.

Reorganization of enterprise units into business associations continued in accordance with the provisions of the new Company Law, which, in January 1989, introduced business organizations similar to those in market economies. The new regulation permitted the formation of business associations with foreign investors as well as Hungarian residents. Foreign investments in JVs were encouraged by generous tax relief. The Bill on Foreign Investments that was implemented in January 1989 provided a 20 percent corporate tax allowance for companies of any size using foreign capital in excess of 5 million forints. The tax allowance could even reach 100 percent if the equity capital was actually beyond 25 million forints and foreign participation was at least 60 percent. Resident shareholders in such associations were typically company managers (rarely employees), and SOEs established their associations behind closed doors and made no particular effort to attract the private savings available in Hungary.

After the new Company Law was introduced, the number of enterprises forming business associations increased. Their motivations became more diverse, and the ways of forming such business associations became more varied. However, due to weak liquidity and near bankruptcy, enterprises often resorted to solutions that, in fact, circumvented legal provisions. The major problem for the founders was to find the financial resources to pay for up to 30 percent of the stock in cash. Several methods were used to overcome the problem. For example, a company could be formed with small initial capital (provided only by the founders) that was to be followed shortly by capital increases. Some entrepreneurs only put up part of the assets required for operation (i.e., materials or machinery as their contributions in kind) and sold or leased all other necessary assets to the company. As a result of the general scarcity of funds, some enterprises were unable to transform all of their units into business associations at the same time. Frequently, the first to be transformed was the unit in which they immediately expected foreign capital investments.

The difficulty in obtaining cash encouraged the undervaluation of in-kind contributions. Setting low nominal values increased the probability of a debt-equity swap and presented less strict dividend requirements. Using undervalued state assets as in-kind contributions favored private foreign or local capital investments since it allowed shareholding arrangements that were different from those that would be possible if in-kind contributions were fully valued. Unrealistic valuation of assets led to the privatization of only a small fraction of state property.

Striking examples of suspected manipulation of state property were noted in the trading and catering industries. Real estate values at favorable locations were underassessed; thus, the founding partners acquired substantial wealth without open competition. The transformation of trading and catering enterprises into business associations was accelerated in the second half of 1989 when the plans for selling shops to private owners were made public.

Despite some progress, privatization elicited a public outcry; for there were suspicions that members of the old regime tried to appropriate state assets at bargain rates. Fixing the value of assets was difficult due to the lack of established capital markets and the shortcomings of the enterprise accounting system. But there was also tension from moral and efficiency considerations. Some SOE managers had entrepreneurial skills and knowledge that were in short supply, and to prevent them from having access to enterprises could have slowed down the privatization process. A political purge would certainly have punished those responsible for previous mistakes, but it would also have created an atmosphere of suspicion that might damage the national economy. On the other hand, allowing corruption would also do much harm. In response to public dissatisfaction with spontaneous privatization and in order to establish clear political goals, the new political regime created the SPA in March 1990. A large portion of state-owned property was transferred to the SPA, which was given responsibility for managing and privatizing these assets. The SPA's top priority was to reverse the lack of competitiveness and openness that characterized spontaneous privatization and to hasten the progress of privatization.[2]

Transformation of SOEs into Business Organizations. The process of forming business associations left public ownership of SOEs unaffected even though some or all of their assets were transferred to the business associations. In most cases this was a reasonable alternative to continuing operation as an SOE. However, in some cases the entire SOE needed to be transformed into a business association. The Transformation Law of 1989 distinguished between self-governed SOEs and those under central administrative supervision. The law required 20 percent (or 100 million forints) outside capital for the transformation of self-governed SOEs. Thus, only 20 percent of the shares of the state were transferred to the organization in charge of managing the state property. The remaining 80 percent could be retained and sold by the transformed company for three years. SOEs under central administrative supervision were not subject to the requirement of bringing in outside capital, and the entire stock was transferred to the SPA. In addition, the law gave two years to self-governed SOEs that had more than 50 percent of their assets as shares in business associations to transform into business associations.

Initially, the Transformation Law had little influence on events. In fact, it was enforced only on a few occasions before the SPA was set up in 1990 and only in 14 cases by the end of 1990. (The total stock of the companies transformed under that law was about 44 billion forints.) Most enterprises chose to avoid the Transformation Law because they generally enjoyed more favorable conditions and greater flexibility under the Company Law of 1988. Self-governed enterprises were often unable to meet the requirement of 20 percent outside capital, and greater control plus the requirement that they transfer part of their stock to the state were additional deterrents.

The provisions of the Transformation Law were applied when government agencies initiated privatization by selling enterprises to foreign investors. Those who "voluntarily" opted for transformation were typically small- and medium-sized enterprises. They could not divide their organizations in an economically viable manner because such divisions would create unmanageable tension and result in the loss of their central functions.

Enterprises that opted for full transformation were not in immediate danger of bankruptcy. Rather, they were influenced by the fear that as SOEs they would lose ground in a few years. Most were able to attract the outside capital necessary for transformation and to have their assets valued realistically. (In the 14 cases approved by the SPA, the assets were transferred to the transformed companies at an average of 48 percent premium over book value.) Because they were not in an emergency situation, some of the transforming enterprises had a choice of potential partners; they sought partners who would not only contribute cash but also bring in marketable products, open new markets, or transfer technology.

In the summer of 1990, the Transformation Law was unfavorably changed for companies that had already been formed. Amendments dropped the requirement that self-governed enterprises raise 20 percent outside capital. Also, the transfer of shares to the SPA was difficult for foreign shareholders to understand, for they had to make their decisions as owners jointly with the SPA. Obviously, the SPA was not the most appropriate partner for making fast, operative, business-wise decisions. To fend off such a situation, foreign investors considering investment in currently transforming enterprises tried to acquire majority control.

In addition, the future of "empty shell" enterprises grew more uncertain. Enterprises were considered empty shells if they had transferred their production assets to business associations, if they were not involved in production, and if their function was simply to manage the property they held. Their validity as holding companies was highly questionable since they did not have to comply with any efficiency criteria and could freely use up available resources. It became important for the managers of these enterprises to take an active part in (and preferably manage) their privatization. For them, the most favorable solutions were ones in which they could select their partners and determine the rules by which they would operate. Provisions of the Transformation Law now offered the most appropriate path for enterprises that found potential partners and required no decentralization.

In terms of the national economy, the Transformation Law offered the obvious advantage that proceeds from the privatization of SOEs flowed through the SPA to the government budget and could then be used to reduce public debt. However, statistics suggest that these transformations only created the conditions for privatization and rarely resulted in the sale of state property.

Transformation of SOEs into Autonomously Managed Companies. In the late 1980s autonomously managed enterprises effectively thwarted the attempts of their productive units to split off from headquarters. Those units wishing to become independent could only do so by becoming a subsidiary or a business association as part of a rehabilitation plan initiated by the government. In 1989 this was changed by Parliament. Enterprise units wishing to become independent could then apply to the founding ministry for approval in cases when the enterprise council (i.e., the decision-making body) rejected their claims. By the end of 1990, more than 30 manufacturing units had applied for independence. Most of the applicants were units of SOEs that had suffered serious market losses or had experienced financial difficulties. In general, SOE units with relatively good market prospects sought independence because they could more likely avert bankruptcy if they remained within the enterprise.

The process of becoming independent was smoothest when it complied with headquarter plans or at least did not jeopardize the survival of the remaining parts of the enterprise. On the other hand, resistance to independence was greatest when headquarters feared that the separation of one unit would set a precedent for others and thus would result in fragmentation of the entire enterprise. Resistance was equally strong when the separation of a financially healthy unit resulted in the bankruptcy of the remaining parts of the enterprise. The ministry approved the applications for separation and issued the document of incorporation for a new company only after it was satisfied that both the independent unit and the remaining parts of the enterprise would be viable.

PRIVATIZATION POLICY DURING THE TRANSITION TO A MARKET ECONOMY

The new Parliament elected in May 1990 pursued privatization and economic reform under favorable political conditions. All six parties advocated the development of a market economy based on private ownership, and that consensus offered an excellent opportunity to craft a sound compromise on privatization policy.

However, the need for social consensus was, in fact, obviated because agreement existed between the two largest parties—one controlling the government and the other forming the opposition—and because legislation relating to ownership was not tied to a qualified majority (two-thirds) vote. In the Hungarian Parliament, government parties had a majority of 58 percent. Thus, they only needed the support of opposition parties for laws requiring a qualified majority. Consequently, the government was given a free hand to implement its privatization proposals.

The government program that was announced in the summer of 1990 promised a rapid reduction in state ownership by privatizing the majority of state property within three to five years. It linked privatization to the reduction of private debts (SOEs to be privatized in the short term were thought to be worth 1,800 billion forints, while public debt accounted for 1,300 billion forints). Economic entities could only acquire state property by buying assets on the market and by assuming the related liabilities. Local governments and the social security program also shared in state property. The government program precluded restitution of nationalized property to previous owners but promised partial compensation.

The government sought the rapid sale of tens of thousands of retail and catering units through small-scale privatization or "preprivatization" and specified three possible ways of doing so. First, special emphasis was given to centrally initiated privatization in which the SPA would periodically identify enterprises to be privatized and select the method and the most appropriate form for managing the process. Second, privatization initiated by enterprise managers could also continue under the supervision of the SPA. Finally, resident and foreign subjects and companies could submit applications to acquire state assets.

In addition, the privatization laws sought to create the necessary financial conditions. The government promised to support the acquisition of state property by bond issues, preferential loans, and tax preferences.

Both the privatization legislation and the government actions pursuant to it indicated that the government preferred the more strictly controlled and centralized methods of privatization. This centralized process clearly slowed down the privatization initiatives of many enterprises; and by mid-1992, privatization managed by the SPA (i.e., the sale of retail units, and the First and Second Privatization programs) was still only at an initial stage. Obviously, it took longer than expected to develop the conditions for privatization loans, but the government's schedule seemed to have been unrealistic.

Since privatization of a totally nationalized economy was unprecedented, there was little opportunity to evaluate the viability of different privatization techniques or combinations of them. But an Organization for Economic Cooperation and Development (OECD; 1991) survey of the initial Hungarian experience came to two major conclusions. First, reasonable demands by creditors, former owners, those who endured environmental harm, and other claimants exceeded the market value of privatized assets; so openness was critical in convincing society of the equity of the privatization process. Second, if Hungarian society was the primary claimant to residual proceeds of the privatization process and if it risked receiving very little or assumed the responsibility for paying compensation to other claimants, then citizens had a right to a social dividend, perhaps in the form of vouchers. But Hungarian authorities decided instead to use residual proceeds to bolster the social safety net. Moreover, any compensation for the general public took place via subsidies to custodians of state assets. For instance, employees were able to buy shares in their companies at a discount, and homeowners could purchase their rental units below market prices. However, potential Hungarian investors were poor in comparison with foreign investors. Thus, Hungarian authorities slowly adopted two policies: Hungarians were encouraged to take part in the privatization process via access to preferential loans that required a small personal contribution; and foreign ownership was restricted to a few well-defined areas of the economy.[3]

In order to ensure efficiency, Hungarian authorities invited foreign experts (well-known international consulting and auditing firms) and organized competitive bidding. Sometimes these proceedings were open to any potential competitors, but in most cases, only selected competitors from a circle of strategic partners were actually invited for a closed bidding.[4]

The actual transfer of state property to private ownership (i.e., privatization in a strict sense) was rather rare in the First Privatization Program (FPP); but there were examples, such as the sale of Tungsram and the Ganz-Vehicle Factory to foreign investors and the public offering of IBUSZ shares. IBUSZ, the largest Hungarian tourism agency, was the very first Hungarian JSC traded on the Budapest Stock Exchange (and at the same time, on the Vienna Stock Exchange).

Tungsram, perhaps the most successful Hungarian company, was an internationally reputed light and vacuum enterprise that produced technical equipment. General Electric (GE) bought 50 percent plus one vote for about $150 million in November 1989 and, at the same time, took an option on another 25 percent. GE bought that 25 percent in mid-1991 for $44 million and thus executed the largest foreign investment in Hungary to date. Ganz-Vehicles, another highly respected manufacturing enterprise in Hungary, was totally taken over by the British Hunslet. Hunslet hoped to sell electric trains to the state-owned Hungarian Railway Company (MÅV) and to modernize the British Rails. Neither aim reached immediate fruition, however, and Ganz Hunslet faced serious liquidity problems beginning in mid-1991.

The major trends in privatization up to that point (i.e., SOEs forming business associations, transforming into business associations, or becoming independent) showed that separation of enterprise units from government control was clearly a favorable course; that solvent buyers were a necessary ingredient for success; and that employee participation, especially in the case of a smaller enterprise, was preferable. In general, the transformation of an entire SOE into a business association was favorable because it was clear to potential buyers with whom they should negotiate; and a corporate or limited-liability organization simplified the technical implementation of a partial sale. However, if the SOE was not decentralized before transformation, it would be more difficult for the buyer to acquire the unit.

It was more doubtful how business associations formed by SOEs could be privatized. These transformations were the source of several embarrassing questions: Who should be the controlling shareholder? Should the holding company or the SPA decide on the sale? Who was entitled to the proceeds of privatization?

ISSUES IN THE IMPLEMENTATION OF PRIVATIZATION

Paradoxically, the pace of privatization slowed measurably because the desired schedule of privatization in Hungary was hotly debated without any social consensus on the basic issue of ownership. An agreement on the objective of privatization and the desired pattern of ownership and corporate structure should have been a precondition for implementing the program. But even though it was an urgent task for the government to pursue such an agreement, essential decisions could only be made on the basis of extensive social debate over such issues as how compensation should be made to previous owners, how employees or citizens could acquire state assets, how property should be allocated to the social security system or local governments, what limits should be set on the acquisition of property by foreign investors, whether or not potential owners should be supported by preferential loans, the extent to which and the cases in which state property should be contributed to new ventures, and the permissible scope of direct state ownership and cross-shareholding among SOEs. The newly elected democratic Parliament, however, preferred to deal with other, mainly political and ideological questions. Therefore, before such basic issues could be settled, privatization inevitably benefited foreign investors, enterprise managers (and occasionally employees), and SOEs.

In addition to those unresolved issues, there were several other major obstacles to rapid privatization: its centralized nature, the absence of the necessary financial conditions, and the large amount of property in state ownership. A substantial part of state property was not attractive to private investors because of its composition, physical state, and excessively concentrated structure. In addition, there were important social groups that were not interested in privatizing state property because it jeopardized their favorable positions.

Other factors that slowed down the process of privatization were the scarcity of private savings, even though various groups of individuals were given vouchers for state assets, and the lack of entrepreneurs who were able to manage property. A real danger was that the need for rapid privatization would transform it from a tool for developing a healthier economy to a goal in itself.

Alternative Processes and Techniques of Privatization

The government followed a process of privatization that depended primarily on centralized control and monitoring but that also allowed other forms. Centrally led privatization was supplemented by investor-led privatization, self-privatization, small-scale privatization, and joint ventures with foreign investors.

Centrally Led Privatization Programs. The SPA, the major actor of the centrally led privatization programs, was established by Law VII of 1990 to help guide and direct the privatization of SOEs; and on September 14, 1990, it announced its FPP that included 20 SOEs (see table 2.1). The SPA was a government agency acting as an administrative body and headed by an 11-member board of directors, 7 of whom were government officials and 4 of whom were independent experts. The president as well as the members of the board were appointed by the prime minister and had a mandate for five years. The operations of the SPA were overseen by its government-appointed managing director. The authority, tasks, and duties as well as the general framework of the SPA's activities were outlined in a series of laws enacted in 1990.

The SPA exercised the state's ownership rights and performed the following tasks and duties: (1) examined the intentions of SOEs for self-initiated transformation; (2) established and sold corporations (business organizations); (3) controlled the transformation and privatization programs determined by the government's privatization strategy; (4) managed SOEs and the companies taken into state administration; (5) controlled the evaluation of the state's assets that

Table 2.1
Major Foreign Companies with Investment in Hungary in 1991

Company	Country of Origin	Industry
1. General Motors	USA	Automobile
2. Royal Dutch/Shell	UK-Netherlands	Petrol
3. Exxon	USA	Petrol
4. Ford Motor	USA	Automobile
5. IBM	USA	Computer
6. Toyota Motor	Japan	Automobile
7. British Petroleum	UK	Petrol
8. Mobil	USA	Petrol
9. General Electric	USA	Electronics
10. Daimler-Benz	Germany	Automobile
11. Fiat	Italy	Automobile
12. Samsung	Korea	Electronics
13. Philip Morris	USA	Food
14. Matsushita Electric Ind.	Japan	Electronics
15. ENI	Italy	Petrol
16. Unilever	UK-Netherlands	Food
17. E.I. Du Pont de Nemours	USA	Chemistry
18. Siemens	Germany	Electronics
19. Nestlé	Suisse	Food
20. Renault	France	Automobile

Source: Népszabadság: February 1, 1992, p. 19.

were to be privatized; and (6) performed other tasks delegated to the SPA by the Privatization Law.

The SPA used different privatization methods for different types of SOEs.

1. *Public offerings* were used to broaden equity ownership and to stimulate the newly formed capital markets. They created profitable investment opportunities, increased the number of investors, and promoted the establishment of financial institutions. Public offerings were best used for the privatization of profitable and well-known companies and could be used exclusively for those medium-sized and large enterprises that were successfully managed and that could be expected to be profitable in the long run even without major changes in management or operations. Public offerings were the only feasible way to

privatize some large SOEs that were not appropriate to sell to another company—especially because of anticompetitive effects.

2. *Private placement* meant that shares were offered to a fairly limited circle of investors (e.g., the issuing bank's institutional clients). It was the preferred method in Hungary and encouraged institutional or individual foreign investors who were likely to play a significant role in the privatization process because the demand for shares at the Budapest Stock Exchange was fairly limited. Therefore, private placement was at least the second-best option if there was no need for a major management change in a company, if it was too small to be listed on the stock exchange, or if there were insufficient demands for its shares on the stock exchange. Also, under this arrangement, enterprises could be privatized quickly, even before the growth of capital markets.

3. A *trade sale* was the best solution if the enterprise's market, financial position, or management was not satisfactory; if it was unlikely to be listed on the stock exchange in the near future; or if the privatization by sale to an enterprise in the same or connected line of business had management, commercial, or technological advantages. Tenders were generally inevitable; but in some cases, it was reasonable to sell additional shares to a preferential partner (e.g., to an outside owner with ownership or to a JV partner or to a licensed partner).

4. A *management or employee buyout* competed with other types of share buying if it exceeded 15 percent of the equities (e.g., managers and employees could form a consortium that submitted an offer for buying a limited part of an enterprise). In case of both public offering and private placement, management or employees were only permitted a maximum of 15 percent of the shares under preferential terms in order to prevent potential managers or employees from gaining an unjustifiably favorable position.[5]

In addition to these four methods of privatization, there were several other more gradual and expensive ones: contracting out the management of an enterprise, selling the assets of an enterprise to a company, leasing state property to a private group or individual, and project financing on credit.

Privatization that began with the so-called spontaneous privatization was followed by the centrally directed "large privatization program." Initial expectations were high. Interest in the prime assets was strong: About 15 bids each were made for 20 of the best companies, and companies such as Hungar-Hotels and Richter Gedeon attracted more than 25 bids each. Only two international banks won bids. Nomura obtained the mandate to privatize both Richter Gedeon Pharmaceutical Works (with a book value of 12.4 billion forints) and HungarHotels Hotel and Catering Co. (with a book value of 11 billion forints); and Credit Commercial de France won the mandate to privatize both Hungexpo (with a book value of 1.6 billion forints) and KNER Printing House (with a book value of 1.5 billion forints).[6]

Early experiences led the SPA to gradually give up the centralized privatization programs, however, because they worked too slowly. The first program was a great disappointment, and none of the 20 companies involved were completely privatized a year later.[7] When the SPA realized that the overcentralization of privatization led to disappointing results, it introduced several other methods while simultaneously engaging in other centralized privatization programs.

In December 1990 the SPA launched the Second Privatization Program (SPP) in order to privatize the "empty shell" companies. Between 1987 and 1990 more than 100 SOEs transformed their plants and assets into business organizations, business associations, JSCs, or LLCs. Under these arrangements the SOE became a trust company that leased or sold its affiliates or plants to private entrepreneurs. But the book value of the assets of the trust company was generally lower than that of its former affiliates. This was the "fast and easy way out" for the large SOEs to transform themselves under spontaneous privatization. The first phase of the SPP included 8 engineering and 4 textile companies with a total book value of 14.2 billion forints. In early 1991 the second phase of the SPP was also launched for the same type of companies but in different industries—including 11 companies with a total book value of 24.6 billion forints.

There was a third group of SOEs that potentially could have been privatized due to their spontaneous transformation into business associations between 1987 and 1990. The 41 companies, registered with the SPA as "potentially privatizeable companies," had a total book value of 22.9 billion forints.[8]

Investor-Led Privatization. In order to accelerate privatization in early 1991, the SPA allowed investors to make an offer for a SOE or to buy shares in an association (or the assets of such an organization). This process, known as investor-led privatization, was open to both Hungarian and foreign investors and was based upon effective regulations and legal rules related to business organizations; therefore, there was no need for separate regulations.

Since only one method could be used to privatize any SOE, it was impossible to provide an offer under the investor-led privatization scheme for those economic entities whose public tender had already been announced by the SPA or in cases of spontaneous privatization in which the SPA had already decided on the desirable method.

The SPA accepted offers for buying any SOE, any interest in a SOE, or shares in a SOE with the following exceptions: (1) SOEs under Law LXXIV of 1990 on the privatization of the retail trade and services; (2) companies involved in the privatization programs of the SPA; (3) companies whose transformation into business associations had been determined earlier; (4) public utilities; (5) financial institutions; or (6) companies dominating more than 40 percent of the domestic market in the given company's main field of activity.

The steps involved in investor-led privatization were as follows: The would-be investor made its intention known to the SPA, which registered the acceptance of the written intention as well as the conditions of acceptance. The SPA appointed a consulting firm that was paid a onetime commission to participate in the transaction. The SPA was obliged to agree on conditions of privatizations with the ministry(ies) and municipality(ies) concerned as well as with the company itself. If the company was self-governed and did not agree with the investor-initiated privatization, the board of directors of the SPA, in accordance with the Asset Policy Guidelines, could take control of the company. The company had to prepare an information booklet as well as the required financial statements, and that took approximately 30 to 90 days.

In order to create competition, the SPA could publicly ask for counteroffers within 30 days through newspaper advertisements or direct contact; and the company had to cooperate by arranging meetings with all the potential bidders. The SPA assessed the offers by comparing them to the asset evaluation prepared during the tendering procedure. After announcing the winner, the SPA transformed the company into a business association, signed a contract with the winner, and made the necessary proposals for the registration of the new business.

There was a special type of investor-led privatization: The employees or management could initiate a buyout of a majority stake in the company. The SPA generally supported employees' attempts to obtain property by selling shares that initially allowed them to obtain a minority stake, but an employee or management buyout had to conform with the general rules of investor-led privatization. There were, however, some major differences. First, during tendering, the SPA and the appointed consultant could seek counteroffers from other potential investors. Second, the SPA could determine whether or not the financial background of the employees or management group making the offer was really sound and check the bank guarantees and loan conditions. Finally, an asset evaluation of the company could be prepared especially for the SPA.

The employees could take advantage of privileges granted by the Asset Policy Guidelines, which were approved by the Parliament annually. In addition, both the employees and the management could obtain the necessary financial resources from the Existence-Credit Facility (a special credit program that was modeled on the postwar German credit policy for promoting private share buying and for launching new ventures) and the special credit program of the National Bank of Hungary (NBH).

The SPA could stipulate as a special condition for the registration of the offer that it cover an amount higher than 10 percent of the asset value of the SOE and a minimum 50 million forints. Employee and management buyouts did not face such limitations.

Self-Privatization. Self-privatization was an important form of decentralized privatization. In fact, self-privatization was an obvious continuation of the former spontaneous privatization, although it really took place under SPA control. This process, however, became the most characteristic form of privatization during the early 1990s. The most successful privatizations were initiated by foreign investors or the managers of SOEs, and the process was initiated by the business organization itself. If an enterprise was operating as an SOE, it first had to be transformed into a business organization whose shares were entirely owned by the state before it could be privatized.

Between September 1991 and March 1992, 347 medium-sized SOEs took part in the self-privatization program. The SPA authorized 84 foreign, joint, and domestic consulting firms to "replace the SPA," that is, to operate and simultaneously supervise the privatization of an SOE. About 30 other companies officially expressed their willingness to take part in the self-privatization program. As many as 66 out of the 84 authorized consulting firms agreed with at least one company about the conditions of privatization.

The major feature of self-privatization was the freedom to choose a consulting firm. SOEs seemed more willing to discuss privatization with another company than with the SPA and were more confident that the consulting firm would agree to a managers' buyout or an ESOP. Because the consulting firms were paid directly by the SPA, the quicker and more effective the privatization, the higher the fee they received.

By March 1992, self-privatization was well on its way: 347 companies had reached agreements with consulting firms; 54 were being transformed into business organizations; 26 were registered; and 10 were fully privatized. The SPA received 1 billion forints from this form of privatization.[9]

However, to the great surprise of the public, the second phase of the self-privatization program, which was declared in March 1992 to begin in mid-April 1992, was almost immediately postponed. This decision was justified by the argument that self-privatization—that is, the cooperation of a SOE and an independent consulting firm—led to the undervaluation of companies. It was evident that the lower the price, the easier and quicker it was to privatize. Under this arrangement, lowering the price allowed the company to be privatized at the earliest possible date, allowed the consulting firm to get its consultation fees quickly, and allowed the SPA to obtain the revenues expeditiously. Nevertheless, the state received a somewhat lower price than expected. The argument, however, discounted certain facts: The lower income was at least better than nothing at all, and many companies either were close to bankruptcy or were merely surviving by consuming assets.

Small-Scale or Preprivatization. Some degree of small-scale privatization began in Hungary as early as 1982 when a large number of small shops were rented to employees and the larger retail and restaurant chains began to run their smaller units under contract. The real estate as well as the equipment and machinery remained in state ownership, but the shopkeepers rented them and managed them on a contract for five to ten years.

Thus, after the fall of the Communist regime, privatization seemed to be easier and faster in the retail trade, restaurant, and personal-services industries. The SPA formulated a special plan and guidelines for the privatization of these industries under the title "preprivatization." Large retail, service, and catering companies (chains) were classified by the SPA as "potentially privatizeable in the short run"—of these 10,000 shops more than one-third were food and beverage trading enterprises, nearly one-quarter produced industrial goods, and the remaining were service enterprises. With great surprise and dissatisfaction, however, the SPA realized that only 40 percent of these 10,000 shops could really be privatized because many were operating on a contractual or rental basis. Only 30 percent were operating in real estate owned by the company. Therefore, the SPA had to privatize these shops gradually: 2,570 were scheduled for privatization in 1991; 1,096 in 1992; and 1,130 between 1993 and 1995.[10]

The number of potentially privatizeable shops was also diminished because the law on preprivatization exempted the so-called trade and service chains from the shop-by-shop privatization process in order to keep the chains together—a decision that was later criticized by those who noted that the chains were established in the first place by nationalizing and combining smaller companies. According to the SPA, 5,074 shops were to be privatized and as many as 2,570 might be privatized in 1991. But in the first half of 1991, there were only 503 auctions, of which only 172 were successful; and there were only about 1,000 successful auctions the entire year. The average auction price was 124 percent of the valuation; although in two-thirds of the cases, not the shop itself but only the possibility of renting it was actually auctioned. In this type of privatization, the SPA accepted the law of supply and demand: The initial prices were generally 20 to 30 percent lower than the capital valuation of the official auditing companies.

Thus, three major problems arose in preprivatization (not taking into account its slow pace): the untouched "pseudo-chains," the frequent auctioning only of the rental rights ("concession"), and insufficient credit. The amount of approved and effectively borrowed credit was fairly low because commercial banks required 200 to 250 credit guarantees (mainly mortgages).[11] As of November 1991 there were only 622 approved credits in the amount of 1.3 billion forints—about half were for ownership rights and half for rental rights. Less than half of the credits went to employees and individuals, and the rest, to entrepreneurs; and while 328 were for private ventures, 294 were for business associations.[12]

There was also a political preoccupation with offering ownership opportunities to as many former commercial and service employees as possible. In March 1992 the two types of credit were unified under the Existence-Credit Facility. According to new regulations, this E-credit could be used for all kinds of privatization; and the maximum amount of E-credits was equal to the state debt, which was diminished by privatization. E-credit could be used by individuals and by such legal entities as business organizations, cooperatives, and ESOP groups. There was no upper limit (at least in forints—the real upper limit was double the statutory capital), and the interest rate was 60 percent of the NBH basic rate plus 4 percent banking fees—17.2 percent in April 1992. E-credit could be used to buy shares under the general rules of the Law on Financial Institutions. The most heavily debated point of the E-credits was the bank guarantee: Banks required 200 to 250 percent guarantees.[13] Banks had a major responsibility to the E-Credit Facility; for it was up to the banks to decide on the feasibility of the project and business prospects as well as the possibilities for repayment and the necessary guarantees. Sixteen banks participated in providing E-credit; for it was not simply the profitability that attracted banks (it was no better than the average) but the possibilities for acquiring new clients.

The Finance Ministry intended to propose a new institutional credit-guarantee scheme and hoped to have the Law on Unified Privatization Promoting Credit Guarantee Scheme become valid in 1992.[14] This would help consolidate the credit system and the facilities. But as of mid-1992, there was little sign of success. Without easier credit conditions and lower auction prices, there was little chance of speeding up the pace of privatization; and with softer lending and lower prices, badly needed budget earnings would decrease.

Joint Ventures. By mid-1992 it became clear that the major obstacle to faster privatization was the lack of domestic demand. Although the amount of private savings in Hungary was enough to purchase as much as 15 to 20 percent of all state assets, private investors had other preferences. Credit facilities were not attractive enough for domestic investors, but foreigners were willing to invest in Hungary because of low production costs as well as the opportunity to enlarge their markets. Thus, foreign capital dominated the privatization process.

Of the total 40.1 billion forints received by the government in 1991 as the result of privatization, 32.5 billion forints came from purchases in hard currency; only 5.2 billion forints came from purchases in forints. Less than 1.4 billion forints resulted from purchases with credit.[15] This meant that more than 80 percent of all privatization earnings in 1991 actually came from foreign investors. The same was true in the first two months of 1992. Of the 14.2 billion forints the state received from privatization, 11.3 billion forints came from hard-currency purchases.[16] Hungary attracted more than half of the total working-capital inflow to Central Europe ($2.8 billion of $5 billion) and about $812 million in direct privatization income in hard currency.

The number of JVs increased substantially after 1990. In 1972 there were only about 250, and 1,000 new ones were established in 1989. But in 1990 and 1991 more than 9,000 new JVs, representing a capital inflow of more than $1.4 billion, were created.[17] By the end of 1991, every fifth business in Hungary was a JV; and the share of foreign equity was about 8 percent of the total corporate capital and 40 percent of the JVs. Most of the JVs were small: Half of them had no more than the legal minimum of 1 million forints investment, less than 8 percent of them had statutory capital between 10 and 100 million forints, and only 2.4 percent of them had greater than 100 million forints as statutory capital (at the exchange rate of $1 = 70 forints in 1992). Fifty-four percent of the JVs operated in domestic and foreign trade, 19 percent in industry, and 14 percent in services. JVs were especially active in export: The average export earnings were 23.3 percent of the total turnover, whereas the average earnings for Hungarian companies were no more than 14.2 percent.[18] The listing in table 2.1 of the 20 largest foreign investments indicates the importance of JVs in the Hungarian economy. More than half of the direct foreign investments were concentrated in and around Budapest; and their major motivation was, of course, the expectation of profit. But profits were not to be earned exclusively on the domestic market; the former socialist countries could be easily reached from a Hungarian base of operations.

Direct foreign investments through newly established JVs remained the major tool for privatization and the main engine of economic development. But this overwhelming role of foreign capital was hotly debated in Hungary, and there was stronger pressure to promote Hungarian ventures to avoid foreign domination of the national economy. On the other hand, neutrality, that is, treating domestic and foreign investors in the same way, was a precondition for creating a liberal economic policy.

The previous government realized that in order to promote direct foreign investment and increase the number of JVs a modern and internationally competitive legal and regulatory framework was necessary. Both the Bill on Business Organizations and the Bill on Foreign Investments in Hungary, approved in 1988 and put into effect in January 1989, intended to fulfill this aim. These laws were accompanied both by a Cabinet decree that allowed foreigners to buy real estate and by several regulatory decisions concerning the exchange mechanism.

Beyond these general rules, Hungary concluded mutual investment-protection agreements with Austria, Belgium, Cyprus, Denmark, Finland, France, Germany, Greece, Italy, the Republic of Korea, Spain, Sweden, Switzerland, the United Kingdom, and Uruguay. Hungary joined the Multilateral Investment Guarantee Agency (MIGA), and Overseas Private Investment Corporation (OPIC) guarantees were extended to Hungary in 1989.[19] The establishment of the legal framework for foreign investments was so successful that Hungary became a tax haven.

Officials of the Ministry for International Economic Relations declared that although foreign investment activity became very active between 1989 and 1991, the share of foreign capital in the Hungarian national economy was no more than 3 to 4 percent (while the international average was about 20 percent). It would have been more effective to promote the improvement and growth of strategically important economic activities rather than capital investment. Therefore, changes were proposed to channel direct foreign capital into fields with the greatest need for new technologies and marketing skills as well as the improvement of management.

Because tax reductions had been limited to ten years, bureaucratic obstacles to establishing a JV or even a fully owned foreign company would end; and only a simple registration process would then be needed. Customs allowances were offered only if the imported equipment or machinery served productive purposes and were not sold in less than three years. Furthermore, the government no longer allowed any special advantages for any particular foreign or joint company.[20]

It was inevitable that JVs would grow in number and importance; they were a potentially advantageous way of developing the economies of Central European countries. Establishing JVs as a major form of importing direct foreign investment successfully decreased foreign debt; improved technologies in host economies; imported badly needed managerial, organizational, and marketing skills; and provided access to the world market. The current political situation and economic reasoning were also favorable for importing working capital to establish large numbers of JVs. But some economists raised questions about whether or not extraordinarily generous tax holidays had been given to foreign investors and whether or not some sectors should be given priority for direct foreign investment.[21]

LESSONS OF EXPERIENCE FROM HUNGARY

Despite criticisms of its slow pace and complex procedures, privatization in Hungary was occurring by the end of 1991, when as many as 216 SOEs (worth 342 billion forints in book value and 459 billion forints in effective value) were privatized. Another 307 large-scale enterprises and 373 small-scale firms were in the process of being privatized. As many as 2,120 shops with a total book value of 3.6 billion forints had been returned to private management under the preprivatization process. The SPA received 40 billion forints cash income in both forints and hard currency. Foreign investors purchased and capitalized state enterprises in the amount of more than $770 million, which accounted for roughly 60 percent of the total direct foreign investments in Hungary.[22]

Privatization remained high on the government's policy agenda during the early 1990s. The transformation of a command economy, in which 95 percent of the companies were owned by the state, into a market-oriented economy, in which 70 to 80 percent of activities were in private ownership, remained the long-term goal of Hungarian policies.[23]   By mid-1992 and despite many difficulties, contradictions, and obstacles, 10 to 12 percent of Hungarian state assets had already been privatized. "Although the next few years will be difficult ones for Hungary," Dr. Lajos Csepi pointed out, "I believe that we now have the infrastructure in place to allow both domestic and foreign investors to invest in Hungary to the benefit of both the Hungarians and foreign companies. The SPA will continue to play a key role in supervising the privatization process and in overseeing all aspects of the transformation of Hungary into a modern market economy."[24]   In another interview Csepi stressed: "Much of the process will be driven by foreign investment in the first phase. The longer-term privatization process, which will be driven principally by the Hungarian owners and managers, will last until the end of the decade. The Hungarians have a very entrepreneurial character and in spite of the difficulties, people want to get the money together to start up business."[25] This emphasis on the spontaneous regeneration of the economy by individual effort was a hopeful sign in a country that still faced enormous economic problems.

Although the government intended not to give preference to foreign investors over domestic ones, nevertheless, JVs were given a preferential position because foreign equity participation implied much more than just capital inflow. It held the promise of obtaining new technology, market access for the more sophisticated export goods, and access to global networks—all of which were essential to the transformation and further development of the Hungarian economy. By mid-1992 there were almost 12,000 JVs in Hungary, and about 60 percent of all JVs operating in Central and Eastern Europe were actually registered in Hungary. This brought nearly $3 billion in direct foreign capital investments to Hungary. The selling of state assets to domestic buyers and foreign investors was combined: In several cases, foreign buyers acquired a majority stake in a Hungarian SOE, and managers or employees bought a minority stake. The foreign equity owner was generally the former foreign trade partner of the SOE whose management and staff were well known to the investors.

Hungary's success in attracting foreign investors was due to several factors: As early as 1988 the legal framework for JVs had already been established; the necessary financial services (i.e., commercial banking, insurance, auditing, and consulting) existed; a stock exchange was operating; and Hungarian managers were eager to take part in the establishment of JVs.

Slow Pace of Privatization

These signs of success do not imply that Hungary's privatization process was flawless or that serious problems were all resolved. Transformation of an almost totally nationalized and state-run command economy into a modern market economy was obviously a difficult and unprecedented task. But privatization policy emerged step-by-step and case-by-case, for it was obvious that privatization was essential for economic transformation.

Privatization was, of course, an internal economic affair. It was up to the government and the financial institutions to establish the necessary preconditions for rapid and effective privatization. Nevertheless, it was obvious that without major international assistance the transformation of the former socialist command economies into market economies could not be realized. International assistance for Hungary was required to end the recession and help stimulate the Hungarian economy to provide favorable conditions for investment; to open foreign markets for both industry and agriculture, for the traditional exportable goods, and for the products of the new JVs and foreign-owned companies; to generate direct foreign investments in order to modernize the Hungarian economy as well as to speed up privatization; to provide technical assistance in order to promote the development of managerial skills and to improve organizational capacities; and to implement modern, marketlike managerial practices. But even if all of these goals were achieved, privatization would take longer in Hungary than was initially expected.

By the middle of 1992, the major debates on privatization were focused on its slow pace as well as the prices for which companies were sold, the choice of foreign buyers, and the potential foreign dominance among buyers (80 percent of the assets had been sold to foreigners, and 90 to 95 percent of the current privatization earnings came from foreign buyers). Debates continued about decentralized privatization. Spontaneous privatization was severely criticized because it preserved the economic power of former political leaders and state enterprise managers through ownership of privatized companies. Parliamentary opposition parties criticized the government because the new management was not professional enough and because assets were given to supporters of the current government. Criticism of foreign investment in the Hungarian privatization process diminished somewhat, but the lack of credits and subsidies for domestic buyers remained a problem.

An economic climate hostile to privatization remained. Hungarian economic policy focused on monetary restrictions since 1979; Hungarian agriculture and manufacturing industries faced crucial market problems; the management of Hungary's $21 billion foreign debt hampered foreign trade; and high inflation pushed interest rates up to 40 percent. Political conditions were not entirely advantageous either. The new, democratically elected Parliament and most of the political parties paid little attention to the need to integrate the Hungarian economy into the world economy and instead debated issues like compensation and such historical symbols as the national coat of arms. Important economic legislation (e.g., the Law on Concessions, the Law on Financial Institutions, and the Law on the Central Bank) was approved only after long delays; and other important proposals (e.g., the Law on Telecommunication, the Law on the Mass Media, and the Law on Public Finances) had not yet been taken up by mid-1992. The possibility for foreigners to buy real estate remained limited; therefore, more extensive foreign investment was hampered. Decentralized privatization was stopped, later restarted, stopped once more, and restarted again under somewhat different conditions. The privatization of the major commercial banks was postponed several times. These delays reflected the uncertainties and the irresolution of the government about some major strategic issues of overall economic development.

Foreign dominance of privatization remained since there were no effective domestic demands and since crucial budgetary constraints (the 150 billion forints forecasted as the 1992 budgetary deficit compared with the 70 billion forints agreed to with the IMF in December 1991) limited major, new credit facilities. Decentralized privatization could not be accelerated with "hidden domestic savings." Without further export prospects, easier market access in the West, and the successful reopening of the former socialist markets, the short-term prospects for the Hungarian economy were not too bright. Therefore, while criticisms were motivated by the common desire to promote privatization and to speed up the process, many groups in Hungary were not content and argued that

1. Decentralized privatization had to proceed under easier and less compli-cated methods and with the involvement of more consulting-auditing firms and fewer government bureaucracies;
2. The government and the SPA needed to give priority to rapidly privatiz-ing medium-sized SOEs;
3. Investor-led privatization had to be simplified, and domestic buyers had to be supported by new and enlarged credit facilities;
4. Ownership of real estate had to be clarified among the state and local governments as well as former private owners in order to make privatiza-tion easier and faster;
5. Manager buyouts had to be promoted, especially in such services as foreign and domestic trade;
6. ESOP-type privatization (the decisive method for smaller enterprises in which the overall production and marketing process could be overseen by the employees, and "communitylike" management was acceptable) had to play an important supplementary role;
7. A clear industrial policy was necessary to guide privatization; sectoral and regional development policies would have to specify which sectors and industries would remain in state ownership and which would be privatized;
8. Direct foreign investment should remain decisive in foreign buyouts and in the establishment of JVs; and
9. Bureaucracy must be limited, and there must be better cooperation among state agencies, ministries, and banks.

In Hungary, as in other Central and Eastern European countries, the unprecedented task of transforming a centrally planned economy into a market economy had to be realized in a politically uncertain climate by inexperienced state and local administrations and by inexperienced entrepreneurs. The weaknesses of the privatization process in Hungary were easily understood; nevertheless, faster privatization was essential. Obstacles to and mismanagement of the privatization process had to be carefully examined and the weaknesses overcome. Many Hungarians believed that "at the end of the day" the entrepreneurial spirit would prevail, but many other Hungarians wondered how many years it would take to see "the end of the day!"

NOTES

1. Organization for Economic Cooperation and Development, *Economic Surveys: Hungary 1991* (Paris: OECD, 1991), p. 110.

2. Ibid., pp. 10–111.

3. Ibid., pp. 107–108.

4. Ibid., p. 109.

5. For a detailed description of the State Property Agency's activity, see State Property Agency, "Information on the Privatization of State-Owned Enterprises 1990" (Budapest: SPA, Information Office, 1990), pp. 3–5.

6. "Privatization Get Tough with Tenders," *Euromoney* (March 1991), p. 46.

7. Nicholas Denton, "Privatization: Race against Time," *Financial Times* (October 30, 1991), p. vii.

8. György Matolcsy, "Years of Our Reconvalescence: The Hungarian Privatization: Trends, Facts, and Experiences of Privatization" (Budapest, 1991), p. 212.

9. Reported in *Népszabadság* (April 17, 1992), p. 11.

10. See Matolcsy, "Years of Our Reconvalescence," p. 207.

11. Adrienne Kurcz, "Egisztencia-hitel: Alapvetô a banki részvétel" [E-credit facility: banking participation is a basic issue], *Figyelö* (April 2, 1992), p. 11.

12. Reported in *Heti Világgazdaság* (November 16, 1991), p. 80.

13. See Kurcz, "E-Credit Facility."

14. "Egységes hitelgarancia-intézmény várható a privatizáció támogatására" [A unified deposit guarantee-institution is to be established in order to promote privatization], *Magyar Hirlap* (April 9, 1992), p. 10.

15. Reported in *Népszabadság* (January 25, 1992), p. 8.

16. Reported in *Népszabadság* (April 17, 1992), p. 11.

17. Reported in *Heti Világgazdaság* (February 22, 1992), p. 9.

18. András Kovács, "A vegyesvállalatok fele a kereskedelemben mûkddik" [Half of joint ventures are operating in trade], *Magyar Hirlap* (January 31, 1992), p. 10.

19. Mihály Simai, "Foreign Direct Investments in the Hungarian Economy—1990" (Budapest: Institute for World Economics of the Hungarian Academy of Sciences, Manuscript, 1990), p. 33.

20. Although Suzuki, the Japanese carmaker, obtained a special (full) tax reduction in late 1991, a quantitative limit on car imports was introduced in January 1992 to protect the Suzuki assembly plant as well as the General Motors engine and assembly plant that began production in April 1992.

21. András Inotai, "Foreign Direct Investments in Reforming CMEA Countries: Facts, Lessons and Perspectives," in Michael W. Klein and Paul J. J. Welfens, eds. *Multinationals in the New Europe and Global Trade* (Berlin-Heidelberg: Springer Verlag, 1992).

22. "Privatizációs tények" [Facts about privatization], *Figyelö* (January 16, 1992), p. 39.

23. Béla Csikós-Nagy, "Privatization in a Post-Communist Society—The Case of Hungary," *Hungarian Business Herald* 4 (1991), p. 37.

24. "Hungary: In the Vanguard of Reform," *Euromoney* (March 1991, Supplement), p. 48.

25. Quoted in Gary Humphrey's "Privatisers Get Back on Track," *Euromoney* (March 1991), p. 48.

3

Privatization of the Alföld Group Ltd.[*]

Erzsébet Poszmik

The private enterprise analyzed in the following case study emerged in the early 1980s and was privatized in the early 1990s as Hungary was undergoing the transition from a socialist to a market-oriented economy. The Alföld Group (AGL) operates as a holding company in which both the parent company and the firms owned and directed by it are organized as limited-liability companies (LLCs). The companies include a development and trade firm fully owned by the AGL and two manufacturing companies that operate as joint ventures (JVs). In one JV an Austrian firm owns 30 percent, and the AGL retains 70 percent; and in the other, a different Austrian company owns 39 percent, a Czech company holds 10 percent, and the AGL retains 51 percent.

The primary activities of the AGL are the development and production of hardware and software for small engineering and electronic equipment; but as a minor activity, it also engages in trade and services for customers of the equipment. Its product mix includes special electronic and mechanical devices used in financial institutions: stamping machines; coin and money counters; accounting machines; electronic measuring, regulating, and steering devices; special computer peripheries; and extension cards for IBM-compatible personal computers (PCs). It also produces software in various programming languages.

The AGL's headquarters are located in a small town on the Hungarian plains, and the company also has a plant in northern Hungary. In 1991 the AGL had about 200 employees, and most of them were graduate engineers working in technology development. In the same year the total annual turnover was about 450 million forints, which included about 90 million forints in pretax profit. By Hungarian standards, the AGL can be described as a medium-sized company; but

---

[*]The name of this company was changed to ensure confidentiality.

before the massive privatization of state-owned enterprises (SOEs) during the early 1990s, it would have been considered a fairly large private company. Characteristically, since the early 1980s, most new major ventures in Hungary have been begun by engineers who were part of the most mobile social stratum and were employed in large SOEs where they were not allowed to use their personal abilities or capacities to the fullest extent.

THE EVOLUTION OF AGL'S ORGANIZATIONAL STRUCTURE

The Alföld Group was established by four mechanical engineers while they were working at a state-owned mechanical engineering company in a small town in the Alföld region, the lowlands in middle Hungary. After working hours, they turned their attention to developing machines commissioned by the Postal Experimental Institute as part of an in-company economic work team (IEWT). Their task was to design and make a prototype of a small stamp-vending machine for use in post offices. This work began and was successfully concluded in 1982. In January 1984 the four engineers quit the SOE and established a private economic work team (EWT). Before describing what subsequently occurred, it would be helpful to briefly explain the organizational structure of IEWTs and EWTs in which the founding owners of the AGL operated.

Structure of IEWTs and EWTs

The IEWTs and EWTs were small government-regulated enterprises that the Hungarian government authorized in 1982 to provide incentives for the emergence of a market economy. The analysis of the activities and effects of these small enterprises is not the subject of this study, and all that will be given here is a sketchy outline of these organizations in order to provide a context for the emergence of the AGL.

EWTs were the most widely used form of private entrepreneurial activity in Hungary during the first half of the 1980s. These enterprises were not legal entities but could be established by at least 2, and at most 30, individuals who used them as a source of primary or supplemental income. The EWTs could engage in any activities, except commerce, that were not prohibited by law for private individuals. Members of the team were obliged to contribute financially and to participate actively in the work team, and their liability for the enterprise extended to all of their private property.

In 1982 there were 2,341 active EWTs, and by 1985, there were 9,312 (statistics indicating their rapid proliferation). The activities of the EWTs made a great contribution toward inspiring genuine entrepreneurial activities and toward strengthening entrepreneurial thinking when Hungary began to shift from a socialist to a market-oriented economy several years later. The ratio of young people and intellectual professionals involved in EWTs to those involved in other small-enterprise structures was high. The EWTs provided opportunities for many people who had not previously had a means of applying their ideas and capitalizing on their entrepreneurial propensities. In the early 1980s the creation of EWTs in Hungary represented a significant step forward despite the fact that only very small-scaled units could operate for any length of time within the severe restrictions placed on their ability to accept new members, accumulate capital, or attract additional funds.

The IEWT was a special kind of economic working team and could be organized exclusively by employees or retired workers of any SOE or budget-maintained institution. While a modest financial contribution was expected from members, basically, the IEWT members united to work together. Any kind of service or productive activity could be pursued either for the host company in which members worked or for outside customers. The equipment of the SOE could be used if members of the IEWT made use of it after regular working hours. The financial liability of members extended only to the amount of their capital input, and the amount of their annual income from the IEWT. Any liabilities in excess of this remained the responsibility of the host institutions.

The number of IEWTs increased from 2,775 in 1982 to 21,490 in 1986. By 1985, 80 percent of SOEs had such working teams. Most IEWTs supplied their host companies; only a handful entered the outside market even though they had the right to do so. Favorable regulations made the IEWTs attractive because they could take on additional work and pay their members a better return than could be earned through overtime work. But for this reason, many people did not regard them as true enterprises.

With the adoption of the Company Act (officially, the 1988 Act on Business Organizations), which was implemented in January 1989, the importance of both EWTs and IEWTs dramatically declined in the Hungarian economy because the new law offered a wider range of options through which entrepreneurs could establish companies.

The Genesis of the AGL

The engineers who founded the AGL had begun working in an IEWT. They were not working for their host company, as the majority of IEWTs were, but for the outside market. Having successfully completed the commission of the Postal Experimental Institute, they only received a little less than 20 percent of the proceeds that the institute paid to the host company—a share that they found unacceptable. In 1984 they decided to quit the SOE and establish an independent EWT, which was the forerunner of the AGL. They established the EWT with a capital contribution of 10,000 forints each, a small amount that involved very little financial risk. What was notable was that they resigned their positions as state employees to earn their livelihood in the private sector—an action that at that time in Hungary still required some courage. The decision to enter the private sector and establish a firm was basically motivated by their circumstances. In a relatively less industrialized small town, this was practically the only way for innovative and enterprising educated people with engineering training to engage in creative activities, to see the results of their efforts, and to gain a reasonable income from successful research and development work. This motivation was reinforced by the fact that the company that had formerly employed the engineers was liquidated in 1984, the first such case in Hungary in 35 years.

The now-independent EWT continued its development work for the Postal Experimental Institute. At first its members devised a tabletop date-stamping machine of which ten prototypes were made. When these proved successful, the engineers obtained a production license; and from the money they received for developing the stamping machine, they expanded production capacity. From this point the incipient private enterprise started to grow.

Early Restrictions and Roadblocks

Any enterprise attempting to establish itself in Hungary in 1984, however, faced quite a few stumbling blocks and difficulties despite the economic reform rhetoric that was so popular at the time. Even the well-intentioned reforms promulgated by the central government created serious restrictions on the operations and growth of these private enterprises. The Alföld EWT was also beset by the difficulties arising from the deteriorating economic conditions in Hungary and from the economic policies that were enacted to deal with them; it experienced more than its share of problems.

First, it faced delays in establishing itself as a private EWT (e.g., it had to register with the Company Court as well as obtain the permission of the local council). All of this took a long time because these government organizations lacked experience in these matters and used ineffective bureaucratic methods. EWT members were also required to produce "certificates of good character," and this process was another source of delay. The excessive regulations on the EWT's operations caused further difficulties. EWTs did not qualify as legal entities, and the complex and gap-ridden Hungarian regulatory system allowed officials to treat them sometimes as businesses and at other times as private citizens. As a result, the rights of EWTs became the subject of endless litigation. Provisions of the law were interpreted differently by members of the civil service who possessed very little relevant expertise at that time.

Obstacles to growth also arose from restrictions on membership to a maximum of 30 and from limits on the number of employees to half the number of members. In addition, a burdensome employment tax made it difficult to hire workers. Another obstacle to growth was the rule that only after-tax profits could be retained as capital within the company. Furthermore, the year-in and year-out tax increases in the early and mid-1980s and the frequent changes in business regulations adversely affected the EWTs. Not infrequently, regulations were introduced in a haphazard fashion and, in some instances, were enforced retroactively. Increasing international indebtedness and Hungary's resulting debt service added to the burdens on the economy and on private businesses as well. The progressively worsening economic situation and the increasing problems of state ownership undermined central government policies that were meant to provide incentives for creating new enterprises and to strengthen existing ones.

Growth and Development of the AGL

The Postal Experimental Institute continued to provide a market for the equipment produced by the Alföld EWT, which, in addition to producing mechanical machines, had begun to develop and manufacture electronic ones. This shift in its product mix brought about an upgrading of the firm's technical output. Furthermore, it enabled the company to enjoy preferential taxation for several reasons: The central government favored the design and production of electronic products because the growth of this sector stimulated the development of high technology in Hungary, and these products were a promising substitute for hard-currency imports.

With the shift in its product mix, the number of owners also increased. In 1985 two engineers working in another town joined the company to develop new electronic products, and the company grew to ten employees. From about this time, a dynamic growth period began during which sales turnover doubled every year and profits amounted to 20 percent to 30 percent of turnover.

As the company grew, ties were broken with the Postal Experimental Institute, whose orders had, until then, provided a stable market, because state specifications would have set back the firm's technical advancement. For example, the Postal Experimental Institute stipulated that the EWT could only build components developed by the institute for products it ordered. But the members of the Alföld EWT contended that these components were not sufficiently up-to-date and were of poor quality. The divorce required the EWT to search for new markets, of course; but development work on small machines needed by post offices and financial institutions continued.

The Company Act and the various enterprise structures that were authorized by it provided a fresh opportunity for the Alföld EWT to change its organizational structure and to privatize its operations completely. It could eliminate many of the government constraints connected with EWT status by re-forming itself into an LLC involving co-owners from abroad. In March 1989 the EWT was transformed into an Austro-Hungarian joint-venture LLC, now owned by six private investors. An Austrian firm, already a co-operating partner, was reorganized into an LLC and entered the company as a new owner with a 30 percent share of the base capital. This move was very favorable for the company; for it could now make good use of the tax rebates offered by the Hungarian government since it met three conditions that entitled it to tax preferences: (1) Western capital exceeded the required share; (2) production exceeded 50 percent of the company's activities; and (3) its sphere of activities—electronics—was a preferential sector of the Hungarian economy. As a result of all this, the firm received total tax relief for five years beginning in 1989.

A further step in improving the firm's organizational structure occurred in August 1990. The property management and investment holding company—the Alföld Engineering and Electronics Group—was formed, which was, from then on, in control of the three LLCs. In addition to the Austro-Hungarian JV, two new corporations were created. One of these was engaged in manufacturing and trade, like the already existing unit, and its product mix was similar. Among the owners of the second firm were both an Austrian and a Czechoslovakian investor who together bought 49 percent of the shares, with the majority retained by the parent holding company. The third member of the group of companies owned and managed by the AGL was a research and development (R&D) and trading firm. Thus, the basic activity of the company—R&D of mechanical and electronic equipment—was now separated in an independent company focusing only on that work. Direct revenues of this company came from its commercial operations.

COMPANY ACTIVITIES AND OPERATIONAL FEATURES

As noted earlier, the company produced small mechanical and electronic machines. In the course of the first three or four years of its existence, postage-stamp vending, rubber-stamping, and banknote and coin-counting machines had been developed and manufactured for the use of the Public Telephone and Telegraph (PTT) Company and other domestic financial institutions. Later, the choice widened: Automatic selling and checking tickets were made for transportation companies; and bookkeeping machines and check-controlling devices enriched the variety. Some of these machines were of original design; others were variants of Western ones adapted to local conditions. Other than the first few products, all the later ones were electronically controlled and represented up-to-date technology. Likewise, the production techniques and equipment were new and high-tech.

Market Position

This product mix largely determined the market position of the firm. It had become a manufacturer of narrowly specialized goods with relatively narrow markets. The small size of the domestic market did not constitute an obstacle in the early years of the firm's operation in view of the small capacity with which it began; and for the small firm that it was, even a narrow market could offer dynamic growth. State-owned financial institutions were safe customers whose ability to pay was assured. Deliveries were made directly to the user, which meant that distribution and wholesale trade were not part of the company's operations. No competition appeared because, until the end of the 1980s, imports were very strongly restricted in Hungary. Side by side with the gradual growth in capacity, opportunities to sell equipment to the Czech PTT arose. This significant enlargement of the market took place in 1989, a year that also brought with it, as was noted earlier, the change in organizational structure that allowed a sizable increase, to about 60, in the number of people employed. The company employed 180 by 1990.

However, this expansion was followed by an unfavorable turn in the company's market position because as an economic result of accelerated political changes, the Czech market was lost and the home market rapidly declined. In order to survive, new markets had to be found, and that required a dynamic marketing strategy. Marketing, however, was a fairly undeveloped area within the company. Given its narrow range of production and its near-monopoly position in supplying its products to SOEs, the company had no reason to develop marketing activities of its own. Until this drastic change in the economic and political situation in 1989, big buyers had existed, and no serious effort had been made to search for smaller customers or to determine the direction in which the product mix should be shifted.

The year 1990 was the first year that the company's ability to utilize its increased production capacities came into doubt (in spite of the already mentioned foreign cooperation); and even getting new customers, however small, became vital. For this reason, the firm then tried to make marketing activities livelier and to introduce a business brokers' commission. At the time, these efforts failed to expand the company's markets. This, again, was one of those typical difficulties that appeared for entrepreneurs not used to operating in a market economy. Marketing failed to become an organic part of the activities of companies that had become comfortable operating in safe markets. The much-too-sudden economic changes found companies unprepared, even if they were much more sensitive than SOEs.

During its early operations, the Alföld Group had always remained liquid and financially stable. During the phase of gradual growth, however, the greatest problem, and the major limitation, was the shortage of capital. The opportunities offered by the market could only be exploited to the limits imposed by the company's own financial resources and accumulating profits. The owners of the AGL were reluctant to avail themselves of credit because they did not find loan conditions sufficiently favorable. In 1991, however, trusting in the government's promises of support through its privatization program, the company sought a "soft loan"; and its financial position was shaken after it became clear that the company was not eligible to purchase the plant of a SOE even though the premises qualified for privatization by the State Property Agency. Thus, having been deprived of credit facilities with "soft" conditions, the firm once again faced financial difficulties.

In-House and Human Resource Management

The management of the AGL was well equipped and organized to high standards. The financial, accounting, and information systems were computerized and capable of providing up-to-date information on company operations. Since its establishment, company activities had yielded a profit every year; and the sum grew proportionally with the growth of output. In 1991, 20 percent of the approximately 450 million forints of sales income was profit. Since the establishment of the holding company, the profits were divided among the component firms. This meant that the less profitable components were being supported from the returns of the more profitable ones.

Human resource management was also quite modern and up-to-date. From the very beginning the owners had placed great emphasis on employees' abilities in the areas of technical and human development. An important contribution in this area had been made by the present managing director, who had played a leading role in founding the company and had been the head of the R&D division of a SOE after graduation. In that capacity, he had tried to create a situation in which he was allowed to pick his own colleagues. When the private company was established, these people also resigned from the SOE and followed him to the private EWT. Thus, right from the beginning there was a very high-level, talented, creative team working together in a company whose members had been long acquainted. This individual selection of workmates continued until the sudden increase of employment in 1991. Then increased hiring was carried out in a slightly more routine fashion. However, candidates for leading technical or executive posts continued to be selected on individual assessment of their skills and knowledge. This care in the field of manpower management was a fairly common feature of private companies that started prior to the demise of the socialist regime. The state sector, where requirements were fairly low, could not satisfy the aspirations of the more talented, creative workers who sought more demanding challenges in the private sector. It goes without saying that the higher level of performance was recognized in the private sector with higher remuneration. In the AGL, employees in key posts worked in a project-manager system that ensured the independence needed in solving technology problems.

After having carefully selected the work force, the managing director put great emphasis on continuous training. The firm was in permanent contact with six or seven institutes of advanced studies whose services were mainly used to acquire current computer techniques, business practices, and languages. The early economic reforms in Hungary allowed the emergence of a fairly large number of competing training companies that offered high-level courses in which practice-oriented, tangible skills and knowledge could be learned. This also meant that it was fairly easy to train employees to adapt to changing conditions, and this versatility became an important contribution to the early success of the AGL.

Other Operations

In spite of the fact that a great proportion of the materials and spare parts were imported from the West, the AGL had no procurement difficulties. All the companies in the group had the authority to make foreign trading transactions, thereby making procurement easier. Computerization of the entire accounting and inventory systems allowed purchasing and storage activities to operate with great efficiency.

Quality-control operations deserve special attention. Contrary to the general practice of Hungarian SOEs, there was no special division or person set apart for this responsibility in the AGL. Every worker was responsible for his or her own work. In addition, attempts were made to build objective quality-control methods into the manufacturing process by checking finished products with specialized instruments. The acceptability of the quality of incoming components and material was also controlled with instrument tests by the worker using them.

From the very beginning of the AGL, technical development had always been assigned a leading role. This can be observed both in the production process and in the operations of the company. R&D activities were financed with 8 to 9 percent of sales revenue compared to an average of 4 to 5 percent in Hungarian enterprises. Other than in the development of finished products, great attention was also paid to the use of up-to-date manufacturing technology. Machines were modern, and computer techniques were applied. In determining the scope of its activities and business management and in deciding on the introduction of necessary changes, the firm always had confidence in the knowledge of its employees and did not hire outside consultants (with the exception of the aborted attempt to participate in the government's privatization program).

In analyzing operations, it is necessary to touch upon questions about how the level of infrastructure affected the success of its operations. It is common knowledge that Hungarian infrastructure and public utilities networks unfavorably affect the operations of businesses. However, this situation did not cause inordinately great difficulties to the AGL. It always remained focused and developed its own energy supply system and telecommunications facilities in proportion to the growth of the company. Substantial financial resources were allocated to this, and problems arising from infrastructure bottlenecks were largely avoided. Because its activities did not require a great deal of transportation or an excessive use of energy or water, there was no reason to worry about the lack of roads, railways, water supply, sewage, and electric power. The company would not have had the means to develop these even if it had been necessary.

A review of the evolution of this private firm and the metamorphosis of its organizational structure indicate the factors that made important contributions to the success of the activities. Also, the major stages in the development of the Hungarian market economy can be easily identified in the history of this company because the owners had the entrepreneurial sense to react instantly to these changes and never failed to seize new opportunities in order to move ahead. Before looking closer at the firm's business operations, let us recapitulate the major steps in its progress.

1. The possibility of creating small enterprises in Hungary became broader in January 1982. The talented, enterprising engineers immediately started successful activities within the IEWT for a market outside the company. Although this form of activity cannot be regarded as more than a quasi-enterprise, it did make a contribution by helping the participants evaluate their own capabilities and collect information about the market.

2. When it became obvious that their products could be sold, the engineers did not hesitate to switch over to the private sector and thus gave up the employment security they had enjoyed in a SOE. Of course, this also provided opportunities for making a higher income. The EWT, the first organizational structure of this private firm, was among the highest-risk forms of entrepreneurial activity then available. Restrictive regulatory measures did not allow for significant enlargement of the firm.

3. The Company Act of 1989 provided new possibilities in a rapidly emerging Hungarian market economy. This opportunity was also immediately seized by the firm; in 1989, it transformed itself into an LLC. This opened the way to involve external investors and foreign capital and, thereby, to attain significant tax rebates. After its incorporation, the company grew rapidly.

4. Thus, it can be seen that during the period between the firm's establishment until the present, the leading role in shaping its form and size was played by changes in government regulations and by economic reforms. Growth of the company was closely linked to changes in regulatory legislation aimed at encouraging a market economy in Hungary. To a certain extent, because the firm was established in a fairly early phase of the development of the market economy, it almost developed along with it.

CHANGES IN STRATEGY AND DECISION MAKING

The market position of the firm in 1991 was quite favorable. The work team that started its activities as a private EWT in 1984 displayed an accurate assessment of the market when it began the development of mechanical, and later electronic, small machines that were not yet available in Hungary. Because of this timely reaction, for a long time they remained in an almost monopolistic position with these special types of machines.

In the early years, the company's strategy had been to develop small machines that were in demand domestically by the PTT, the National Savings Bank, and other major financial institutions. The company's owners were conscientiously striving to work for big and safe SOEs whose solvency was secure. For Hungarian financial institutions working at a very low technical level and being very poorly equipped, the modern, high-tech products developed by the private company were bound to be very useful. During the first few years the company sought only a narrow circle of customers among a few SOEs with secure payment capabilities. After five or six years of operation, and primarily because of economic conditions in Hungary, the prime strategy of the firm was to sell machines of its own development in the home market. Such a segment of the market was targeted because it allowed almost monopolistic production of small machines used by financial institutions. This strategy ensured rapid growth and success.

As a result of the evolution of legislation regulating the forms of enterprise, it became possible in 1990 for the company to assume a new structure that allowed for growth and the involvement of external capital. However, the demise of the socialist regime in Hungary in 1989 occurred during a strong economic recession in which the ability of companies to purchase equipment was vastly reduced. For this reason, as early as the end of the 1980s, the company was faced with severe constraints on the development of new machines to be used in the home market of financial institutions. At this point, the company diversified and produced a few small electronic machines that could be used by transportation and commercial companies. The owners also realized that in order to maintain growth, it would be necessary to export and to penetrate Western markets. The sooner-than-expected collapse of the Council for Mutual Economic Assistance (COMECON) only added to the urgency of exporting. This change in strategy was facilitated by the Austrian co-owner who used his own connections in securing orders until markets were found in European countries. In essence, this meant that the AGL had to engage initially in assembly operations for Western firms that were attracted by the low Hungarian wage level. For the AGL, on the one hand, it was important to secure enough work to absorb its production capacity at all times and, on the other hand, to provide its employees with experience in producing the precision and high-quality work required in the West. Therefore, even though its profits from the assembly contracts were no more than 5 to 6 percent of the sales value, the contracts were important in preparing the company to export its own products.

In order to ensure the success of the new market strategy as well as further growth, the company purchased the premises of the SOE from which the founders had resigned in 1984. After the liquidation of this SOE in 1984, its place was taken by another SOE that was then being privatized; and this restructuring made the purchase of its facilities possible. This purchase allowed the AGL to consolidate operations that had previously been carried out at several sites and also precipitated better organization and more rational operations. Buying the premises led, however, to severe financial difficulties that very clearly reflected the weaknesses in the privatization laws during the early 1990s. Counting on a special kind of credit earmarked to support privatization in Hungary, the AGL went ahead with the deal but later found out that the conditions of this loan did not apply to it as a company. Such loans were given only to private individuals who wished to buy state property and not to holding companies. Another obstacle was that the actual date of the purchase preceded the enactment of the credit law by a few days. To obtain some other type of credit was not possible except at very unfavorable interest rates of nearly 40 percent. In this case, government economic reforms did not support this kind of effort at private development. The controversial and lengthy process of adopting a credit program to support privatization yielded a complicated scheme full of disqualifying clauses that, in fact, did not effectively encourage the participation of potentially successful private companies. Despite these difficulties with the government's credit program, the owners of the AGL saw the difficulties surrounding the purchase of the new facilities as their own mistake: Instead of taking matters into their own hands, they had hired an advisory firm in Budapest to assess the potential for their participation in the government's privatization program. But the consultants could not carry out the task in a way that would help the company.

The main reasons for the shift in the company's strategy were the rapid changes occurring in the Hungarian economy. The demise of the socialist regime and the adoption of economic policies designed to increase the share of private ownership in Hungary took place during a deep recession. Thus, participation of the AGL in domestic privatization brought with it unfavorable financial consequences, for the owners had to finance the purchase of a state-owned plant with their own funds instead of with the expected loan. A bit too late, they realized that it had been a blunder to make the decision to purchase before appropriate legislation had come into force.

Most companies, like the AGL, continue to struggle with market problems. The disintegration of the socialist countries' markets and the shrinking domestic market equally hurt the new Hungarian private companies. Shrinking demand in the internal market and in neighboring Czechoslovakia was very difficult for the AGL. For this reason a fairly swift change in strategy was needed at a time when the company did not have products that could be sold in Western markets and did not have the experience to penetrate European markets. Thus, the previous strategy of increasing output had to be replaced by a strategy aimed at protecting the existing level of production.

In this difficult period of transition, maintaining production was the main worry of most Hungarian companies, whether they were state owned or private. Penetration of Western markets was a serious problem for companies like the AGL that sought to turn out modern, high-technology products. The strategy that proved to be a success in the first period of economic transformation—to develop and adapt to home-market conditions machines that were not yet being produced in Hungary—no longer worked in the early 1990s. Starting production in a market in which it was the sole producer was a good initial strategy for the AGL and resulted in rapid growth for the firm. But during that period, nothing was done to prepare for eventual changes in economic conditions brought about by the collapse of the socialist regime and the demise of the COMECON market. For the AGL, the security of the domestic and socialist market turned into a disadvantage under conditions of accelerating change. This was a negative side of working under nonmarket conditions—private firms gradually patterned themselves after SOEs, tried to establish a monopoly or near-monopoly position, and frequently became a bit smug.

THE EFFECTS OF CHANGES IN THE ECONOMIC ENVIRONMENT

As a result of rapid political changes taking place in Hungary and the demise of its export markets in the COMECON countries, the economic recession continued to deepen during the early 1990s. To a great extent, this negatively affected the success of the Alföld Group, which had depended on secure markets in Hungary and in nearby socialist countries. In 1991, for the first time in its existence, it was struggling with problems of sales and capacity utilization. (Since this is a recent problem, for the time being it is hard to say when and with what success these difficulties can be overcome.)

The regulatory system of the 1980s had been unfavorable for the company because, due to large budget deficits, an ever-increasing portion of profit was taken by the Treasury. In addition, other aspects of the regulations changed very quickly and in incalculable fashion. There were no measures in the government regulatory system to alleviate the capital shortages that had consistently been a problem for the company. The capital investment required for operations was the one area in which the firm competed with SOEs. A company that occupied a monopolistic position in the market, that was not engaged in competition for inputs, and that had a favorable competitive position in the labor market (owing to its well-trained, well-organized work force, which was paid higher-than-average wages) found itself clearly at a disadvantage in the capital market. In the undeveloped Hungarian capital market, SOEs enjoyed advantages in obtaining money for development and investment. Banks failed to assist private companies by providing only incremental capital. When the AGL was transformed into an LLC, new avenues opened for external capital investment (by the entry of either foreign or local co-owners); but that would have meant reducing the control of the original owners—something that they wished to prevent.

The government's policies to create a market economy as well as the regulations geared to implement them can be evaluated as partly positive and partly negative from the point of view of the firm. The taxation of profits increased—something that should have been expected as the government's budget deficit grew. Incentives for companies to grow would have been stronger if they had been allowed to use an increasing portion of their own profits to expand their capacity and markets, but with increasing taxes this could not work. Conditions for acquiring additional capital through bank loans did not improve either. Representatives of the AGL also viewed government policies to liberalize imports negatively because this led to the deterioration of market potential for domestic firms. They believe that it would have been more expedient to retain a certain degree of protection for domestic industry until economic conditions improved.

The Company Act and the act regulating investment of foreigners were regarded positively inasmuch as the freedom of applying up-to-date organizational structures and the possibility of involving foreign capital, together with the significant tax rebates attached to it, somewhat alleviated the shortage of capital. But the investments of new co-owners threatened to relegate the founding owners to a minority position, so many companies sought only limited foreign or external participation.

In retrospect, it is clear that from its establishment until 1990, the company that evolved into the Alföld Engineering and Electronics Group enjoyed undisturbed development and made a profit. Success was both the result of a well-selected product mix commanding a safe market and the good sense of the owners who reacted quickly to the gradually improving entrepreneurial opportunities. However, the fast pace of political transformation after 1989 led to basic economic difficulties when traditional markets dramatically vanished. A company based on production for domestic and socialist markets was not in a position to make rapid adjustments or to penetrate new markets quickly. Government policies and regulations that sought to build a market economy were enacted during a time of economic recession and did not adequately underpin the process by supplying private enterprises with the support they needed during a difficult period of transition.

4

The GDK Automotive Parts Company of Hungary

Erzsébet Poszmik

The Hungarian enterprise GDK has operated (with Swiss-Hungarian ownership) as a private limited company since 1990. The progress of GDK provides a good example of how the private sector has fared in Hungary since the demise of the Communist regime in 1989. The executive director—who is also the majority owner—began work as an artisan in Budapest about 20 years ago almost immediately after passing the apprenticeship examinations that qualified him as a skilled worker. In the beginning, he produced automotive parts primarily for cars manufactured in socialist countries and sold his products to private retailers of automotive parts in Hungary. The market for automotive parts was very promising in the early 1970s, for the number of privately owned cars had just begun to grow significantly. Naturally, the bulk of these cars consisted of models manufactured in socialist countries. The number of Western cars had begun increasing a bit faster in Hungary only in the late 1980s following favorable changes in customs regulations. But because imports depended on international trade agreements, the supply of spare parts and components was irregular and unreliable. Thus, the domestically produced parts were—and still are—genuinely needed.

In spite of changes in business laws and in economic conditions in Hungary, GDK's product mix remained unchanged for a long time: It produced, primarily for the domestic market, parts for cars manufactured in socialist countries. Production provided 95 percent of the turnover, while trading made up the remaining 5 percent. Ninety percent of production consisted of automotive parts, and the rest (10 percent) was of tools. GDK's annual sales totaled 350 million forints in 1991, of which 10 to 12 million forints was the net profit produced by about 120 workers. Almost 20 percent of the sales were made abroad, mainly in Italy, Germany, the Netherlands, and Greece. The firm has its own sales office in Budapest, while production is based in a nearby small township. The present plant, formerly a unit of a state-owned engineering firm, was acquired in the course of its privatization. At this production plant (the renovation and modernization of which required considerable investment), efficient manufacturing meets high-quality demand—a fact acknowledged by the Grand Prize that GDK won at the Budapest Autumn Fair in 1991.

The career of the executive director illustrates the difficulties faced by someone who has been in private enterprise under socialist conditions for a relatively long time. For private companies, the acceleration of economic and political changes in 1989 created a new situation demanding considerable efforts to survive, even for those managed by businesspeople accustomed to enterprise and risk taking. Analysis of the situation and of the attitudes of these entrepreneurs is important because their role is essential to the success of economic transformation.

ECONOMIC POLICY AND PRIVATE ENTERPRISE

From the early 1970s until 1982, a period in which Hungarian privately owned businesses were few and far between, the firm operated as an individual private enterprise. Private enterprise was barely tolerated in an economy strongly influenced by the socialist ideology of state ownership and control, and economic policy made private enterprise difficult for various reasons. It is not the objective of this study to discuss these reasons in detail, but it is necessary to point out that operational conditions were much more difficult for private enterprises before the change of regime than for state-owned enterprises (SOEs) and cooperatives. Although, officially, the operation of the private sector was not limited, the de facto situation in which private enterprises were merely tolerated remained unchanged until 1982.

Even though private enterprise was not encouraged, a special type of entrepreneur evolved from the period when state ownership was dominant. The people who chose to work in the private sector instead of in a secure state job faced more difficult conditions and took more responsibility upon themselves. It is obvious, in comparison, that these individuals were ready to venture more bravely, to work harder, and to face clashes and conflicts. Those who endured as business owners have played important roles in the current development of the market economy. They were capable of such leadership because of personal qualities and their experience as well as by virtue of the assets they accumulated. These qualities were fundamentally different from those of successful private businesspeople of developed market economies, however, in that the private enterprises operating during the era largely followed patterns set by the dominant state sector. While the private sector worked to more exacting standards than SOEs, it did not have the competition generated by a genuine market economy. It learned to adjust to changing government regulations but not to changing market demands.

These successful private entrepreneurs, however, played an important role in the economic transformation because they were the ones who had the financial means to buy part of the state's assets. However, private funds were rather limited when compared with the size of the state's assets to be privatized or to the private assets that citizens of Western countries could use for similar purposes.

Setting the Stage for Change

While operating as an artisan, the executive director of GDK was motivated by his family background in the choice of his trade: His father and grandfather had been ironworkers in a similar field. He began his independent business in a very small way—completely with his own resources and working side by side with his wife. Car parts, which were constantly in short supply, guaranteed a safe and stable market; thus, the business grew continuously and securely. After a few years the business received a sizable order from the Hungarian division of a foreign automaker and then met orders procured by Kisipar Termeltető Vállalat (a business maintained by a representative organization of Hungarian artisans that endeavors to help members of the private sector by coordinating and procuring orders for them).

The owner relied exclusively on his own funds to develop his business and took out no investment loans. He explained his reticence to borrow—which even he regarded as a bit conservative—by pointing to the economic situation. It was safer and more useful for private enterprise owners, who had long been pushed into the background, to rely on their own strength because they received no substantial credit allowance and because the frequent and unexpected changes in economic regulations could cause them unpredictable difficulties that unforeseen debts could only aggravate. All of these uncertainties arose under circumstances in which private business could only be conducted in a form involving unlimited risk; thus, forms of business association that made the limitation of liability possible were not available to private individuals. Possibilities for growth and progress for the Hungarian private business sector were extremely limited.

The market position of the firm during the 1970s and early 1980s was influenced by the development of some 20 other firms of similar size and production, and they divided the market among themselves. Thus, in spite of impediments and difficulties caused by central regulations, they became accustomed to the conditions and adjusted to the economic situation.

Participation in Privatization

A new phase in the life of GDK began in 1982. The government considerably eased earlier restrictions on establishing and operating private enterprises, and new forms of business organization were introduced. However, they did not provide the types of individual business associations well known in market economies; rather, they offered opportunities for private individuals (either as full- or part-time workers) to engage in small-scale enterprises that were operated within larger SOEs. The entrepreneurial opportunities for these businesses were quite limited.

At that time the executive director of GDK was an independent artisan already employing a modest work force and overseeing substantial production increases. But in order to achieve even further growth, he chose one of the new organizational forms. Thus, in 1982 he transformed his business into a special cooperative group. This form required that a cooperative take responsibility for the firm; and so GDK became attached to a cooperative farm. Its labor force increased considerably, and as many as 50 workers became engaged in the production of automotive parts. The former executive director became the president of the company, and the cooperative farm carried the risk of the business in return for part of the profits. The location of production remained unchanged, for the cooperative farm leased the workshop and machinery from the former artisan, now the new president. The company worked very efficiently and showed outstanding results. The market situation remained just as favorable as before; production increased without problems; and the president-manager (who as a private owner had been used to performing better-than-average work and demanded as much from his workers) guaranteed quality products.

The period from 1982 to 1988 was an interesting time for private business owners in Hungary. The various available business forms created opportunities for setting up and operating new businesses. These forms allowed small-scale enterprises that were attached to SOEs to expand with limited individual risk. Workers were stimulated to perform better; but they did not emerge as owners because opportunities for obtaining capital were limited. Even though private enterprises were more prevalent than ever before, the government sought to relegate them to an auxiliary role while maintaining the dominance of state ownership. Privatization had not yet emerged as a major objective of economic reforms.

The Company Act, which permitted modern forms of business association for private individuals by eliminating most of the impediments to enterprise growth, came into force in 1988. GDK converted to the private limited form in 1990. The ownership composition of the new company was as follows: The original artisan, then president of the company, became majority owner with 70 percent of the 51 million forints in initial capital, and the other 30 percent was supplied by a Swiss businessman. Thus, a Swiss-Hungarian joint company was established in which the Swiss owner held preferential shares. Under those terms, he received dividends but took no part in decisions and did not exercise his ownership rights in the management of the company.

In addition to the changes in organizational form and in ownership, other changes also took place. The size of the company increased considerably. When

GDK bought a division of an engineering enterprise that had been owned by the state, GDK relocated its plant to a small town near Budapest. When the plant was purchased, GDK's product mix became diversified. The former SOE had also manufactured simple forged tools, and the new owners continued that activity.

The purchase of the plant was motivated by several factors: its favorable location, its suitable size, and the forging capacity it offered to expand GDK's manufacturing capacity. On the other hand, most of the buildings and equipment were outmoded; and their replacement required considerable investment.

STRATEGY AND DECISION MAKING

Prior to the fall of the Communist regime, only about 20 artisan groups in Hungary had been engaged in the production of automotive parts. They had become accustomed to the semimarket conditions of the Hungarian economy and had successfully maneuvered around the constraining economic policies and central economic regulations that had created unfavorable conditions for them. Prior to 1989, GDK had produced about 40 percent of the manufacturing parts and components for socialist-made cars in Hungary. This made up about 95 percent of its activities, while the remaining 5 percent came from direct sales of the products in a retail shop.

During the socialist era, GDK gradually grew in size and profits under essentially secure conditions. The competitors and cooperating partners knew one another and were already accustomed to pseudomarket conditions. The situation was easier to deal with than uncertainties brought about by the accelerated changes produced by economic reforms after 1989. During the period of economic reform after 1989, however, market conditions changed drastically. A number of GDK's former competitors withdrew (failed or switched to some other business). This was partly responsible for the increase of GDK's market share from 40 percent to 90 percent, which was almost a monopoly. This greatly increased share, however, yielded some 40 million forints less in sales than before.

A number of factors accounted for the drop in sales, and the most important was the decrease in demand. During the late 1980s and early 1990s, the general deterioration of the standard of living in Hungary reached a stage where the use of cars decreased. The middle class, which mostly had Eastern European cars, was forced to hold back consumption and use their cars only when it was absolutely necessary. This recession was optimistically judged as temporary. However, another quite decisive trend was also occurring. Not only had the use of cars dropped, but there also had been a change in the composition of the stock of cars. This was partly because new customs regulations allowed the more affluent people to buy Western cars under more favorable conditions. It was also partly because the manufacture of traditional socialist-type cars ceased within a few years due to the rearrangement of economic relations with former socialist countries and the conversion of the car industries in various countries. Thus, no one even bought the stock on hand, and the Hungarian stock of older cars continued to age even further. This broadened GDK's market for a few years because more parts had to be replaced in the older cars; but, unfortunately, this effect was reduced by the growing impoverishment.

Because of this loss in sales, a change in GDK's production pattern was unavoidable. New products had to be manufactured in order to ensure long-term survival; so the production of small agricultural machines was planned and then gradually implemented. Ownership of agricultural property was also about to change radically in Hungary. Parallel with the partial distribution of the still-dominant cooperatives and state farms, the number of smaller privately owned farms was expected to grow; and some forms of cooperation based on looser ties (e.g., jointly doing some of the work needed in a given phase of production) were expected to develop. Thus, manufacturing small agricultural machines was a sound decision that ensured a marketable product for GDK. In order to strengthen this line, establishing connections with Italian firms of similar profile became a real consideration. For the time being, GDK was only selling the products of these Italian manufacturers; but it intended gradually to start production. Efforts were also being made to develop connections with Western firms that were involved in the production of automotive parts. The company had already done some commission work but also began to sell parts. In 1990 and 1991, about 20 percent of sales were made in Western countries.

Privatization Period

Changing the production pattern in order to survive was the major force behind GDK's development strategy after 1989. The failure of GDK's competitors also indicated how difficult the economic situation had become in Hungary. Development of a new strategy was required because of decreasing market demand and the extensive process of privatization. New owners appeared, and the old cooperative methods disintegrated. Although GDK developed stable and reliable relationships with customers and suppliers—most of them private entities—in the course of 20 years in business, the diminishing number of SOEs created new uncertainties for the company. The least favorable circumstance was the large number of failures among earlier customers (most of them private businesses). The result was, therefore, that a circle of predominantly privately owned buyers and suppliers evolved slowly under limited market mechanisms.

GDK's situation was favorable when the Hungarian economic reforms began. It was one of the first to participate in the privatization process by buying the manufacturing plant near Budapest; however, the economic and social changes that came with political and economic reforms after 1989 made its position uncertain.   Development of the market economy and radical changes in ownership created difficult economic conditions, even for entrepreneurs who had survived the discrimination of socialist economic policy. The reforms demanded an ability to adjust, but the situation was uncertain because temporary effects also asserted themselves. These uncertainties created dispirited entrepreneurs who had been accustomed to safer, though disadvantageous, circumstances under the state-managed economy. In spite of that, the emerging difficulties were successfully overcome; and the most serious worry of the owner of GDK was that he would need a suitable partner for managing the company in order to ensure long-term efficiency.

The president of GDK, who controlled a majority interest, was solely responsible for the company's development strategy. But he had worked as a one-man entrepreneur for such a long time that he was used to making his own decisions, and his strong personality was not an advantage in the collective management that was generally exercised in business associations. The ownership composition of GDK made possible one-man management, a goal he had set in establishing the company. Nevertheless, he became a little less self-confident amid the fast-paced economic changes. He increasingly felt the need to have a deputy of similar qualities, but he could not find a suitable man. The president never called on outside consultants and did not plan to use their services because he had little confidence in them and considered these experts to be outsiders who were not committed to his company. After making his own decisions for a long time, he became unaccustomed to cooperative decision making.

OPERATION OF THE COMPANY DURING THE TRANSITION TO A MARKET ECONOMY

As noted earlier, GDK primarily manufactured automotive parts; and various hand tools (e.g., axes, hammers, and cutting tools) were added to its range of products in 1990. In order to counterbalance partial market losses, the company accepted commissions from Hungarian and foreign interests for forging, cutting, and heat treatment. It accomplished this by using the equipment at the engineering plant that it had purchased from the state. Apart from production, the company also retailed the parts and components made in its own shop. Sales there, however, represented only a minor share (about 5 percent) of annual revenue.

This product mix resulted in material-intensive activity, a rather unfavorable feature considering Hungarian prices. For example, iron was very expensive and sold at about three times the price charged for it in Germany. This greatly reduced the international competitiveness of GDK's products even though they were of high quality because of above-average labor discipline and skills.

Marketing

For a long time there was no real need for intensive marketing by GDK because of its secure market. However, GDK's president consciously made the point to always have precise and up-to-date information concerning his business. He regularly followed information on television and radio as well as in publications; and he regularly took part in domestic and foreign trade fairs, which he considered necessary for establishing business contacts that were indispensable for Hungarian business executives. It must be added here, however, that while participation at fairs also constituted a very important advertising medium for businesses in developed market economies, the Grand Prize won by this firm in 1991 created no particular attention in Hungary. Nor did it attract attention from government organizations or from purchasing representatives of other businesses. However, the president of GDK believed that personal contacts were still the most successful means of conducting business and pushed the importance of advertising far into the background.

As in the past, the company sold the bulk of its products to private retailers. Bulk supplies were sent from the manufacturing plant, while smaller quantities were sold in the retail shop. Sales posed no problem for businesses producing goods in short supply. Thus, GDK's president was not particularly concerned about his sales, which were made with few problems.

Finance

The general state of the Hungarian economy strongly influenced this aspect of GDK's operations. Difficulties arose from the widespread insolvency of businesses, for even producers of readily salable goods had financial difficulties because their debtors did not pay their bills. The company was trying to avoid this trap by paying cash but also by demanding cash in payment. Naturally, this could not always be achieved. Because of the president's conservative views, the company never took out loans and did not intend to do so because of high interest charges. The company, therefore, had no debt.

Labor Management

When GDK bought the division of the state-owned engineering enterprise, it also absorbed about 700 employees. After a very strict selection process, however, only about 100 of them were kept; and 600 jobs were scrapped within a year. This explains why the Hungarian work force, accustomed to full employment for the past 40 years, feared privatization.

GDK's president had very strict standards for selecting his workers; being skilled in most of the trades needed in the company, he was therefore a keen judge of these abilities. His general practice had been to ask the recommendations of two workers when employing a new one, but he mainly needed the worker recommendations to verify appropriate character qualities. GDK's junior executives and foremen were generally products of training within the company. The greatest problem was that there was no partner or successor in leadership.

This situation was, again, slightly contradictory. GDK's president had always believed that the most important issue of the company's long-term survival was whether or not it would succeed in finding a top associate executive with the appropriate knowledge and decision-making capability. On the one hand, he knew that he had borne the burden of making decisions alone during his 20 years in business; and he wanted to share leadership or at least see at his side a possible successor maturing to the task. On the other hand, he did not consider himself able, either because of his nature or because of his long-standing work as sole leader, to adjust to a similarly strong personality. This reluctance indicated the entrepreneur's loss of confidence in Hungarian society—a typical problem that affected people who had been active in the private sector for a relatively long time and had become accustomed to being their own masters under semimarket (or pseudomarket) conditions. The changing economic environment and its novel influences often had adverse effects.

Training and Development of Human Resources

The president of GDK did his best to increase the professional standards of his labor force: He was ready to help or to finance whatever training and studies his workers wanted. The managers in GDK were leaders in using extension training and in attending various special courses. But to the president's regret, the demand for further training was low even though the company had initiated and organized training abroad (particularly in Italy). Training had been available in plants that operated at considerably higher technical standards, and yet workers' interest remained below the president's expectations. These opportunities were not taken in spite of the fact that the company paid expenses and the participants visited such plants as the famous Ferrari works.

Quality Control

For a long time GDK operated under the philosophy that production of faulty goods was no sin in itself, but these goods should never reach customers. Thus, the prestige of the firm was considered to be of primary importance. Well-selected workers with appropriate skills were always employed. Good work was expected from them, yet occasional errors were tolerated. Thus, quality control automatically functioned as self-control for the workers, who were paid high hourly rates in compensation. But some changes occurred after 1989. Owing to commission work carried out for Western clients, Japanese-type quality control was introduced at the insistence of the foreign partner. The president of GDK regarded this as a significant step forward, which contributed to the company's adjustment to increasingly strict demands posed by the changing market.

The president believed that GDK was suitably competitive and also capable of carrying out the necessary changes in its product mix. The most pressing points at issue after 1989 were the fast-changing legal rules for doing business and the officials who enforced them. The difference was that the major constraints were no longer the discriminations of socialist ideology but the inconsistencies of government officials and the rapid decline in the size of the state budget.

THE EFFECT OF ECONOMIC REFORMS ON THE COMPANY

Beyond general limits already discussed, the economic and political changes modified the position of the company in the Hungarian market but in a somewhat unfavorable direction. The complete liberalization of imports forced domestic producers to compete with products from the more-developed Western European countries. This fact primarily affected the production of hand tools and the planned production of small agricultural machines. The comparatively higher cost of raw materials, energy, and tools in Hungary than in the West also had to be taken into consideration.

Another adverse effect in the short term was that the quantity of goods sold by foreign tourists had greatly increased as a result of the liberal visa policy and the loose control of tourists coming into the country. Besides hosts of other goods, tourists also sold automotive parts on the black market for far less than domestic prices. These products of uncertain origin and uncontrollable quality created serious competition for GDK and resulted in a considerable drop in sales. (Only in mid-1992 did Budapest police begin a drive to restore order in public squares and places where black markets operated.)

Finally, mention has already been made of the general loss of confidence caused by the changing economic environment after the initiation of economic reforms in 1989. It appeared that government intentions concerning the development of a market economy triggered an unfavorable effect in traditional private businesspeople. They did not feel free to enjoy the lifting of restrictions because of worries arising from growing uncertainty. One would think that the initial advantage held by private businesspeople of 20 years' standing was a considerable asset in the midst of rapid privatization. Very likely this was correct. Their advantage was quite considerable compared with newly emerging entrepreneurs, yet their earlier position was easier than the present one. They became accustomed to the old environment, found their way easily in semimarket conditions, and developed the necessary contacts. But their expertise in business could not as easily be applied during the reform period.

5

Decentralized versus Centralized Privatization: The Case of Slovenia

Joze Mencinger

The transition from a socialist to a market economy, an essential counterpart to sweeping political and ideological changes in Central Europe, has proven to be a painful process with many setbacks. Of course, the economic, social, and political tensions emerging from the redistribution of income, wealth, and power should have been expected. The transition started without a clear picture of the actual situation, without a fully worked-out scheme for the new economic system, and without economic and social arrangements for the transition period. Instead, illusions prevailed that the market mechanism would instantly transform socialist countries into welfare states. Former Communist countries with the weakest market institutions declared the strongest faith in a capitalist market system. General recipes for macroeconomic stabilization, supply-side restructuring, and privatization became magical potions; but the first results were very disappointing. Many people suffered substantial reductions in their standard of living; production declined; unemployment increased; and the distribution of income worsened. The enthusiasm of Western countries for political freedom and economic reform in Central Europe waned as it became clear that the amount of money needed to meet demands to continue communism's cradle-to-grave social benefits exceeded the Central European financial resources.

It also appears that the differences among Central European countries were neglected. Political and social environments, existing institutional frameworks, degrees of monetization of the economy, industrial structures, levels of incorporation into the world economy, macroeconomic performance, and other characteristics of Central European countries differed enormously. In some countries, planning institutions had to be dismantled; in others, they had already been displaced by market institutions. Some countries had weak links with the world market, while others had already developed trade relations and other forms of cooperation with Western countries. These differences were important when choosing the ways in which macroeconomic stabilization, supply-side restructuring, and privatization should be enacted and implemented if economic and social costs of the transition were to be minimized. "The trick to avoid losing too much of the old building while replacing the foundations quickly," S. K. Chand and H. R. Lorie observed, "is to support those parts of the building that can be retained."[1]

The belief that the differences among countries matter and that the macroeconomic environment is important for economic transition in general, and for privatization in particular, is reflected in this chapter. It analyzes the creation of market institutions and the economic and political conditions that led to the collapse of Yugoslavia as well as the efforts of Slovenia to bring about a double transition—that is, from a socialist to a market economy, and from dependence to independence. This chapter focuses on the problems of privatization, which proved to be more of a political issue than an economic one, and concludes with an epilogue on the outcome of debates over the most appropriate approach to privatization in Slovenia as of mid-1992.

INITIAL CONDITIONS FOR ECONOMIC TRANSITION IN YUGOSLAVIA

Economic reforms in Yugoslavia (and Slovenia) started nearly 40 years ago, long before those in Central Europe. Since 1945, four distinct periods of transition can be distinguished: administrative socialism from 1945 to 1952; administrative market socialism from 1953 to 1962, which gradually led to market socialism from 1963 to 1973; and contractual socialism from 1974 to 1988, which ended in collapse. The reasons for the transitions from one form of socialism to another differ: Political factors were dominant in abandoning the Soviet-type, centrally planned system in the early 1950s and in the adoption of contractual socialism in the early 1970s, while the reforms of the 1960s were prompted predominantly by economic considerations.[2] Although these reforms remained halfhearted efforts to implement policies promoting free-market exchange of goods and services and failed to diffuse political and economic power, they nevertheless created preconditions (unthinkable in other Central European countries) for a rather swift transition to a market-oriented economy.[3]

The economic situation of the early 1980s developed into a profound economic, social, political, and moral crisis that prompted attempts at new reforms. Economic deterioration turned into stagflation and, after 1983, into hyperstagflation (see table 5.1). The annual growth of gross national product (GNP) declined from 5.7 percent from 1974 to 1980 to an average annual rate of -0.3 during the 1980s. The unemployment rate ranged from 13.5 percent to 17.5 percent during the 1980s and reached 19.6 percent by the end of 1990. The average inflation rate increased from 20 percent during the 1974–80 period to 2,600 percent in 1989. Real wages dropped to two-thirds of those in 1979, and

Table 5.1

The Performance of the Yugoslav Economy in the 1980s

	Internal Balance		External Efficiency Balance		
Year	GNP Growth Rate	Inflation Rate (percent)	Unemploy- ment Rate	Export/ Import Ratio	Capital/ Output Ratio	Labor/ Output Ratio
1974–1980	5.7	20.1	13.3	55.6	2.64	1.86
1981	1.5	44.8	13.5	70.2	2.69	1.79
1982	0.5	31.0	14.1	77.8	2.82	1.84
1983	-1.0	38.1	14.6	81.6	2.96	1.89
1984	2.0	56.3	15.3	84.5	2.95	1.89
1985	0.5	75.4	16.0	87.2	2.97	1.91
1986	3.5	88.1	16.2	84.1	2.95	1.91
1987	-1.0	118.4	15.7	91.3	3.01	1.97
1988	-1.7	251.2	16.4	95.7	3.13	2.01
1989	0.6	2665.0	17.5	90.2	—	—
1990	-7.6	121.7	19.6	75.8	—	—

Source: Statistiki Godinjak Jugoslavije, various years.

Kosovo, for example, widened from 5:1 in 1955 to 7:1 in 1988. From 1986 to 1988, the economic situation worsened, partly due to eccentric economic policy pursued by the Mikuli government.

In May 1988, however, a market-oriented economic policy finally emerged. It was based on the liberalization of prices, imports, and foreign exchange markets as well as on restrictive fiscal and monetary policy and wage controls. However, it soon became apparent that the government was unable to assert discipline over fiscal and monetary policy. In October 1988 the last of the three anchors—wage controls—slackened, and urgent measures were added to ease social tensions and prevent further reduction of real wages. Before the end of 1988, the Mikuli government resigned and was succeeded by the Markovi government, which eagerly continued economic reforms and launched a new stabilization program.

In 1988 the Mikuli government initiated the transition to a market system by establishing a commission that launched a program of economic reform. Contrary to expectations, the reform proposals of the Mikuli Commission were radical, although theoretically confused and inconsistent. The proposals began with the premise that social ownership of the means of production was at the heart of Yugoslav economic problems and urged that the concept of social property—by which everyone and no one was the owner—be abandoned. They also demanded that the existing relationship between management and labor be replaced by a recognition that those who provide the capital are also entitled to management and profit-sharing rights. However, while recognizing the need for private property, these proposals insisted that social property remain the predominant form of ownership.

The legal conditions for the reform were created by amendments to the constitution adopted in November 1988. "The Principles of the Economic System Reform," a document containing a general outline of economic changes, was adopted in October 1988; and systemic laws, which regulated the economy and labor relations adopted in 1988 and 1989, were much more radical. The two most important laws, the Foreign Investment Act and the Enterprise Act, were passed in late December 1988 and formally abrogated the existing economic system based on self-management and social property. They reestablished enterprise as a legal entity that could engage in economic activities and be fully responsible for its business operations. Four types of ownership of the means of production were introduced: social, cooperative, mixed, and private. The Law on Social Capital, enacted in 1989, gave Workers' Councils the power to sell companies to private owners. It specified that revenues from sales be paid into a special Development Fund. Privatization agencies were established in each republic to assist enterprises in transforming themselves. The laws were amended in August 1990 in several important ways, but the most important provision allowed employee buyouts through the purchase of "internal shares" at a discount and with prohibitions on the resale of these shares in the securities market.

In December 1989 a "shock therapy" was adopted in the form of an economic stabilization program that called for fixed exchange rates, tight monetary policy, and wage controls. In fact, the initial overvaluation of the dinar, weaknesses in wage controls, and a fiscal overhang existed from the very beginning. In the first two quarters of 1990, economic performance was satisfactory; in April the rate of inflation was even negative. But in June, fatal mistakes were added to those committed in December 1989. Policymakers started to pump money through selective credits for the agricultural sector and nearly doubled the wages of federal employees. The program was left without an anchor and began to drift; the whole burden of reform was placed on the fixed exchange rate. This made price stability unsustainable. Private consumption and public sector spending increased dramatically during the summer and stayed on the same level until the end of 1990 when economic activity dropped to less than 90 percent of the 1989 level. In the last two quarters, prices jumped again. Severe monetary restrictions that followed in the last quarter of 1990 pushed the economy into critical illiquidity, large-scale bartering, and recession without deflation. With fixed exchange rates for the dinar highly overvalued, exports were left without support, imports increased, and trade deficits started to grow. In October 1990 a politically enacted speculative attack on foreign exchange deposits depleted foreign currency reserves, the last element of the stabilization program.

In the political realm, the legalization of political parties in 1989 created the preconditions for free elections and parliamentary democracy in the republics. The results of the elections divided the country into parts; and this division, together with the emergence of nationalistic governments and quickly growing animosity between Croats and Serbs, led to the disintegration of Yugoslavia as a nation. The federal government tried to reverse economic deterioration, but all the attempts were blocked by the republics. In autumn 1990, Yugoslavia, in fact, ceased to exist as an economic unit: Taxes were not collected; money was printed elsewhere; and tariffs and special levies were introduced for "imports" from other republics. In addition, the republics started to build differing economic systems. Under these circumstances the collapse of economic reforms and of the stabilization program was unavoidable.

Despite the failure of systemic change and macroeconomic stabilization on the federal level, the former constituent republics, compared with other Central European countries, retained many advantages for economic and social transition. Most of the preconditions for transition (decentralization, price reform, openness to the outside world, and diversification of ownership) were at least partly met before the political and ideological collapse of socialism.

ECONOMIC POLICY OF SLOVENIA IN 1990 AND 1991

The economic policy goals of Slovenia's government after general elections in May 1990 were set on the supposition that both economic policy and the economic system were inadequate and unstable. Consequently, the government decided to pursue an economic reform policy aimed at achieving three major goals: first, the survival of the economy in the period of stabilization and transformation; second, the construction of a market-oriented economic system; and third, the gradual takeover of economic policy from the federal government. Pragmatism and gradualism were the pillars: They were to ascertain the socially bearable costs of transition, facilitate the rapid adaptation to highly uncertain political decisions, and generate proper responses to the economic policies of the federal government.

From the very beginning, the government of Slovenia implicitly supported the federal stabilization program by imposing relatively efficient wage controls and by reducing (compared with the rest of Yugoslavia) public consumption. Increasing discrepancies in federal economic policies that adversely affected the export sector, however, soon prompted demands for changes in the stabilization program.[4] They included devaluation of the dinar, reduction of federal government taxes and spending, efficient control of wages, corrections in monetary policy, and redemption of Iraqi debt to enterprises by the federal government. Requests urging a limited use of the economic policies that were left to the republics' governments were ignored. Proposals to prevent bankruptcies by postponing tax payments and export subsidies as well as to prevent them by a partial redemption of the Iraqi debts by government bonds were introduced during 1990.

In January 1991 following the disintegration of the fiscal system in September 1990 (Serbia failed to transfer proceeds of federal sales taxes and customs duties to the federal budget), a trade war began (in October 1990, Serbia imposed special taxes on Slovene and Croat firms and on deposits of all payments to these two republics); and finally, because of a raid on the monetary system in December 1990 (Serbians broke into the Treasury and printed unauthorized currency that they distributed to groups in Serbia), Slovenia requested changes in economic policy, rejected federal proposals for centralized government, and for the first time, proposed principles for the division of financial and nonfinancial assets and liabilities between Slovenia and the rest of Yugoslavia. The requests were ignored. When the National Bank of Yugoslavia ceased to intervene in the foreign exchange market, Slovenia reacted by introducing its own quasi–foreign exchange market with a flexible exchange rate, and a Slovene ECU (European Currency Unit) as a measure of account. Thus, to a limited extent, Slovenia established sovereignty in the fiscal and foreign exchange system long before the formal proclamation of political independence.

Systemic changes were made cautiously as well. Two types of statutes were introduced: those facilitating the functioning of a normal market economy and those needed for the transition to an independent government. In the first group, a system of direct taxation introducing simple, transparent, uniform, and nondiscretionary taxes was introduced in December 1990. The first normal budget of an independent country was presented to Parliament in February 1991, and a new system of simple indirect taxation was being prepared. The statutes regulating the monetary and financial sector—such as the Bank of Slovenia Act, the Banks and Savings Institutions Act, and the Rehabilitation of the Banks and Savings Institutions Act—were prepared to enable swift adjustment toward (at a still uncertain time) political independence. Provisional notes were printed to allow for the introduction of a Slovene currency. In short, Slovenia was, at least in part, economically and institutionally prepared to face the uncertainties of political independence.

Economic policy based on pragmatism, gradualism, firm but flexible wage controls, and restrictions on government spending also proved to be relatively successful. In one year, the productivity of the Slovene economy, as compared with that of the rest of the country, grew by 16 percent; and relative competitiveness increased by 35 percent. In May 1991 the bottom of the cycle was reached, and productivity and investments in fixed assets started to grow. The restructuring started as well: Unemployment increased rapidly as enterprises started to adjust to new economic conditions.

On June 26, 1991, Slovenia and Croatia proclaimed independence, and Slovenia immediately started to implement it. The proclamation coincided with the unresolved disputes over customs duties, and federal authorities attempted to take control of the borders. The army units that were sent to the borders were, however, surprised by the resistance. In a week the army gave up, and the federal presidency decided that the army would withdraw if Slovenia would postpone the implementation of independence for three months. At the same time, animosities between Croats and Serbs culminated and escalated in an extremely cruel civil war of unforeseeable duration and outcome with disastrous economic results. Slovenia became economically independent on October 8, 1991, after the three months' moratorium. A new currency, the Slovene tolar, was introduced; and dinars were converted to tolars at the rate 1:1. The initial value of the tolar was set to 32 Slovene tolars = 1 deutsche mark, which implied a real devaluation of 16 percent. Internal convertibility and floating exchange rates were introduced.

The relevant economic arguments for independence differed considerably from the populist notion of "being exploited" by the rest of Yugoslavia. The issues were linked to the prospects for economic transition. Political disintegration deprived Yugoslavia of all systemic advantages for a swift economic transition, and the differences between the "West" and the "East" became an unsurmountable barrier to the implementation of systemic changes and for a sound economic policy. In such circumstances, the price of the "secession" became lower than the economic and social costs of sharing the Yugoslav chaos.

For Slovenia, however, the economic price was very high. The loss of the Yugoslav market; the diminished supply of raw materials and of cheaper, finished products from the rest of Yugoslavia; the consequences of a small currency area; the termination of foreign trade links that Slovenia had through companies in other parts of Yugoslavia; the embargo on financial flows until debt issues were settled; and the weaker interest of foreign investors in a smaller market were only some of the predictable consequences of independence. Other issues (i.e., foreign debt; domestic debt in foreign currency deposits; vanishing foreign currency reserves; the allocation of nonfinancial assets of the federation; and the status of 2,500 different bilateral and multilateral agreements on export quotas, transport licenses, and air controls signed by the Yugoslav government) might take years to resolve.

THE DILEMMAS OF PRIVATIZATION

The privatization issue caused a major controversy within the government, divided politicians, and became the root of political instability. Two major concepts known as the Korze-Mencinger-Simoneti law and the Sachs-Peterle-Umek law competed with each other.

The Korze-Mencinger-Simoneti Decentralized Concept

A concept of decentralized, monitored privatization was brought to Parliament in June 1990. According to this concept, privatization should be country specific and based on the advantages of the Slovenian economy: the relative independence of enterprises, regional dispersion of industry, the existing industrial structure, close links with foreign firms, and the relatively large financial resources of the population. Advocates of the Korze-Mencinger-Simoneti decentralized approach argued that Slovenia had a relatively well operating, though not very efficient, economy and that the crisis in 1990 and 1991 was produced by the federal government's hazardous economic policy supported by international financial institutions and Western scholars and was exacerbated by the problems of political independence.[5]

The illusions that privatization would increase efficiency overnight and that it would be socially just were dismissed in the Korze-Mencinger-Simoneti concept. Advocates of a decentralized approach argued that privatization could only create conditions for economic efficiency. They assumed that privatization had to be a continuing process; that its economic, social, and political consequences were unknown (except in theoretical models); and that many solutions would turn out to be wrong and would have to be changed. The claim that a centralized model of free distribution and provisional nationalization would immediately create private owners was questioned by those who argued that free distribution only looked like it was socially just and that nationalization only seemed to make control of the process possible. Adoption of the centralized method of privatization would, instead, nullify the advantages of decentralized decision making. Defenders of the decentralized approach argued that through temporary nationalization the state would have to assume all functions of the owners and would, thereby, establish a powerful state business sector. This would be a slow process requiring an enormous administrative apparatus.

Supporters of the Korze-Mencinger-Simoneti concept argued that decentralized decision making had been the advantage of the Slovene economy, when compared with other Central European countries, and that Slovenia had other characteristics that were conducive to this method. For one, industry dispersed over the country allowed strong links to develop between employees and their firms; and this minimized the social costs of transition to private ownership. Also, there were many medium-sized firms with well-established commercial and capital links (joint ventures) to foreign firms. The population was relatively wealthy; and most financial resources (estimated at U.S. $2.5 billion) had been kept "under mattresses" or in foreign banks, while U.S. $1.2 billion of assets had been frozen in the Yugoslavian banking system. The characteristics of the Slovenian economy in 1989 are described in table 5.2.

With these characteristics in mind, the government of Slovenia put forward the concept of decentralized privatization to be implemented by firms in which

Table 5.2
Basic Socioeconomic Data in 1989

Data	Slovenia	Percent of Yugoslavia	Yugoslavia
Population (millions)	1,996.0	8.2	23,690.0
Area in 000 km	20.2	7.9	255.8
Employment	851.0	12.4	6,875.0
Unemployment	28.0	4.5	1,201.0
GDP (millions of 1972 dinars)	6,593.0	18.1	39,625.0
GNP/Capita (YU = 100)	202.0	—	100.0
Exports of Goods (millions of US$)	4,118.0	28.7	14,308.0
Imports of Goods	4,727.0	25.0	18,871.0

Source: *Statistini letopis Slovenije*, 1991.

workers, managers, creditors, former owners, and foreign and domestic companies could participate. Several methods were stipulated for ensuring the flexibility required by diverse forms of social ownership. An enterprise might choose from different methods of transformation laid down by the law and could combine them. Both the Privatization Agency and the Development Fund were to help in the process. In short, the government would determine the rules for privatization and monitor it but would not, except in special cases, administer it. Thus, privatization would be gradual; and there would not be a free distribution of shares at the beginning of the process. Consequently, enterprises were to be transformed into joint-stock or limited companies in two years.

Four principal types of ownership restructuring were stipulated: first, by sale of existing equity capital; second, by raising additional equity capital; third, by transfer of equity capital to the Development Fund; and fourth, by debt-equity swaps. Three different levels of involvement by the Privatization Agency were distinguished: autonomous privatization in which only the Agency monitored the procedure, privatization with the participation of the Agency, and privatization carried out by the Agency. All four types of ownership restructuring could be used in each of the three levels of involvement.

Proceeds from sales would go to the Development Fund. Initial privatization by sale could be full or partial. If partial, the unsubscribed shares would be temporarily transferred to the Fund in a form of purchasable nonvoting shares. Each consecutive year the privatized enterprise would be obliged to buy back 10 percent of the shares that were not initially subscribed; if not, the Fund could turn them into common shares and sell them. If privatization took place by raising additional equity capital, the new capital would remain with the enterprise. Purchasable nonvoting shares for the existing social capital would be transferred to the Fund; all other rules of the sale would apply. In both cases, a preliminary valuation was required. Valuation was not necessary if an enterprise issued ordinary shares and transferred them to the Fund.

The Privatization Agency participated in ownership restructuring in cases it considered important and in all cases in which buyers were not domestic companies or citizens. To prevent "spontaneous privatization," the Agency had to be notified of such transactions as the sale or leasing of parts of an enterprise. Finally, using any of the authorized methods, the Agency would privatize enterprises that were partly or entirely owned by the Republic of Slovenia.

Citizens of Slovenia would be entitled to a 30 percent discount on the purchase of shares up to a value of 20,000 deutsch marks; and the employees, to an additional discount of 1 percent for each year in service. The total discount, however, could not exceed 50 percent. The proceeds of the sales were to be used for pension and disability insurance, social development and environmental programs, restitution, and payment of debts. It was also stipulated that in the future—according to a separate act—shares of the Fund were to be given to pension and investment funds and other financial institutions and that some shares of these funds and financial institutions were to be distributed free of charge to citizens of Slovenia.

The decentralized approach to privatization tried to avoid shocks by leaving to the enterprises the right to decide on the pace and the method of privatization. This was done within limits, for the process for deciding was originally to end by the close of 1993. This approach would allow the relatively rapid creation of an incomplete ownership structure and, afterward, its gradual completion. Priority was given to speeding up privatization of management. Owners would become those citizens or legal entities who wished to be active owners of the enterprise and who were willing to pay for it. More important, it was believed, the concept would avoid the need for extensive government administration and potential political interference.

The decentralized approach had some major shortcomings. It did not privatize and restructure enterprises with poor performance or losses. These enterprises would most likely decide to transfer common shares to the Development Fund and, thus, opt for voluntary nationalization. The state might be stuck with their shares and forced to carry out their privatization. Also, the valuation of the enterprises might be subject to manipulation and corruption—processes whereby buyers might make windfall gains. This could give rise to considerable political resistance. The incentives to employees to buy shares would stimulate the creation of inside investors who, particularly if they owned a minority of shares, might pursue policies that were only in their own interests and not in the interests of other owners. Moreover, they could continue to siphon profits into salaries at the expense of other shareholders.

The Sachs-Peterle-Umek Centralized Concept

The competing concept was derived from macroeconomic distributive models and would apply solutions proposed in other countries of Central Europe, notably Poland. This approach, advocated by Harvard economist Jeffrey Sachs and others, required massive and speedy privatization administered by the central government and relying on the free distribution of company shares. The concept underwent many changes since it was first introduced in May 1991.

According to the Sachs-Peterle-Umek centralized concept, privatization would be carried out in two stages. In the first stage, 10 percent of capital based on book value would be distributed among employees in all companies free of charge. In large companies (with more than 500 employees), 70 percent would be transferred to the Development Fund in the form of common shares; and 20 percent, in the form of purchasable preferential shares. The government would also create a list of large companies to be sold to foreigners. In the medium-sized companies (125 to 500 employees), at least 30 percent of the capital in the form of common shares and 42 percent in the form of participatory preferential shares would be transferred to the Fund, while 18 percent would be privatized by an immediate workers' buyout. In small companies (with less than 125 employees), 49 percent of capital in the form of participatory preferential shares and 20 percent in the form of common shares would be transferred to the Fund; and 21 percent would be left for an immediate workers' buyout. All proceeds from sales would go to the Fund. In the second stage, 15 percent of the shares of the Fund would be transferred to the Slovene Compensation Fund; 35 percent, to five newly established investment companies; and 20 percent, to the Pension Fund. The shares of the investment funds would be distributed among citizens of Slovenia.

The assumed advantages of this concept were that it would immediately create the ownership model established in Western economies and that it would improve corporate governance in a way that would be fair to all citizens. Additional benefits of the option were that it would reduce the need to raise taxes to pay for pensions and that institutional owners would monitor and control enterprises to ensure their efficiency and profitability. Opponents argued, however, that the transfer of ownership to institutional owners and the distribution of shares to citizens would be a two-stage "paper privatization" that would not address real issues and would postpone rather than promote real privatization. Critics argued that Slovenia needed active instead of passive owners; it required strategic partners instead of merely thousands of small financial investors.

Furthermore, the ownership structure created by such privatization would not at all resemble the ownership structure in Western Europe. Investment companies and pension funds, which would be the first-level owners, would be passive investors that would diversify risks and that would not have enough ownership interest in a given company to actually restructure it. The companies would be established by government decree, and ownership would be administratively distributed among numerous institutional investors. The operations would, therefore, resemble a reorganization or a reform of state ownership that might have been a step forward in the former centrally planned economies of Central Europe; but such an approach would represent a step backward in Slovenia. The boards of the institutional owners would be nominated by the government, and the managers of the companies would be appointed by the boards of institutional owners. Both would lack private ownership interests and would become obedient public servants. Thus, critics contended, instead of privatization, the transformation of social to state property would be complete; and real ownership would stay firmly in the hands of the politicians.

The second stage of privatization—that is, the distribution of ownership to the entire population—would be a politically attractive sideshow of "fairness" that would have nothing to do with efficiency and social equity. It would only strengthen political control because it would reintroduce the "everybody and nobody" concept of institutional ownership of property. It might take decades before reasonable concentration emerged. The macroeconomic consequences of giving away the shares of institutional owners would be similar to those of a voucher scheme. Savings on the national level would be reduced because financial assets would flow from those with a high propensity to consume.

CONCLUSION

The controversy over the decentralized versus the centralized approach to privatization became a political rather than an economic issue—the root being control over the economy. The first concept presumably enabled the control to remain in the hands of managers and thus in the hands of the old political elite. The second concept would, on the other hand, transfer control to the government and thus to the new political elite. Although two out of three required drafts of the decentralized version of the privatization act were passed by Parliament, the political leaders of the coalition parties prevented the final draft from coming to Parliament for a vote. After a year of battles in Parliament and in the mass media, by May 1992 the privatization controversy in Slovenia appeared to be resolved by the proposal of a new act that was considered to be a compromise between the two concepts. Namely, while allowing for institutional ownership, the proposal would allow the enterprises to make crucial decisions and to enable insiders, together with those who bought shares, to attain majority control over the enterprises.

According to the draft of this new privatization proposal, ownership restructuring would occur by granting restitution to former owners through the Denationalization Act and the Cooperatives Act; by debt-equity swaps; by the transfer of shares to the Restitution, Pension, and Development funds; by an internal sale of shares to employees; by manager and worker buyouts; by the sale of shares or of the company; and by raising additional capital. Privatization would begin by changing the existing social enterprises into joint-stock companies. Ten percent of the capital left to former owners after restitution and voluntary debt-equity swaps would be transferred to the Pension Fund; 10 percent, to the Restitution Fund; and 20 percent, to the Development Fund, which would transfer the shares to newly established mutual funds. All Slovene citizens would be entitled to buy shares of these funds up to 160,000 tolars per person (about 3,000 deutsche marks) with a 90 percent discount. Up to 20 percent (and up to 300,000 tolars [about 6,000 deutsche marks] per person) of the capital would be sold to the employees at a 90 percent discount, and the proceeds would remain in the company. The rest of the shares of a company (up to 40 percent) would be sold in 18 months or transferred to the Development Fund in the form of preferential or common shares, depending on the choice of the company. If a company decided to use manager and worker buyouts, the workers and managers would have to purchase the shares within five years. The shares would be salable, except for those purchased by 90 percent discount; and those could not be sold for 12 months.

NOTES

1. S. K. Chand and H. R. Lorie, "Fiscal Policy," in V. Tanzi, ed., *Fiscal Policies in Economies in Transition* (Washington, D.C.: International Monetary Fund, 1992), p. 11.

2. J. Mencinger, "The Yugoslav Economic Systems and Their Efficiency," *Economic Analysis* 19, no. 1 (1986), pp. 31-43.

3. See A. Katz, "The Adaptability and Feasibility of Market Socialism: Lessons from Yugoslavia," mimeographed (Pittsburgh: University of Pittsburgh, 1987).

4. "The Memorandum on Economic Policy in the Rest of 1990" sent to the federal government in August 1990.

5. A. Bajt, "Trideset godina privrednog rasta," *Ekonomist* 38, no. 1 (1984), pp. 1-20.

6

Decentralization of Administrative and Political Authority to Promote Regional Economic Development: The Case of Ljubljana

Pavel Gantar

The political changes that occurred in Yugoslavia in 1990 and the subsequent declaration of autonomy by the Republic of Slovenia in 1991 brought about a major transformation in the republic's economy as well as in the economic conditions of various regions of the country. The economic performance of the Ljubljana region, for example, declined rapidly after 1990, although the problems associated with the decline were merely strong manifestations of trends already detectable in the late 1980s.

A study by the Ljubljana Regional Chamber of Economy assessing the economic performance of the Ljubljana region listed a myriad of problems.[1] Between 1990 and 1991, industrial production fell by 15 percent to a level not seen since 1975. The largest decreases were in the machine, industrial equipment, and construction industries. Companies in the region experienced serious problems in obtaining supplies of raw materials and other intermediate production goods, particularly from abroad and from other Yugoslav republics. Exports and employment also declined by 15 percent from January to November 1991. Unemployment rose to more than 13 percent. Payment delays, particularly from other Yugoslav republics, increased enormously. Active debts of organizations in the other Yugoslav republics to firms in the Ljubljana region were 3.6 times higher than these same organizations' claims on companies in that region. Military hostilities that accompanied the breakup of former Yugoslavia made these debts virtually impossible to collect. As a result, 333 companies in the region became insolvent and had their accounts blocked; many were on the verge of bankruptcy and were kept active only by help from the state.

The investment of industrial firms in the Ljubljana region also dropped substantially. In 1991 the regional economy had only 14 percent of its total industrial investment in the Republic of Slovenia even though the region's contribution to the republic's total output was substantially higher. Thus, by

1992 the economy of the Ljubljana region was experiencing one of its deepest depressions in history.

This severe economic downturn could be attributed to several factors. First, the substantial loss of markets in the republics of former Yugoslavia and markets abroad weakened the position of many companies in Ljubljana.[2] Second, the gradual introduction of market criteria in managing firms caused either restructuring or close-downs that produced higher unemployment. Third, the relatively harsh state monetary policies aimed at reducing inflation and limiting investment in socially owned industries weakened their capacity to recover. Finally, the government's short-term economic policy of providing tax relief to those enterprises thought to have the financial and technological potential for restructuring was designed to avoid the severe social costs of closing unprofitable firms as well as to allow inefficient enterprises to continue operating.[3]

The most serious immediate outcome of the depression in the Ljubljana region was rapidly increasing unemployment.[4] In 1991, unemployment grew on average by 1,034 people a month. At the end of December 1991, registered unemployed in the Ljubljana region reached 26,566, a level almost 99 percent higher than in 1990. The degree of relative unemployment, that is, the relationship between those seeking employment and those working in private and socially owned (state) businesses, rose to nearly 11 percent in November 1991—a 100 percent increase over the level in December 1990. The number of requests for unemployment support increased in 1991 by 84 percent and made heavy demands on the state budget.

If the Ljubljana region is to benefit from the reforms that were adopted by the state in 1990 and 1991 to transform socially owned enterprises into private ones and, thereby, create an institutional setting for the development of a market-oriented economy, there also has to be an appropriate restructuring of the administrative and political system in Slovenia to allow various regions of the country to cope with their economic problems.

This chapter examines the challenges that faced the region of Ljubljana during the early period of economic transformation in the Republic of Slovenia from 1989 to mid-1992. It also identifies the changes that are needed in the structure of local and regional government in order to create a stronger institutional base for the development of a market economy and to deal effectively in the future with the problems of social change accompanying such a transformation.

CHARACTERISTICS OF THE LJUBLJANA REGIONAL ECONOMY

The development of modern Ljubljana dates back to the second half of the nineteenth century when it was an Austrian provincial town of some 30,000 residents. The major impetus for the economic and demographic growth of

Ljubljana was the construction of the southern railroad connecting Vienna, the capital of the Austro-Hungarian monarchy, with the Italian port of Triest. The southern railroad brought Ljubljana into the European rail network and made it a more attractive location for capital investment and trade. Another impetus for Ljubljana's growth was the reconstruction of the city after the earthquake in 1895. The new urban plan for Ljubljana gave the city a modern spatial pattern of development, created new sites for industrial location, and provided such modern infrastructure as roads, water supply, sewage, and electricity.

After World War I, Ljubljana became part of the new state of Yugoslavia and grew in size to about 100,000 inhabitants. During that time, Ljubljana was one of the most important economic centers in Yugoslavia and a seat of provincial administration. After World War II, Ljubljana was subjected to all of the changes that came with the Communist economic and political system. The Communist program of "socialist industrialization" created an enormous need for labor, and Ljubljana grew very rapidly to its current population of more than 300,000 residents. The city of Ljubljana was also the cultural and political capital of the Republic of Slovenia, which was part of postwar federal Yugoslavia. On October 8, 1991, the Republic of Slovenia declared itself an independent and sovereign state and was subsequently recognized as such by most nations of the world. The city of Ljubljana became the capital of the new nation.

The Ljubljana region is a largely urban economic area divided adminis-tratively into five municipalities—Bežigrad, Center, Moste-Polje, Šiška, and Vič-Rudnik—that function as political and administrative units. Two of the munici-palities, Šiška and Vič-Rudnik, include large rural areas. These five municipali-ties delegate some of their responsibilities to the city administration that makes decisions about issues that affect the whole city. Each of the municipalities has a communal assembly with authority to make decisions about local public services.

The city administration is organized in the same way as the municipalities. A city assembly exercises the responsibilities that are transferred from the municipalities, but the system is complicated because the city assembly must obtain the consensus of all five communal assemblies to pass many types of legislation or directives. For example, the city budget, major investments in infrastructure, and new development programs have to be approved by all five communal assemblies as well as by the city assembly.

Such a local political system functioned quite smoothly when Yugoslavia was under one-party rule. But in the pluralistic political system that emerged after the demise of the Communist regime, it was much more difficult to obtain consensus from the various political parties or coalitions that ruled the municipalities. For example, the coalition that won the city elections in 1991 quickly fell apart; and the city's Executive Council, which is the executive body of the city assembly, did not have majority support. Therefore, the assembly could not approve the city budget for 1992. The mayor, who was a member of DEMOS (Democratic Opposition of Slovenia), refused to introduce a vote of confidence in the Executive Council; and Ljubljana was without a budget. This caused severe problems in operating public services.[5]

Population Growth and Characteristics

The population of Ljubljana's municipalities, with the exception of Center (the central city), grew rapidly from 1948 to 1981 and then slowed down during the 1980s (see tables 6.1 and 6.2). Center, the central municipality that encompasses the most urbanized area of Ljubljana, experienced a substantial decline in population during the 1970s and 1980s as the area was transformed into a central business district with commercial, banking, trading, cultural, and political activities and institutions. Table 6.3 indicates considerable differences in population characteristics among Ljubljana's municipalities, particularly in the two that include large rural areas (Šiška and Vič-Rudnik). Table 6.4 shows differences in population density (population per square kilometer) among the municipalities. Despite its large population decline, Center is still the most populated area of Ljubljana; and Šiška and Vič-Rudnik manifest all of the characteristics of a rural area. Tables 6.5, 6.6, and 6.7 show the number of households and dwellings as well as the average size of households in 1971, 1981, and 1991 and further illustrate the differences bewteen urban and rural municipalities.

Table 6.1
Population Growth in the Ljubljana Region, 1948-91

	Bežigrad	Center	Moste-Polje	Šiška	Vič Rudnik	Ljubljana
1948	17,538	38,362	25,274	29,949	45,904	157,027
1953	20,839	42,076	27,095	37,637	48,290	175,973
1961	31,239	43,484	32,724	46,593	53,265	207,305
1971	41,318	40,134	44,717	65,884	65,747	257,800
1981	55,609	32,285	61,493	81,543	74,281	305,211
1991	58,243	28,921	72,235	83,310	80,582	323,291

Source: Statistical Yearbook of Republic Slovenia, various years.

Table 6.2

Indexes of Population Growth in the Municipalities of Ljubljana

Commune	Index 1991/1948	Index 1991/1981
Bežigrad	332.10	104.74
Center	75.39	89.58
Moste-Polje	285.81	117.47
Šiška	278.17	102.17
Vič-Rudnik	175.54	108.48
Ljubljana	205.90	105.90

Source: Statistical Yearbook of Republic Slovenia, various years.

Table 6.3

Number of Settlements in the Municipalities of Ljubljana

	Bežigrad	Center	Moste-Polje	Šiška	Vič-Rudnik	Ljubljana
1971	19	1	60	62	189	331
1981	11	1	61	56	192	330
1991	9	1	39	54	189	292

Source: Statistical Yearbook of Republic Slovenia, various years.

Table 6.4

Population of the Municipalities of Ljubljana per Square Kilometer

	Bežigrad	Center	Moste-Polje	Šiška	Vič-Rudnik	Ljubljana
1971	898	8,027	294	422	121	286
1981	12,090	6,457	405	523	137	338
1991	1,266	5,784	475	534	148	358

Source: Statistical Yearbook of Republic Slovenia, various years.

Table 6.5
Number of Households in the Municipalities of Ljubljana

	Bežigrad	Center	Moste-Polje	Šiška	Vič-Rudnik	Ljubljana
1971	14,089	15,872	15,048	22,639	20,989	88,637
1981	20,068	14,392	21,847	29,018	24,640	109,965
1991	21,918	11,537	25,044	29,885	27,797	116,181

Source: *Statistical Yearbook of Republic Slovenia*, various years.

Table 6.6
Number of Dwellings in the Municipalities of Ljubljana

	Bežigrad	Center	Moste-Polje	Šiška	Vič-Rudnik	Ljubljana
1971	11,922	13,204	12,357	19,140	19,108	75,731
1981	19,353	12,347	20,111	28,060	24,055	103,926
1991	22,336	11,601	25,536	30,605	30,107	120,185

Source: *Statistical Yearbook of Republic Slovenia*, various years.

Table 6.7
Average Size of Households in the Municipalities of Ljubljana

	Bežigrad	Center	Moste-Polje	Šiška	Vič-Rudnik	Ljubljana
1971	2.9	2.5	3.0	2.9	3.1	2.9
1981	2.8	2.2	2.8	2.8	3.0	2.8
1991	2.7	2.5	2.9	2.8	2.9	2.8

Source: *Statistical Yearbook of Republic Slovenia*, various years.

The Ljubljana region is not formally organized as a political and administrative unit but is really only a collection of municipalities that sometimes cooperate on issues of mutual interest. In addition to the five Ljubljana municipalities, it includes an additional eight adjacent municipalities. The population of this region reached 470,130 inhabitants in 1981, and by 1991 it had grown to 504,387 residents as a result of suburbanization. The concentration of population in the central urban area ended in the 1970s, and since then the region experienced faster population growth in suburban areas.

Employment in Ljubljana is relatively high, and women make up almost half of the labor force (see table 6.8). But a closer look at the region's employment characteristics offers a less optimistic view of the region's economic growth potential. The high rates of employment from 1969 to 1990 were not so much the result of strong regional economic performance as they were the outcome of socialist development policies. The highest rates of employment were seen in the 1970s when economic development in Yugoslavia was based on industrial expansion through foreign borrowing. After the debt crisis of the 1980s, the rates of employment in Ljubljana slowed down substantially and actually declined from 1985 to 1990. Moreover, the great majority of jobs were created in the state-controlled sector. In 1990 only a little less than 7,000 people were employed in the private sector as compared with more than 177,000 in the socially owned sector. And yet employment grew from 1985 to 1990 only in the private sector, while it declined in the socially owned sector.

Economic Structure of the Ljubljana Region

Table 6.9 shows the employment structure of the major socially owned business sectors and public services. If employment is taken as an indicator of the relative strength of different sectors of the economy, then industry is clearly the most important one in Ljubljana. The heavy decline in employment in the

Table 6.8
Employed Persons in Ljubljana, 1979–90

	Total	Socially Owned Sector	Private Sector	Share of Women
1970	126,718	122,421	4,297	55,047
1975	158,678	154,696	3,982	71,765
1980	182,772	177,635	5,137	84,877
1985	190,160	184,125	6,035	88,663
1990	184,301	177,367	6,934	88,127
Index 1990/70	153	125	164	169
Index 1990/80	101	99	134	103
Index 1990/85	96	96	114	99

Source: Statistical Yearbook of Ljubljana, 1991.

Table 6.9
Employment in Major Socially Owned Business

	1979	1981	1983	1985	1987	1990
Industry & Mining	49,937	50,986	51,751	52,441	55,323	48,278
Agriculture *	543	481	570	661	659	493
Construction	16,738	17,599	14,859	15,906	15,426	11,719
Transportation/ Communication	10,283	10,663	10,808	11,040	11,555	11,880
Trade & Retail	25,108	27,114	26,015	26,034	26,763	24,879
Tourism	4,777	5,474	5,589	5,684	6,069	5,884
Small Business **	5,804	5,907	5,678	5,072	6,560	5,884
Finance	12,922	10,917	14,681	15,913	15,943	16,303
Housing & Infrastructure	4,614	4,923	5,145	5,363	4,580	—
Education	17,792	17,760	18,811	19,054	19,818	20,328
Health	12,174	12,621	13,473	13,974	14,713	15,202
Administration	9,370	9,643	9,763	9,378	9,448	8,826

* Farmers are not included.
**Privately owned small businesses are not included.

Source: *Statistical Yearbook of Ljubljana*, 1991.

construction industry indicates the slowdown of investment activities in the city. social and public sectors such as education, health, and administration remained relatively stable from 1979 to 1990 with a slight tendency to grow; whereas employment in industry and construction declined. The high growth in employment in the financial sector indicates that Ljubljana was becoming the center of finance for Slovenia.

Table 6.10 shows the structure of the national social product in Ljubljana. The data confirm again that the most important sector of economic activity is industry. Its share of social product has increased, which suggests that the level of productivity is rising even though the rate of employment in the sector is declining. The second-most important contributor to social product in Ljubljana is trade and retail activities.

Table 6.10
Structure of the National Social Product in Ljubljana

	1985	1986	1987	1988	1989
All Sectors	100.0	100.0	100.0	100.0	100.0
Industry & Mining	40.8	38.8	39.7	44.0	43.7
Agriculture	1.1	1.2	1.1	1.1	1.1
Forestry	0.2	0.2	0.2	0.1	0.2
Water Management	0.2	0.3	0.3	0.2	0.3
Construction	5.9	7.1	6.3	5.7	4.0
Transportation/ Communication	6.8	7.6	6.8	6.3	6.0
Retail & Trade	25.1	25.9	24.9	23.4	25.1
Tourism	3.9	2.9	3.5	4.2	2.9
Small Business	5.3	5.6	5.5	5.1	4.5
Infrastructure	1.1	1.2	1.5	1.3	1.1
Finances *	7.8	7.2	7.9	6.7	8.6
Education **	1.5	1.5	1.9	1.6	2.1
Health	0.2	0.2	0.4	0.3	0.4

* Technical and business services are also included.
** Science, culture, and information are also included.

Source: *Statistical Yearbook of Ljubljana*, 1991.

THE NEED FOR ECONOMIC AND ADMINISTRATIVE RESTRUCTURING

Clearly, industry remains the most important sector in the economy of the Ljubljana region. In the future, economic conditions in the region will depend heavily on industrial performance. Therefore, the prosperity of the city and its surrounding region will require substantial industrial restructuring and will also mandate substantial changes in the local and regional administrative system.

Regional Administrative Changes

Local and regional administrative and political restructuring must achieve at least two objectives. First, the legitimate activities of the nation-state at the local level must be differentiated from the responsibilities of local governments. One common characteristic of Communist systems was that they did not recognize the differences between local self-government and the local administrative activities of the nation-state. In Communist systems these two activities were integrated into a single state administrative system. Differentiating between the two levels of government would, of course, limit the role of the state at the local and regional levels and make localities responsible for their own development and prosperity.

Second, differentiation between national and local government must be accompanied by administrative and political decentralization. Decentralization implies the withdrawal of the state from direct regulation of local economies and the creation of a local political and administrative system that is able to provide both the infrastructure and the public services that are required in a market economy.

From 1974 to the late 1980s, Yugoslavia was relatively decentralized because of the sensitive multiethnic character of the country. Some degree of self-administration was granted to the republics; and municipalities—the basic units of local government—had substantial responsibilities for providing such public services as elementary schools, medical care, unemployment support, cultural activities, local roads, and parks. They were authorized to introduce special taxes (so-called contributions) to finance them. The idea was that each public service would have its own financial resources from a particular "contribution" paid as a tax by all employed residents in the municipality. This led to a very complicated and somewhat uncontrollable taxation system. In some municipalities the average citizen had to pay more than ten different contributions to the national government, the republic, and the municipality. Such a taxation system became a heavy burden for the economy because it continually generated demands for higher wages. Despite this official system of decentralization, the federal government always found ways of controlling local public expenditures and of redirecting financial resources to the republic or federal government levels. Such a system also created a huge "self-management bureaucracy" that was unable to organize efficiently the provision of public services.

Yet this relative autonomy of local administrative units in former Yugoslavia had some important advantages. It stimulated local incentives and entrepreneurship more than in other Central and Eastern European countries, and it produced a cadre of "nonpolitical" local managers who were much more aware of modern public management than the Communist party officials. These local managers were able to adapt very quickly to changes in political power and to the democratic, multiparty political environment after the collapse of the Communist regime.

One of the first tasks of the new democratically elected government in Slovenia was to change the complicated taxation system and to adopt practices common in Western Europe. The first step was to abolish the complicated system of contributions and to replace it with a single income tax that was collected at the national level. But if one looked at the formal responsibilities of local government units in Slovenia in 1992, they were far smaller than was the case in the former Communist system. Under the new system, financial resources for local public services were collected by the national government and then allocated to the municipalities. This approach was adopted as a provisional solution until the new Act on Local and Regional Self-Government could be formulated and passed by Parliament. Thus, the first step in adjusting the local administrative and political system to the requirements of a market economy in Slovenia was not decentralization but rather the opposite: The government of the republic reassumed control over local expenditures by centralizing the taxation system.

Because the city of Ljubljana is divided into five municipalities, the responsibilities of the city administration remain few even though in 1992 the city assembly did manage to consolidate some responsibilities previously held by municipalities, particularly in the field of urban planning, communal infrastructure, transportation, and environmental protection. The local government units coordinate their activities regionally only on public works that are financed by the municipal authorities.

By the early 1990s, the Ljubljana region had developed a considerably higher level of services in health, education, culture, and sports than the rest of the country. But the deteriorating economic situation adversely affected the financing and maintenance of these services. The city administration, according to Zinka Venta, adopted three main strategies to adjust to the worsening economic conditions.[6] First, it developed a strategy of rationalization that consisted of searching for "internal reserves" that would finance reorganized service activities. This involved restricting wage increases for public service workers, reducing investments in public services and infrastructure, and raising eligibility criteria for access to some services. According to local administrators, this strategy proved to be relatively successful even though it shifted the financial burdens to public service employees and clients.

The second strategy involved the "commercialization" of services, that is, shifting more of the costs to those who used them. As a result, for example, the costs increased for those using health services. Among local administrators, the commercialization of public services was not assessed positively because it produced greater social and regional differences in service costs and coverage. Yet such an assessment may simply have reflected traditional socialist perspectives that were still strong among many public and social services administrators.

The third strategy, according to Venta, was one of "externalization." This consisted of shifting responsibility for some public services to social or informal self-help groups such as the family, volunteers, or community organizations. This process started only in 1992, but it is clear that it is not an effective alternative for providing all institutional public services. And yet many residents of the city believe that it can be an important supplement to the rigid institutional system of service delivery.

Regional Employment Promotion Programs

In the emerging market economy of Slovenia, local and regional governments are expected to play an important role in alleviating unemployment problems and in sustaining those business activities that offer more jobs. But this is quite a difficult task, for many local administrators were not trained to promote economic support activities in the municipalities. Indeed, in the Communist regime they were supposed to block and suppress private incentives. In 1991 the municipalities in the Ljubljana region initiated 92 projects that were expected to provide jobs for 600 people for a three-month period. Most of the programs focused on repairing roads and infrastructure. However, the projects have not met expectations; in fact, only about 300 people obtained short-term employment. Still, an increase in public works programs is expected in 1992 because the implementation of many of the projects initiated the previous year met unexpected difficulties.

In a market-oriented economy, local politicians and administrators need retraining and a better understanding of how to achieve closer cooperation between the local administration and the state-run bureaus of employment. In the Ljubljana region, the Bureau of Employment started 44 retraining programs (particularly for those occupations having greater possibilities for self-employment) that eventually involved nearly 2,000 people.[7] In 1990 the bureau also started a program of individual counseling that was based on experiences in the United States with incubators for fostering entrepreneurship.

The most important way of alleviating unemployment was through cofinancing first jobs. In 1991 the bureau cofinanced the initial employment of 2,274 people for a period of from six months to one year. The bureau also started a self-employment program that offered free seminars on "Entrepreneurship for Beginners"; the seminars provided all of the information that potential entrepreneurs needed to start a business. Twenty-one seminars in which 456 people participated were organized in 1991. However, no results have been reported on how many participants actually started their own business. Another important program for actively promoting employment sought to create 1,000 new jobs. Every firm that offered a new job to an unemployed worker for at least three months was given 60,000 (at that time, Yugoslav) dinars. Through this program, 579 people found new jobs.

All of these programs were carried out at a time when only a small portion of the population in Ljubljana was unemployed. Moreover, all of these measures were financed by the state and organized by the regional bureaus of employment that were units of the Ministry of Work. The local and regional administrations were only indirectly involved by pressing the state to offer more funds and programs for their own regions.

Industrial Restructuring

During the early 1990s it became increasingly clear to local officials that the only real option for alleviating the serious social problems caused by growing unemployment was to stimulate a new "economic takeoff" in the region. The possibilities of economic recovery in the Ljubljana region are closely linked with the restructuring of existing industries and the opening of new small- and medium-sized firms. The problem of restructuring is, in turn, linked with the forthcoming privatization of state-owned firms. These firms, which account for the great majority of jobs, now have serious financial problems. They are obliged to prepare programs of restructuring that the banks and the Ministry of Industry will review and decide upon. If there are possibilities to restructure the firms, then the banks and the state will help with financial and other services. Yet the prospects of privatizing socially owned firms, particularly those involved in industrial production, are poor. Privatization will accelerate the closing of those state enterprises that are unable to restructure.

More optimistic prospects may be found in the private sector. A "company boom" appeared in Yugoslavia after the so-called Markovic Act on Privatization.[8] Within two years some 3,000 private firms (most of them involved in financial, commercial, technical, and other services) were established in the Ljubljana region.[9] However, only half of these new private firms are operating; many of the others, called "sleeping firms," will probably never become active. Also, these firms have not been strong employers; most of them have hired only a few people. The 500 firms that are socially owned account for 92 percent of all employees. Despite the small contribution that the new private firms make to the regional share of national social product and their low level of employment, these new companies are financially sound, profitable, and operating in fields where the former socialist economy was not involved. These firms may be regarded as a good base for regional economic recovery.

Again, the role of local and regional governments in assisting these new companies was relatively small. The company boom was an unexpected event for them; therefore, they remained inattentive to it. The most they could do was to provide locations for new firms; other forms of support simply did not exist.

CONCLUSION

Although the governments in the region will have to reorient themselves and take on new responsibilities in order to stimulate regional economic growth, the present structure of local government is not conducive to such a task. The fact that Ljubljana is divided into five municipalities complicates decision making in the city. Therefore, many reformers propose restructuring Ljubljana into one municipality with decision making concentrated at the city level. The main question is how to transform some important services such as physical infrastructure provision that are now the responsibility of the city administration. The present city administration has decided to form public enterprises that will manage physical infrastructure and services such as water provision, sewage, communal heating, and city lighting. Although this is considered a better alternative than having the city administration manage them, a policy of giving concessions to private enterprises to provide some community services and infrastructure would be a much better way of ensuring more effective service for clients.

Because of administrative dualism between municipalities and the city administration, there is now a great deal of duplication. This produces decisions that often cancel each other and contribute to inefficiency. According to some assessments (no one has exact data), there are more than 2,000 people employed in the city and municipality administrations, not including those employed in providing public services and infrastructure. At least one-third of these people would lose their jobs if local governments were consolidated.

One of the most important problems pressing on regional and local governments is providing private businesses with adequate sites or space in the Ljubljana region. Ljubljana has a long-term spatial plan in which alternative uses of space are identified, but the procedures for obtaining construction permits are long and complicated. As a result, for example, Ljubljana was not able to provide a location for a new hotel that was very much needed in the city. It will be essential to develop less complicated procedures in order to make the city attractive to foreign investors. But above all, if industry in Ljubljana is to be restructured to participate more effectively in a market economy, the region needs a less complicated political and administrative system allowing efficient decision making and effective control by citizens.

NOTES

1. Regional Chamber of Economy, *Assessment of the Economic Performance of the Ljubljana Region for 1992* (*Ljubljana, Slovenia: Regional Chamber of Economy Ljubljana, 1992*).

2. In less than six months, the firms lost from 20 percent to 70 percent of their markets in former Yugoslavia.

3. The state allowed firms incurring losses to write off their taxes and other obligations to the state budget. Also, it provided some funds to alleviate the problems of workers with very low wages. The policy was temporary, and

decisions will still have to be made about which firms are able to restructure and which have to be closed down.

4. Robert Mulej, "Employment, Unemployment, Retirement . . ." (Ljubljana, Slovenia: Regional Chamber of Economy Ljubljana, Special Analysis, 1992).

5. The elections for the city assembly were won by DEMOS, which consisted of the Slovenian Farmers party, the Slovenian Christian Democratic party, the Social Democratic Party of Slovenia, the Slovenian Democratic Alliance (which eventually split into the Slovenian National Democratic party and the Democratic party), and the Green party. The Social Democratic party, the Democratic party, and the Green party left the coalition; and by 1992 the impacts of the internal split in DEMOS were still uncertain.

6. Zinka Venta, "Strategies of Public Services Development," in Niko Toš, ed., *Public Services in Ljubljana—Strategies for Their Further Development* (Ljubljana, Slovenia: University of Ljubljana, Faculty of Social Sciences, 1991), pp. 14–17.

7. Robert Mulej, *Employment, Unemployment and the Measures of the Active Policy of Employment in Ljubljana Region for 1991* (Ljubljana, Slovenia: Republic of Slovenia Ministry of Work, Bureau of Employment, 1992).

8. Markovic was the former Yugoslav prime minister who started transforming the socialist state into a market economy in Yugoslavia in 1989. This program was stopped by ruling Communists in Belgrade and subsequently by the disintegration of the Yugoslav state.

9. Vinko Gobec, "7,612 Firms—Half of Them Operative," and Robert Mulej, "Company Boom in the City," both in *Slovenian Business Report*, vol. 4 (Ljubljana, Slovenia: CIOS Business Incubator, December 1991).

7

Privatization of Tobacco Company Ljubljana (TCL)

Uroš Korže and Marko Simoneti

In October 1991, the Development Fund of Slovenia (hereafter referred to as the Fund), acting on behalf of the government, sold 76.5 percent interest in Tobacco Company Ljubljana (TCL) to a group of two foreign tobacco manufacturers and marketers: Reemtsma from Germany and Seita from France. That was the first trade-sale transaction in Slovenia not structured in the joint-venture (JV) format and the first foreign investment after Slovenia declared its independence from former Yugoslavia. Negotiations with several foreign investors were taking place in 1991 despite the military intervention in Slovenia and great uncertainty about its future international status. The closing of this business deal not only broke the financial blockade imposed on Slovenia by the international financial community but also helped change Slovenia's risk rating and encouraged other potential investors to go on with their proposals for new JVs and acquisitions.

The TCL sale was a rather complex deal and, therefore, a great learning experience for the staffs of the Agency for Privatization (Agency) and the Fund. This was also an important demonstration for the public about how privatization should be executed in a fair, transparent, and competitive manner and about how the interests of all concerned parties (employees, management, government, consumers, and foreign partners) can be met successfully.

TCL'S BACKGROUND

TCL was established 120 years ago as a state tobacco monopoly and as one of the first large industrial facilities in Slovenia. The company, with a long tradition in tobacco manufacturing, had been run for four decades within the system of workers' self-management. Managing directors and heads of various organizational units were elected by the Workers' Council, which was chosen by the employees. Traditionally, the Workers' Council did not interfere with management decisions and almost always agreed to proposed policies.

In 1991 the company was the seventh largest cigarette factory in former Yugoslavia with a market share of 7.1 percent, with about 1,600 employees, and with a domestic sales volume close to 4 billion. TCL manufactured an additional 1.1 billion units for other tobacco companies and exported 0.2 billion units. In addition to cigarette production, the company was also a cigarette wholesaler and had retail outlets in Slovenia, Croatia, and Serbia. TCL distributed 80 percent of all cigarettes consumed in Slovenia. Additionally, TCL had acquired a small leather-goods business for which it used the same distribution network.

During the late 1980s and early 1990s, TCL's profits had gradually declined; and the company began losing its market position to competitors. The share of TCL's brands in the Yugoslav market fell from 17 percent to 7 percent during the 1980s, primarily owing to the lack of attractive new brands to meet consumers' changing demands. There was also a great danger of losing export sales because TCL's old brands were not of internationally acceptable quality.

TCL's business plan immediately before the privatization stated the following strategic objectives:

1. To produce a new international brand of cigarettes with rich American-blend taste and with low tar and nicotine content;
2. To gain better access to international markets for cigarettes and tobacco as a substitute for shrinking markets in Yugoslavia;
3. To increase the quality of existing TCL brands;
4. To obtain new machinery and equipment for the production of high-quality cigarettes; and
5. To introduce modern management techniques in the production and marketing of the cigarettes.

At the end of 1990, TCL's management came to the conclusion that these developmental objectives were attainable only through a strategic alliance with one of the big international cigarette manufacturers. Setting up a JV was considered to be the best way to provide for the long-term prosperity of the company. Other privatization techniques, such as a management and employee buyout complemented by a public offering of shares, had been considered as well. But neither a management and employee buyout nor a sale of the company to financial institutions or individual investors could solve the company's fundamental problems. The new owners would simply not be in a position to provide a new brand of cigarettes, access to international markets, or new technology and managerial skills.

THE NEGOTIATING PROCESS

The privatization process was initiated by TCL management. In its search for potential strategic partners, the management soon focused on two potential investors that expressed strong interest in purchasing the company: Reemtsma from Germany (in alliance with French Seita) and a large multinational company from the United States. At the beginning of 1991, both the Agency and the Fund were invited by the management of TCL to advise on the anticipated transaction. The two institutions had a double role in this deal. The staffs of the Agency and the Fund served primarily as consultants in preparing the privatization plan, in designing tendering procedures, in analyzing the offers, and in negotiating the deal with the winning bidder. At the end of the negotiations, the legal role of the Agency was to approve the transaction, whereas the Fund had to sign the contract with the foreign partner.

The management of TCL saw advantages of the active involvement of the Agency and the Fund, not only in providing professional support but also in minimizing the danger of speculation that a transaction was structured "under the table" to benefit the existing management. Foreign investors were also pleased to work with the Agency and the Fund because they had confidence that all steps, being in compliance with legal requirements, would minimize the problems of getting necessary approvals and guarantees.

A complex and fragile institutional arrangement—with the company initiating the privatization, the Agency approving it, and the Fund having the final say as the seller—had to be effectively managed throughout the entire process. A special committee composed of representatives of TCL, the Agency, and the Fund was set up to prepare the necessary steps and select the winning bid. Each of the parties in this arrangement had different goals, and moreover, each was legally and practically able to block the transaction at any time. Therefore, the negotiations took place, not only with the foreign partner but also among the parties on the "domestic" side.

Both of the interested bidders were given the opportunity to have their financial and technical advisers analyze the company thoroughly. The advisers spent many weeks in TCL. The developmental objectives for the company were carefully explained to foreign investors by the management. Both bidders used international accounting and auditing companies to appraise the value of the company. On the seller's side, the valuation report of the appraiser, who was licensed by the Agency, was prepared according to Slovenian valuation standards and principles.

When this analytical work was completed by all parties in April 1991, both potential investors were given a formal invitation to submit their offers and explain the financial and commercial arrangements through which they would take a stake in the company. They were also asked to prepare a detailed program on how they could contribute to fulfill the developmental objectives of TCL by developing new products, modernizing technology, developing marketing strategies, introducing changes in internal organization, developing human resources, and stabilizing local supplies of raw materials. They were told explicitly that the price would be important but not necessarily the main criterion for deciding on the preferred bidder. It was announced to both of them that, in evaluating proposals, future prospects of the company and the overall economic implications for the Republic of Slovenia would be taken into account as well.

Both offers were received on June 10, and both investors were given the opportunity to present their offers to the Selection Committee on June 17 and 18. These presentations were organized to clarify various aspects of the offers, and there was no negotiation with the bidders at this point. The main conclusion after the first round was that both proposals were satisfactory from the point of view of further development of the company, but the offered purchase prices were too low in comparison with the appraised value. A decision was made to start negotiations with both bidders in order to increase the price and modify some financial and legal arrangements that were not acceptable to the Slovenian side. An additional objective of the negotiations was to make final offers more easily comparable with each other by insisting that (1) nonbusiness assets and the leather business be excluded from the transaction; (2) job security, employees' remuneration, and employee ownership be addressed properly; (3) the value of the company and all financial instruments be denominated in foreign currency; and (4) adequate investment and employment guarantees be given.

Discussion with foreign partners started in July during the military intervention of the Federal Army in Slovenia. The willingness of the foreign partners to continue discussions during the war was an important signal for the Slovenian side that the bidders had a genuine interest in investing in TCL. The philosophy of a discounted cash flow was followed during the price negotiations. The Slovenian negotiators first discussed with bidders their projections about future sales, various costs, and investment expenditures in order to reach mutually acceptable cash-flow projections. Next, the discussion moved to the required return on investment in Slovenia. The key issue was how much the rate of return should be increased to accommodate for the political risk in Slovenia. The Slovenian negotiators' position on this point was that political instability was a short-term problem and that, in the long run, political and economic risks in Slovenia would be much lower. They were backing their view on the acceptable range of discount rates with the results of more than 50 appraisal reports prepared for privatization of Slovenian companies in the previous year. Firm determination was shown to postpone the deal if large discounts were needed to attract foreign interest in TCL. The representatives of the Agency and the Fund were in a relatively strong position; for while they were simultaneously negotiating with two interested potential buyers, their position was further strengthened by the fact that the survival of TCL was not directly threatened by postponing the transaction altogether.

After two rounds of negotiations, both investors submitted their new proposals to the Selection Committee at the end of July 1991. Both offers were significantly improved (the offered prices increased by 40 percent and 20 percent), and they became acceptable from the financial point of view. But the following issues were also taken into consideration in selecting the winning bid.

1. From the point of view of the future development of the company, industrial specialists from TCL thought that both offers were very strong; but the advantage was on the side of Reemtsma/Seita, which proposed a partnership that would preserve the identity of TCL and continue the business tradition of one of the oldest Slovenian companies.
2. The offered price for the company and proposed payment arrangements made by Reemtsma/Seita were clearly better.
3. From the macroeconomic point of view, the committee looked into employment generation, additional investment in Slovenia, fiscal implications, and immediate impact on foreign exchange generation; on this point the American proposal was stronger.
4. From the strategic point of view, the committee considered how the proposals would contribute to the international promotion of investment opportunities in Slovenia; and neither of the bids had any edge in this respect.

At the beginning of August, the Selection Committee unanimously decided that Reemtsma/Seita had the winning bid and that the negotiations should continue only with them. No agreement in principle was signed because it was assumed that a final contract could be concluded in a couple of days. Basic financial elements in the winning offer were accepted as given, but many issues were still to be resolved. It was decided that if the agreement could not be reached shortly with them, negotiation would be reopened with the second bidder from the United States.

Nevertheless, it took two months to prepare a final draft of a sale contract that was acceptable to all parties and approved by the board of directors of Reemtsma/Seita, by the Workers' Council of TCL, and by the boards of the Agency and the Fund. The contract was finally signed in October 1991, approximately seven months after the investors were formally invited to submit their proposals. It took the parties an additional two months to fulfill the conditions for closing and to close the deal.

THE STRUCTURE OF THE DEAL

The transaction was structured as a Reemtsma/Seita purchase of a 76.5 percent share of TCL from the Development Fund. Beforehand, the socially owned company was transformed into a limited-liability company (LLC) with the Fund as the only shareholder. In the bidding stage, both of the bidders were required to make an asset transaction, that is, the purchase of TCL assets by their newly established Slovenian subsidiaries. Following the awarding of the contract, these assets would be cashed in, the old company would be liquidated, and the residual money would go to the Fund. Other than for tax reasons, the main argument behind such proposals was the fear of unknown and contingent liabilities or potential future claims in case of a share purchase. Because asset transfers are slow and cumbersome (assets were located in many cities of Yugoslavia), this approach was rejected by the Slovenian side. The winning bidder finally accepted the share deal, but the Fund had to agree to provide necessary guarantees and indemnifications for potential claims to the company.

Foreign partners were not interested in the purchase of employees' flats and other nonbusiness assets. Therefore, these were transferred free of charge to the Slovenian Housing Fund (SHF). Employees were guaranteed (by SHF) all the privileges the new Housing Law granted to the tenants and buyers of the state-owned apartments. Similarly, foreign partners were not interested in the leather business. This business was not ready to be spun off or sold prior to the closing; so a special arrangement was agreed upon in which TCL accepted the obligation to consolidate, temporarily manage, and then sell the business within one year on behalf of the Fund. But TCL would bear no risk for its financial performance. To guarantee against such risk, the Fund was obliged to extend to TCL a one-year deposit against which the potential current losses of the leather business could be offset; and at the same time, the Fund reserved the right to audit TCL's financial records.

The new privatization law being debated in Parliament contained provisions for sale of shares at concessionary terms to employees. In order to allow the employees of TCL to take advantage of proposed benefits, the remaining 23.5 percent of the shares was reserved by the Fund for the future discount sale or even free distribution to employees. Foreign partners were willing to accept employees'-share participation only on the condition that employees' shares stayed indivisible. The contract, therefore, established a new joint-stock company (JSC) in which individual employees would be shareholders and for which the sole purpose would be to hold and manage the shares of TCL.

Financial and Tax Issues

The agreed purchase price was paid in cash. Additionally, the Fund was contractually allowed to reduce (prior to the closing) the equity of TCL by converting a substantial part of it into senior debt. Debt was denominated in deutsche marks with a maturity of five years, at an annual fixed interest of 8.5 percent, and with a mortgage based on real estate of the TCL. The Fund obtained the right to demand from TCL the exchange of this debt for bonds of the same maturity and interest and the right to register the shares for public offering. In order to support development of the capital market, this option would be exercised quickly with the bonds traded on the Ljubljana Stock Exchange.

This solution came as a result of TCL's shortage of working capital. Therefore, substantial investments had to be carried by foreign investors in order to build up sufficient inventories of raw materials. That meant less cash for the Fund (or the reinvestment of a part of the proceeds back into TCL). The Fund was willing to accept some long-term debt if an option was given to convert it easily into transferable securities. The foreign partners increased TCL's working capital by extending a similar long-term subordinated loan to the company to be paid in immediately after closing.

A detailed investment program ensuring new technology and modernization of existing facilities for the next five years was included in the contract. For the purchase of the majority stake in TCL and for further development of the company, the foreign partners invested nearly 120 million deutsche marks in Slovenia.

The acquired TCL was not given any special or extraordinary tax advantages, although there was a substantial effort by both bidders to obtain them. The exception was the approval by tax authorities for TCL to raise the book value and the base for depreciation to the fair market value (purchase price)—all of which was unusual with share transactions. TCL was not given tax relief for new businesses because the acquisition did not qualify for such treatment.

Labor Considerations

An agreed-upon modernization plan for TCL was prepared so that there would be no redundant work force. On an average, a 20 percent raise in real wages had been promised so that the lowest salary in the company would not be less than 400 deutsche marks per month. This positioned TCL on the upper-wage-level range of companies. All fringe benefits were preserved. Along with that, an extensive training program to raise productivity and to introduce new standards of quality for employees was proposed. Thus, it should come as no surprise that there was no active opposition to the deal from the trade unions both within and outside the company.

Control over the Company, Minority Rights

After the closing, a new seven-member board of directors was nominated—the chairman being the chief executive of one of the foreign buyers. Three members were nominated by the foreign shareholders, and the other three were divided as two representatives of the employees and one representative of the Fund.

A shareholders' agreement defined specific provisions for corporate governance and minority shareholders' rights. For example, no liquidation could be concluded for five years; and consent would be required for modifications of statutes, decreases of capital, and the admission of new partners. The Fund, in principle, agreed to accept new shareholders. Foreign partners got the right of first refusal for the remaining share of the Fund with the limitation that it was free to transfer these shares to workers, the public, and its subsidiaries or to make any other transfer required by law.

Representations and Warranties

The Fund accepted the obligation to indemnify the purchasers against all potential claims of third parties with regard to the title of the assets, specifically for the restitution claims that may arise. This warranty was limited to a maximum of two years.

One major issue was the demand of the foreign partners that access to the cigarette markets of Croatia and Bosnia and Herzegovina remain unrestricted and that the purchasers were not discriminated against by customs duty, tax, or quantity barriers. During a period when war was going on in Croatia, this request became a major threat to the execution of the entire transaction, especially when Slovenia and Croatia introduced different taxation practices. The problem was resolved only after the closing; the foreign partners eventually relied on a Slovenian government letter of intent regarding this subject.

Another issue that arose was the demand of the foreign partners that they obtain approval of the transaction under the existing federal law (adopted by the Slovenian Parliament), not only from the competent Slovenian ministry but also from the Yugoslav authorities. Slovenia had not yet been recognized as an independent country, and the bidders feared that the Yugoslav army might come back and question the validity of the contract. Although this demand was reasonable from the point of view of foreign investors, it was difficult to satisfy because communications with the Belgrade authorities ceased after the war began in Slovenia. Fortunately, the Belgrade authorities failed to respond to the application on time; and, therefore, the contract became valid automatically under Yugoslav law.

At first the foreign partners demanded that a part of the purchase price be paid to the special escrow account from which it could be released only after two years. The purchasers wanted to be able to compensate themselves directly from the escrow account for damages. This demand was not accepted by the Slovenian side on the grounds that the Fund already offered full-scale guarantees.

DEVELOPMENTS AFTER THE ACQUISITION

The time that has passed since the closing date has been too short to make any decisive evaluations of the deal. There were some charges in the media that the

TCL privatization was carried out without a specific government- or parliamentary-approved strategy as to which companies ought to be sold to foreign investors. Information on details and numbers was relatively scarce because of the confidentiality limitations, and that in itself spurred speculation about what was happening.

After the acquisition, TCL immediately got new orders from the new owners and increased production for export. A new international brand of cigarettes was introduced in Slovenia through an aggressive promotion and advertising campaign never seen before in the country. According to company sources, the results so far have been below expectations.

In spite of the increase in wages, considerable discontent arose among employees because the working load was substantially increased. This was due not so much to increased export orders as to quality problems in introducing the new brand. Nevertheless, the workers did not join the trade union–organized general strike. The managing director preserved his job, but some new executives were nominated. With the exception of the marketing director, no expatriate staff were hired immediately after the acquisition.

The board of directors (interestingly, foreign partners have nominated for their board representative one Slovene, a distinguished economist) had several meetings in which they discussed and approved business plans proposed by the management, and developed and introduced management incentive schemes. The focus was on the training of managers and production foremen. English has been accepted as the official language for the board meetings.

Housing stock has been successfully transferred, and much of it was privatized. The leather business has been reorganized and consolidated and showed positive financial performance, contrary to all expectations.

The consummation of the deal has had a particularly positive influence on the international investment community. The number of deals "in the tube" has increased considerably, and many potential foreign investors have been referred to the TCL case.

CONCLUSION: SOME GENERAL LESSONS FROM A TRADE-SALES CASE

The trade sale is a technique of privatization that is the most appropriate for medium-sized and large companies that need to secure new technology, new markets, know-how, adequate supplies of raw materials, and other essential inputs from strategic buyers. From the point of view of increased efficiency, this is a very appropriate technique of privatization; but on the negative side, the process itself is not very transparent to outsiders because many details of a transaction have to be kept confidential for competitive reasons. It is hard to avoid at least some public skepticism after such transactions are completed. The Agency and the Fund have already been through this process several times and have identified common issues arising during negotiations. Interestingly enough, similar situations are reported from Hungary and from other countries in the region.[1]

1. Each privatization transaction can be structured as an asset purchase or as a share purchase. Foreign buyers prefer to purchase the assets of the company, although this is very time-consuming. There are many reasons for this preference:

   a. To pick up only the assets of the company that are linked to the core business and leave nonproductive and other assets to the old company;

   b. To avoid problems of overemployment in the old company and employ only the people needed for production in the core business;

   c. To protect themselves from the environmental and other hidden liabilities of the old company;

   d. To avoid complicated procedures required by the privatization laws and supervision by the privatization agencies/ministries;

   e. To revalue the purchased assets and increase the depreciation base, which leads to lower tax payments in the future; and

   f. To pay the purchase price not to the government but to the old company that is often commercially dependent on a new company or on the buyer.

2. Most of these companies badly need fresh capital to purchase new machines and to modernize production. Foreign buyers often propose that a JV with the state be formed when the company needs new investments. They often suggest that additional shares representing the majority interest in the company be issued to them and that the money stays in the company for future investments. A foreign buyer actually gets control over the company and control over the cash paid into the company. The government gets no cash but becomes a minority partner in a modernized and potentially more profitable company.

This formula of privatization through recapitalization (purchase of newly issued shares) can easily be abused. New shares are sometimes offered in exchange for transfer of know-how, training, market share, and other contributions that are difficult to appraise properly. Paid-in cash is under the control of the new majority owners, and it might not be spent properly for new equipment and machines. The simple rule used in the TCL case was that the amount of newly issued shares should be limited by the amount of money needed to repay excessive debts of the company and by the amount of money needed for immediate purchase of new equipment and needed inventories.

3. Foreign strategic buyers are mostly interested in a dominant position in the company; and they accept a minority position only if special management rights, off-take arrangements for final products, or long-term contracts to supply inputs are offered to them in addition.

4. Some foreign companies have the policy of 100 percent ownership of their subsidiaries, but many are willing to accept the government as a minority shareholder. The ratio of 49 percent of the shares in domestic hands and 51 percent of the shares in the hands of foreigners is very common. In this situation

a foreign partner has complete control over the management of the company but pays for only half of it. It is unrealistic to expect that this company will ever be highly profitable because the majority owners will channel profits through transfer pricing to the companies where they have complete ownership. The rights of the minority shareholders should be specified in the contract so that they can exercise some management control or leave the company in case of poor financial performance.

5. There are some industrial sectors where many trade sales have already been completed in Eastern and Central Europe. These include hotels and such companies as cement, pulp and paper, auto parts, and home appliances. Information on these transactions can be very useful in the negotiations with foreign partners.

6. The advantage of a foreign buyer in a trade sale is that it understands the industry. Therefore, it is essential to ensure good cooperation of the management of the company with the Agency and the Fund acting as a selling agent. It is very difficult to sell the company in a trade sale against the will of the management. The management has to be cooperative, or it has to be replaced before the process starts.

7. The assessment of fair market value by an appraiser has relatively limited relevance for a well-executed trade privatization. There are many synergies that might exist between the buyer and the company. In the TCL case, the investor's value (what the investor is willing to pay for the company) is much higher than the fair market value. The only way to find out the potential value of the company is to have *a competitive process*. Less time and money should be spent on analyzing the company and much more on attracting potential buyers who will reveal their interest. It is useful to provide special investment memoranda or a company profile for prospective investors and give them the opportunity to visit the company and to meet with the management. Some of the prospective investors usually know the company very well from their past commercial arrangement, but less informed investors should be given a chance to get acquainted with the company. Everything should be done to avoid getting only one serious buyer. And all interested investors or brokers have to be asked to provide basic information about their business references in order to check their credentials.

8. Bidders should always be asked to prepare *a detailed business plan* for the company that covers various aspects of its operations: marketing strategy, production and technology development, investment plans, and human resource development. Valuable information that can be useful in the future development of the company can be obtained from prospective investors.

9. Selection of the winning bid is very difficult because proposals are complex and cover various aspects of the company's operations. Sometimes proposals are practically impossible to compare unless there are some specific guidelines contained in the letter of invitation. It is useful to assign weights beforehand to various aspects of the offer. Macroeconomic implications for job

creation, foreign currency revenues, market structure, and fiscal revenues of the government are particularly difficult to assess properly. It is equally difficult to rank two offers where the first is promising to create 300 new jobs, while the second is offering 30 million deutsche marks more in a purchase price.

10. Special attention has to be given to all essential proposed elements that will become part of a sale contract. *Employment and investment guarantees* have to be included in the contract; otherwise, the company might be sold to a bidder on the basis of promises that will never be fulfilled.

11. Many of the companies in Eastern and Central Europe have serious environmental problems; in addition, their internal working conditions do not meet modern health and safety standards. To continue operating in the future, large investments are needed in these areas; and damages to the environment from past operations should be remedied. There are two ways to deal with the environmental issues. The implicit liability of the company to clean up the environment can be explicitly recognized, and the price of the company appropriately reduced; or this liability can be taken over by the seller. In most cases, foreign buyers perform a detailed environmental audit, and they insist that responsibility for the most serious ecological problems be assumed by the seller.

12. Foreign buyers often insist that special privileges be granted to them by the governments as part of the deal. Sometimes they require that the government commit itself to do everything in its power to change legislation or economic policy. This should be avoided at all cost. Strict application of the principle of national treatment of foreigners in the privatization process can be very useful in removing the requests for changing the economic system or economic policy from the negotiating table.

NOTE

1. See, for example, Lajos Bokros, "Spontaneous Privatization—Hungary" (Second CEEPN Annual Conference: Privatization in Central/Eastern Europe, November 29–30, 1991); or "Joint Ventures, Acquisitions and Privatization in Eastern Europe and the USSR" (*Economist Intelligence Unit/Business International*: Report No 2105, February 1991).

8

Privatization in Practice: Czechoslovakia's Experience from 1989 to Mid-1992

Michal Mejstrik and James Burger

Czechoslovakia began its transition to a market economy immediately after the Velvet Revolution of November 1989 brought an end to 40 years of Communist rule. In order to understand the challenges inherent in such a transition, we should first examine the situation in Czechoslovakia and Eastern Europe before the transition to a centrally planned economy and then examine the reforms that were initiated at the beginning of 1990.

Since the nineteenth century, the Czech lands have been the most industrially developed part of the Austro-Hungarian Empire, which disintegrated in 1918. The market system developed in an independent Czechoslovakia and, except during the German occupation, continued until 1948. The Czechoslovakian financial policy after World War I attempted to revive a wartime economy in which the propensity to save, to engage in entrepreneurial activities, and to work had declined. State paternalism prevailed, as did the rationing scheme and galloping inflation typical at that time in Austria, Hungary, Germany, and Poland. Through restrictive fiscal and monetary policies, Czechoslovakia was able to regain a strong currency and to transform itself smoothly from a war economy. As a result, the per capita gross national product (GNP) of Czech lands rose during the 1930s almost to a level that prevailed in some Western European countries.

From 1862 to 1948, Czechoslovakia had a refined Business Code, corporate law, and other legislative components of a market economy with which people were quite familiar. Even during the Communist era, Czechoslovakia's geographic location in Central Europe did not allow citizens to forget their capitalist neighbors in West Germany and Austria who were seen in the mass media or those who came as Western visitors (of which there were more than 1 million a year in Czechoslovakia). These economic characteristics were quite distinct from those in the former Soviet Union and somewhat different from those in Poland and Hungary. Thus, in 1968 it was Czechoslovakia that first attempted to transform its socialist economy by combining elements of planned and market-oriented policies.

The market economy of Czechoslovakia was weakened at Munich in 1938, however, when Western Allies betrayed Czechoslovakia to Hitler's demands. This resulted in the Nazi occupation of Czech lands (Bohemia and Moravia) and the separation of the Slovak State. For the first time in their history, the less economically developed Slovak lands (formerly Upper Hungary under the Austro-Hungarian Empire) became an independent state, but at the cost of close ties with Nazi Germany. In 1945 Western Allies interrupted the liberation of Europe near the western border of Czechoslovakia and made it possible for the Soviet Union to liberate all of Czechoslovakia, Poland, Hungary, Bulgaria, and Romania and to achieve temporary popularity in the process.

Gradually, after 1945 and, finally, in 1948 under Soviet influence, Communists took power in Czechoslovakia, Poland, Hungary, and East Germany and began to build a socialist economy. They sought to redistribute income on behalf of workers by dismantling the market system, by replacing it with a command economy, and by redistributing property rights through nationalization and collectivization of economic activities. The Czechoslovakian agrarian reforms, for example, created some 10,000 agricultural cooperatives and state farms as the exclusive form of farm organization. Industrial and financial enterprises with more than 500 workers were taken over by the government in 1945 before the Communists actually came to power, but smaller enterprises with over 50 employees were expropriated by the new Communist government in 1948. The process was completed in two final waves of nationalization in 1955 and 1959 when smaller enterprises, such as private craft and service establishments, were either liquidated or nationalized and then integrated into larger state-owned enterprises (SOEs). By 1960, 93 percent of net material product (NMP [the socialist version of gross national product]) was generated by SOEs. The nonfarming private sector's share of NMP dropped by 33 percent during the first 12 years after World War II. By the mid-1980s nearly 97 percent of Czechoslovakia's NMP was generated by SOEs; and only 0.7 percent came from nonfarm private enterprises. The situation was nearly the same in East Germany; but a much smaller share of national product came from SOEs in Poland and Hungary, which paradoxically had a much shorter tradition of private industry.

Under the Communist regime, an economic policy of structural reconstruction sought to concentrate industrial operations based on the "law of increasing returns." The policy exploited available resources to attain the greatest possible economies of scale. This principle was applied, however, with little consideration for optimal plant size. The concept of economies of scale was derived almost mechanically from patterns observed in the West but, ultimately, became only a technical rationale for steadily increasing plant size. Communist authorities were thus allowed to form artificially large, integrated plants that eventually became monopolies or oligopolies.

The hierarchical structure of the centrally planned economy, which required central management and coordination, also provided the rationale for forming administrative monopolies. During the 1950s, Czechoslovakian authorities decreased the number of enterprises while increasing their size. Thus, between 1958 and 1980, the share of employment for industrial SOEs with less than 500 employees fell from 13 percent to 1.4 percent. As a result, in 1988 the average size of the more than 1,600 industrial SOEs, which employed nearly half of Czechoslovakia's labor force, was more than 3,100 workers. This concentration and the subsequent creation of monopolies and oligopolies account for the great difficulties Czechoslovakian manufacturing firms are now experiencing with international competitiveness. Economists currently fear an irreversible decline in export manufacturing because of gradually decreasing productivity and quality as well as the continuing loss of markets (see table 8.1).

THE POINT OF DEPARTURE FOR PRIVATIZATION

Because of the economic conditions that existed after 40 years of Communist rule, radical measures had to be taken in 1990 to restructure industry and meet world standards of production. Reformers faced an economy dominated by large state monopolies and created and maintained by administrative fiat rather than by economic forces. For all practical purposes, there was no private sector in this economy.

Table 8.1
Growth of Total Factor Productivity in Central and East European Countries (average annual percentage change)

	1961-65	1966-70	1971-75	1976-80	1981-88
Czechoslovakia	0.4	2.0	1.5	0.7	0.1
German Democratic Republic	0.7	1.5	1.3	0.8	1.1
Hungary	1.2	1.6	1.6	0.5	0.3
Soviet Union	0.9	2.1	0.7	0.5	0.5
Poland	0.9	1.1	2.2	-0.6	0.2
Bulgaria	1.7	2.2	2.0	1.4	0.8
Romania	1.2	1.0	3.1	1.5	0.7

Sources: Based on *Economic Survey of Europe*, 1984–85 and 1989–90 (United Nations, 1985 and 1990); and on *Statisticka rocenka CSSR*.

The coalition structure of industrial management made possible by artificially created monopolies and oligopolies developed its own system of barter exchange and an informal, resource distribution network where formal monetary costs played a secondary role. The key to success in a barter-exchange system was the ability to deliver deficit products known as "natural revenues" (e.g., industrial materials that were in short supply, scarce consumer goods, or vacation bonuses). In a system where deliveries of many intermediate goods were not always assured by central planning, possession of such goods or access to high-level personal contacts had more value than money. In fact, money often played a secondary role in purchases and was used only for accounting purposes. Unprofitable firms were universally subsidized, and prices were artificially set by central authorities. Therefore, the main goal of an enterprise was not to generate profits but to produce in accordance with the central plan.

It should be emphasized, however, that the traditional assumption of top-down planning was largely a fallacy. The collusion of formal and informal interest groups created an illusion of "plan struggle," so often depicted by Western analysts of centrally planned economies. In reality, collusive oligopolies decided on the distribution of resources as well as on benefits that created internal rewards for the "mafia" who ran them. This coalition structure was deeply rooted in informal networks.

Unfortunately, the behavioral problems associated with collusive practices could not easily be changed by the formal transformation of the command economy to a market-oriented system. In 1989 the reformers faced a hostile environment in which to introduce a market structure. Barriers to entry included not only those common in developed market economies but also those associated with uncertainties in supply and lack of market and resource information. As experience in former Yugoslavia, Hungary, and Poland had already shown, such partial reforms as cuts in state subsidies and liberalization of prices could help reduce the hostility of the environment; but they usually led to a system of mutual lending and subsidization within industrial coalitions. These practices caused other serious problems.

In Czechoslovakia the principal points of departure for reform were the privatization of SOEs and the development of a new private sector composed of small- and medium-sized firms. Privatization was preceded by the breakup of monopolies and by the internal decentralization of management decision making and, thereby, changed the rigid and highly centralized internal organization of SOEs.

Even the formal breakup of SOEs, however, did not immediately dissolve the coalition structure. In such a small closed economy as Czechoslovakia, units of former SOEs could easily become monopolies in their own right. Thus, Czechoslovakian reformers faced a monumental task of creating basic competition, that is, alternative suppliers who provided goods at a wide range of prices and qualities. And renewing the dynamism of the prewar market economy had to be done in the context of a globalized economy, which had already transformed some industries into independent multinational entities.

After 1989 the economic reform and adjustment process in Czechoslovakia was closely supervised by both International Monetary Fund (IMF) and World Bank officials, who provided independent expertise in privatization and in the creation of conditions for Czechoslovakia's reentry (as a founding member) to both organizations. The reformers adopted Western European patterns of economic and legal organization in order to prepare Czechoslovakia for affiliation with the European Community. But because of low levels of efficiency and the ossified, informal power structure that dominated SOEs during the Communist era, many officials and interest groups saw gradual privatization of SOEs as the inevitable way to surmount the many difficulties of reform and to improve the operating efficiency of SOEs without causing social upheaval.

The great controversy over reform in Czechoslovakia after 1989, therefore, was between gradualists and radicals over the speed and means of transition. Some external factors, namely, the decline in oil supplies, the increases in oil prices, and the need to use convertible currency in foreign trade, accelerated the adoption of a radical reform package by the federal government in May 1990. Although the radicals had been in control of policy since the Velvet Revolution, gradualists continued to argue that reforms were being implemented too quickly, were creating unanticipated side effects, and were leading to social problems, like inflation and unemployment, that the public could not bear. They argued that price liberalization (enacted on January 1, 1991) should not have occurred until after monopolies had been broken up and that the resulting inflation was greater than it should have been.

The restructuring of the state sector and the means of establishing private ownership were the focal points of this controversy. The gradualist reformers, rooted in 1960s thinking, preferred a slow process and wanted to postpone changes to sometime in the future. Gradualist arguments against speedy privatization emphasized the danger of large-scale layoffs and unemployment as well as the need for more effectively functioning markets before businesses were forced to operate self-sufficiently. To minimize the problems associated with privatization and to receive maximum returns on the sale of SOEs, they argued, it would be better to restructure SOEs before privatizing them.

The radicals proposed speeding up reforms and minimizing the privatization period for at least some SOEs. Their main argument was that a market economy could not function without a renewal of private ownership. Radicals also noted that in the period preceding privatization, ambiguity about ownership and accountability had led to economic and ecological irresponsibility and nontransparent financial transactions. Under the influence of the more radical reformers, several dozen economic reform laws, including a new Commercial Code governing business activity, were passed by the National Assembly in 1990. The Commercial Code overrode or rescinded many previously existing laws of economic conduct in Czechoslovakia: the old Law on Joint-stock Companies (Act 104/1990), the old Economic Code (Act 109/1964 and numerous subsequent amendments), and parts of the old Act on Economic Relations with Foreign Countries. The new code defined various forms of possible business organization, including the joint-stock company (JSC), a limited-liability company (LLC), general and limited partnerships, as well as contract laws and others guiding business conduct.

The Commercial Code also created guidelines for business activity by foreign investors by allowing foreign legal entities to engage in business activities in the Czech and Slovak Federal Republic (CSFR) under the same conditions and to the same extent as Czechoslovakian nationals unless stipulated otherwise under the law. The government acknowledged that foreign investors could play an important role in the transition process in Czechoslovakia. It assumed foreign companies could start their investments in a stable Czechoslovakian economy in Central Europe and then "go East" (the large Eastern European, and especially the Soviet, markets were well understood by Czech and Slovak businessmen, most of whom could speak Russian) or "go West" (an opportunity considered by the Japanese, among others, who took into account the relatively skilled labor and low wage and transport costs in the CSFR).

The risk aversion of many Czechoslovakians was recognized as a potential obstacle for some foreign investors, but domestic demand for additional convertible capital was high. Even more important than the reliable supplies of technology or innovative products that foreign investors could bring were up-to-date organization and management practices that could help domestic firms restructure themselves to meet higher standards in Western markets and adopt more effective marketing techniques.

Important steps in promoting foreign investment were taken by adopting legislation that amended the joint-venture (JV) regulations and relevant bilateral agreements on protection of foreign investment and profit repatriation. Perhaps the most important change was the elimination of prior approval for the establishment of JVs or foreign-owned enterprises. In fact, the Act on Enterprises with Foreign Property Participation was amended in 1990 to allow up to 100 percent foreign ownership. Furthermore, it became possible for foreign companies to create JVs through the process of large-scale privatization.

The new laws also allowed returns on foreign capital investments—profits from enterprise activity, interest payments, capital growth, returns on bonds, and payments for intellectual property—to be freely transferred abroad. The State Bank only required evidence, that is, financial statements, to document that the amounts in question were actually returns on investment. Czechoslovakia also signed bilateral agreements with a number of countries and thus safeguarded the rights of investors and their property as well as guaranteed the free flow of capital and profits. In addition, 20 countries signed agreements with Czechoslovakia eliminating double taxation.

Foreign investors also received tax benefits. The standard corporate income tax in Czechoslovakia was 55 percent, but enterprises with over 30 percent foreign participation and profits of over 200,000 crowns were taxed at only 40 percent. In addition, a tax holiday of up to two years could be granted if an enterprise paid no dividends during that period. Starting in 1993, there would be one uniform tax rate of around 40 percent. Enterprises in which the share of foreign ownership was greater than 30 percent were also entitled to concessionary rates of depreciation on fixed assets purchased after January 1, 1991. Local currency financing was also made available for JVs in which a minimum of 5 percent of gross profits was contributed to a single reserve fund that was maintained at a minimum of 10 percent of the JV's "basic capital."

As a result of government policies liberalizing and promoting foreign investment, the number of JVs as well as the amount of capital in them increased rapidly from 1989 through the end of 1991 (see table 8.2). The majority of such ventures was with small business units (less than 1 million crowns of capital investment), and most of these relationships were established by German and Austrian firms (see table 8.3). After the approval of privatization projects involv-

Table 8.2
Number and Capitalization of Joint Ventures

	Number of Joint Ventures			
	February 1991	May 1991	July 1991	August 1991
Czech Republic	1,638	2,222	2,261	2,266
Slovak Republic	486	665	676	680
Total CSFR:	2,124	2,896	2,937	2,946

	Capital in Joint Ventures *			
	February 1991	May 1991	July 1991	August 1991
Czech Republic	7.4	20.7	22.7	22.9
Slovak Republic	1.9	3.4	3.7	3.5
Total CSFR:	9.3	23.9	26.4	26.4
Of Which Total Is Foreign Capital	4.8	10.3	11.8	—

* Billion crowns; $1 = 28–29 crowns.

Sources: Based on *Economic Survey of Europe*, 1984–85 and 1989–90 (United Nations, 1985 and 1990); and on *Statisticka rocenka CSSR*.

Table 8.3
Number and Size of Foreign Joint Ventures

Number of Joint Ventures Categorized by Foreign Investor (as of July 23, 1991)	
Country	Number of Ventures
Germany	873
Austria	833
Switzerland	201
Italy	137
United States	133

Size of Joint Ventures Categorized by Capital (as of July 23, 1991)	
Capital	Number of Ventures
Up to 0.1 Million Crowns	1,187
0.1–1 Million Crowns	1,290
1–100 Million Crowns	438
Over 100 Million Crowns	22

Sources: Based on *Economic Survey of Europe*, 1984–85 and 1989–90 (United Nations, 1985 and 1990); and on *Statisticka rocenka CSSR*.

ing foreign participation, these trends were expected to change significantly—to increase in the average size of JVs and to decrease in the level of German and Austrian participation.

The Czech Ministry of Industry reported that by December 31, 1991, there were 84 enterprises under its jurisdiction with foreign capital involvement. This number, of course, only represented former SOEs in the Czech industrial sector and those established before the first wave of privatization. Of these 84 cases, only 3 involved investments of more than 1 billion crowns ($34 million); only 8, over 100 million crowns ($3.4 million); and 9, between 10 and 100 million crowns ($340,000–$3.4 million). In sum, these investments totaled 18.5 billion crowns ($600 million); and through guarantees or conditional promises, they offered the possibility of an additional 18.5 billion crowns of investment in the near future. By the end of February 1992 and the first wave of privatization, 123 more projects promising 23 billion crowns ($900 million) of investment had been approved.

During the first wave of privatization, negotiations were under way with 220 potential foreign investors. The total book value of assets involved in these negotiations was almost 50 billion crowns ($1.7 billion). By mid-April, 50 deals with 15 billion crowns of investment had been closed. Considering that the book value of these properties was only 8 billion crowns, the potential for inflow of foreign capital in the remaining 170 properties (which employed 100,000 workers and had about 40 billion crowns in book value) was quite likely to exceed the estimated book value.

THE CONCEPTUALIZATION OF PRIVATIZATION

The overall objective of privatization in Czechoslovakia was to substantially decrease state ownership of productive assets and to broaden the base of private ownership. Property rights would be transferred from the government to a broad constituency of individual shareholders, including such potential detractors of privatization as managers and employees of SOEs and their customers. Eventually these future shareholders became personally interested and involved in privatization and became a powerful political constituency supporting it and opposing renationalization.

In January 1991 the National Assembly adopted reform policies that introduced a number of changes simultaneously. Some delay caused by nationalist tensions initiated in Slovakia slowed down the necessary adjustments but did not pose a serious threat to reform. An important component of reform within each republic was the creation of two important institutions: the Ministries for Privatization and Property Management and Funds of National Property, which transferred many enterprises to private ownership and accumulated proceeds from privatization; and a coordinating Bureau for Privatization and Property Management in the Federal Ministry of Finance. (The roles of these institutions are described in various detail throughout the remainder of this chapter.) According to the Federal Ministry of Finance, perhaps 70 percent of SOEs were subject to privatization; and this process was carried out mainly by organizations within the Czech and Slovak republics.

Reformers considered various means of privatization but finally adopted an approach that combined such standard methods as public sales and auctions with other processes designed to compensate for factors peculiar to Czechoslovakia. The use of standard methods alone was clearly impossible in Czechoslovakia because public savings were not large enough to buy all of the state property. This problem was especially acute because citizens with a significant amount of savings were thought to be either former Communist party members or black marketeers, neither of whom were very popular.

Efforts to sell SOEs to the first foreign company wishing to purchase them ("spontaneous privatization") were politically unacceptable because citizens feared that the foreign investors would provide existing managers (who were often Communist party functionaries or *nomenklatura*) with "golden parachutes" in return for selling out at low prices. The experience of Hungary, which had done something similar, showed that the effort to reverse the agreements with foreign investors could mean the loss of government credibility abroad.

The Process of Privatization

The Federal Ministry of Finance originally envisioned a structure for privatization that more or less held up throughout the process. The basic concept behind the structure (the implementation of which is described below) was to divide SOEs into three categories and to sell them off in two phases. Companies were first divided into three classifications.

1. Category A consisted of public utilities and other regulated SOEs that were not designated to be privatized in the near future. The provision of public goods and services at the federal, republic, and local levels would involve about 30 percent of the SOEs. A redefinition of what constituted public goods and services at the federal (e.g., defense and foreign service), republic (e.g., some public utilities), and municipal levels (e.g., collective goods of local importance, such as cultural activities) would determine the nature of government budgets and their revenue needs.

2. Category B included state-owned "heavy industries" (B1) and "light industries" (B2) that were to be privatized. In order to allow SOEs to divide their assets, some firms were commercialized; that is, prior to privatization, they were converted into state-owned JSCs whose boards of directors were appointed by the government. These corporations would be self-financed, although, informally, the government allowed some of them to acquire tax exceptions or subsidies. The costs of commercialization, privatization, and settlement of liabilities were to be assumed by the Funds of National Property.

3. Category C covered newly defined municipal property (i.e., national property turned over to municipalities) or businesses (e.g., restaurants, local services, and rental flats) acquired through the small-scale privatization law enacted by newly established, district privatization committees as well as by autonomous local governments and municipal councils elected in November 1990. These units were to be returned to original property owners (if they existed) or to be auctioned (except for flats—the privatization of which had not yet begun by mid-1992).

The process actually occurred in two stages: first, a period of small-scale (category C) privatization; and second, a period of large-scale (categories B1, B2) privatization. Both processes were governed by the restitution and privatization laws. In order to decentralize the process and to clear up ownership rights of small enterprises in 1991, the municipalities were given property that they had owned before December 31, 1949, "historical property," and all buildings on their land. This amounted to 25 percent of property held by the republics—mostly residential and small industrial premises in the Czech lands, and a similar amount in Slovakia.

Phase 1 was the preparatory stage and focused on small-scale privatization. With the final deadline of May 1992, SOEs not producing public goods had to prepare their own privatization proposals beginning in the last quarter of 1991. The firms could choose to submit different types of privatization projects and to use different methods of privatizing. The property claims of the original owners had to be considered and included in the privatization projects. The government estimated that about 10 percent of these firms would be closed down and liquidated.

Phase 2 focused on large-scale privatization and included SOEs in categories B1 and B2. This phase employed such standard methods as public auction or tender, direct sale, or transfer of the property to municipalities, as well as the use of vouchers. Each firm was responsible for preparing its own proposal for privatization subject to the approval of the Ministry of Privatization. The municipal property of category C would not necessarily be converted into JSCs but might be offered directly to the original owners or to single proprietors.

THE SMALL-SCALE PRIVATIZATION PROCESS

As noted earlier, small-scale privatization was accomplished by two means: restitution and auctions. Although these methods were thought to be complementary, the restitution process had higher priority and initially slowed the progress of both small- and large-scale privatization until procedural and legal difficulties were resolved. After the official deadline for the submission of restitution claims, however, privatization accelerated in Czechoslovakia (unlike the experience in Poland and Hungary) because many original ownership rights had been resolved.

By various measures, the government promoted the creation of a new private sector composed of small- and medium-sized businesses, and new legislation helped to register a growing number of entrepreneurs (see table 8.4). Many participants in small-scale privatization were workers or self-employed persons who registered themselves as entrepreneurs for tax reasons. Restitution of smaller business units was governed by Law 403/1990 on the Mitigation of the Consequences of Certain Wrongs Affecting Property, which mandated the restoration of small assets that had been expropriated without compensation in the last wave of nationalization in 1959. Under this law, original owners or their heirs had to produce evidence (which was generally available in local government files) of their claims; and upon proper justification, state agencies had to return property immediately in tangible form or else provide financial compensation. By mid-1992 more than 30,000 claims had been met under this law.

In clear-cut cases, restitution transferred property quickly and uncontroversially to private ownership. But the number of property claims (close to 100,000) created many legal complications, especially in cases where the justification was

Table 8.4
Number of Private Registered Entrepreneurs

	December 31, 1990		June 30, 1991	
Total Persons:	488,361		920,981	
Sector:	Number	Percent	Number	Percent
Agriculture & Forestry	8,302	1.7	21,183	2.3
Industry	135,764	27.8	254,911	27.6
Building	133,323	27.3	228,403	24.8
Transportation/ Communication	14,162	2.9	26,708	2.9
Trade	61,533	12.6	158,409	17.2
Science & Development	977	0.2	921	0.1
Hotels & Recreation	10,256	2.1	18,420	2.0
Repairs & Services	44,441	9.1	72,757	7.9
Education, Culture & Health Care	14,162	2.9	23,946	2.6
Other	62,022	12.7	116,044	12.6

Source: Fund of National Property, Czech Republic, *Telegraf* (February 5, 1992).

not easy to determine. Because restitution of property had priority over other forms of privatization, the legal complexities slowed down the entire process.

The auction procedure for small-scale privatization was outlined in Law 427/1990 and its subsequent amendments and passed in 1990. The Law on Small Privatization made the public auction the only means by which small- and medium-sized enterprises could be privatized. This gave the process a strong flavor of democracy and decentralization because any person could petition that any business unit be privatized by submitting a proposal to the regional privatization office. The current owner of the property could raise objections only if he could show that sale of the unit would threaten his enterprise's activity. This was somewhat of a problem because parent enterprises generally resisted attempts to strip away some of their assets through restitution of their small plants. Proposals approved by the local privatization boards were confirmed by the National Ministry of Privatization and designated for auction.

There was no official limit on the size of business units that could be auctioned through small-scale privatization, although units that had been designated for large-scale privatization could not be sold under the small-scale privatization process.

During debate on this law, one particularly strong controversy arose over the rights of current managers or employees in privatization auctions. Some members of Parliament, and even President Vaclav Havel for a time, believed that current managers and employees should have such privileges as access to special loans or preferential prices in privatization auctions. In the end, however, the right-wing members of Parliament rejected all such proposals, and no preferential treatment was given to current management.

Standard procedures governed the public small-scale privatization auctions.

1. The businesses to be privatized were designated by appropriate republic authorities, and no businesses upon which there were restitution claims could be put up for auction.
2. Lists of businesses to be privatized (including name, assets, price, and information on the auction as well as on the owner of the property) were to be made public at least 30 days in advance of the public auction.
3. In the first round of auctions, only Czechoslovakian citizens or those who became citizens after February 1948 could participate.
4. The successful bidder had to submit full payment within 30 days, and the business unit (but not the existing debt) was transferred to him immediately.
5. Proceeds from small-scale privatization auctions were to go to the Fund of National Property of the appropriate republic. These funds were frozen for two years and could be deposited in banks but not used for budgetary purposes.
6. In cases where no satisfactory bids were made and there were at least five interested buyers, a "Dutch" auction was used in which the starting price of the unit would be decreased gradually but never by more than 50 percent. Units not sold in the first round could be reauctioned. Foreigners were then allowed to participate, and the starting price could be reduced by up to 80 percent.

In most cases, the real estate of the enterprise was not actually auctioned; but the ownership of equipment and an exclusive right to make a rental agreement to use the premises for business purposes were. Generally, the owner of the premises was a state or municipal organization. The successful bidder was originally entitled to a two-year lease, which was later extended to a five-year lease.

The first privatization auction took place on January 26, 1991; and during that year over 20,000 businesses—about 14,000 units in the Czech Republic and almost 7,000 units in the Slovak Republic—were privatized. This generated revenue of over 25 billion Czechoslovakian crowns (U.S. $900 million) (see table 8.5). The steady progress of this process in the Czech Republic is shown in table 8.6. From these numbers it is clear that small-scale privatization was well under way in Czechoslovakia by mid-1992.

Problems and Unique Features of Czechoslovakian Small-Scale Privatization

Although substantial progress was made in restoring small businesses to private ownership, the process was not completely free of difficulties and problems. One problem involved liquidation of the debts of the enterprises that were sold. Once business units were privatized, the new owners were not responsible for previous liabilities, and this created problems for the holders of claims against these small enterprises. The law stipulated that for two years the proceeds of small-scale privatization auctions could be used for the satisfaction of claims; however, the delay in completing the process created problems for the debt holders. In cases where local government institutions owned the businesses, the municipalities sometimes tried to charge excessive rents for property taken over by successful bidders. Furthermore, the original two-year lease period discour-

Table 8.5
Small-Scale Privatization in the Czech and Slovak Republics, 1991

	Number of Units	Starting Price (billion crowns; $1 = 28–29 crowns)	Sale Price (billion crowns)
Scheduled for Small-Scale Privatization	21,940	22,096	—
Sold in Privatization Auctions	14,726	11,549	18,122
Of Which:			
Sale Includes Real Estate	3,814	10,490	14,000
Sale of Rental Rights Only	10,912	1,059	4,122
Slovak Republic (through November 24, 1991)	6,723	6,134	7,486

Source: Fund of National Property, Czech Republic, *Telegraf* (February 5, 1992).

Table 8.6
Small-Scale Privatization in Czech Republic (by month)

	Units Sold (cumulative)	Revenue (million crowns) cumulative)
1991: February	—	—
March	228	88
April	1,349	914
May	2,948	1,525
June	4,749	2,696
July	6,478	3,898
August	8,016	5,288
September	9,514	6,879
October	10,201	9,790
November	12,911	10,130
December	13,230	15,621
1992: January	13,935	16,869

Source: Fund of National Property, Czech Republic, *Telegraf* (February 5, 1992).

aged the new operators from investing in their businesses, and the law had to be amended to increase the term of leases to five years. This amendment also led to increased sales prices.

According to the Minister of Privatization, the most serious problem was the reaction of the management of small enterprises. Seeing privatization as contrary to their interests in many cases, current managers tried to stall or sabotage the small-scale privatization process. They often refused to provide necessary information to privatization commissions, provided incorrect or deliberately falsified information, overvaluated unsalable stocks, and appropriated usable stocks. The pace of small-scale privatization was also slowed in many areas by logistical problems in establishing local privatization commissions. Apparently, in some areas there were delays in naming members of the commissions as well as organizational problems, difficulties in finding office space, and complexities in clearing up restitution claims on enterprises designated for auction.

The policy toward foreign participation was also criticized by those who questioned the logic of denying foreigners access to the first round of auctions. And it was not clear to many observers that foreigners had actually been excluded. There were allegations of widespread "shadow buying" by foreigners who provided financial backing for Czech bidders. Critics argued that if this was in fact the case, then the policy of excluding foreigners really only excluded reputable foreign buyers (i.e., those who were willing to abide by the rules).

The use of Dutch auctions was also criticized because of suspected collusion—several bidders agreed among themselves not to bid in order to lower the price of the enterprise—and because of alleged cases of payoffs in which potential buyers paid others not to bid or to remain in the bidding only to have the necessary five participants required for the Dutch auction. Such problems were compounded by some public resentment against the idea of "giving away" public property, that is, of selling off enterprises for bids below the initial price.

LARGE-SCALE PRIVATIZATION

The privatization of large state enterprises was also progressing by mid-1992, although more slowly, because it was a more complicated process. The restitution law passed in February 1990 covered assets expropriated through the nationalization effort that began February 28, 1948. It also covered property nationalized through forced gifts and illegal restitutions and rehabilitations during the 1950s and 1960s. This law gave the original owners the full rights to property or to other forms of reimbursement and generated more than 20,000 demands for restitution. Many claimants accepted financial reimbursement or ownership of shares rather than the actual return of property.

In adopting the Large Privatization Program (Law 92/1991), Parliament decided to speed up the privatization of SOEs and authorized two waves of large privatization. Each SOE that was selected by the government for the first wave of privatization had to present its own "basic privatization project"—its plan for transforming itself from a SOE to a private company. Other enterprises were expected to participate in a second wave of privatization or not to be privatized at all. The structure of the privatization project was obligatory. Because there had been no Workers' Councils operating since April 1990, the company management took primary responsibility for the formulation of the firm's basic privatization project. Following the submission of basic projects, any other person or enterprise was allowed to submit a "competing privatization project," that is, an alternative to the company's plan.

In order to increase the supply of technology and to improve organization and management through direct foreign investment, potential foreign buyers were permitted to collaborate with Czech firms on preparing privatization proposals or to submit their own competing proposals. Approvals were made by the Ministry of Privatization, which also received advice from the "founding" ministries (i.e., the Ministries of Industry, Agriculture, or Trade) and from the government's Economic Council. As will be seen later, the number of competing projects submitted was much larger than anticipated; thus, severe strains were created on the Ministry of Privatization.

Many state-owned JSCs were created through the commercialization of SOEs, and other enterprises could propose commercialization as part of their privatization projects. Enterprises could suggest the portion of their shares that would be privatized through such means as direct sale, public auction, or public tender or through more unique methods such as distribution of shares through the voucher system. Within the framework of the voucher method, a significant amount of state property would be transferred to private ownership in exchange for investment coupons. Each citizen would get coupon booklets—1,000 points of investment vouchers with limited maturity—for a registration fee of 1,000 crowns ($34, or 25 percent of the average monthly wage). These vouchers entitled citizens to bid for ownership of shares of any company privatized by the voucher method.

The voucher method had a number of advantages. First, it solved at least two immediate problems: inadequate public savings to purchase state property and the lack of knowledge among the public about how to purchase companies or securities. The sale of state property for investment vouchers was organized in a way that was simple enough for every Czechoslovakian citizen to understand. Voucher privatization would, above all, guarantee that a large volume of state property would pass quickly into private ownership. Second, the voucher method also guaranteed that a maximum number of Czech and Slovak citizens could participate in the process. Third, it was widely perceived to be a fair process. Each individual would be able to participate in decisions about capital investment according to his own preferences. Also, mutual funds could emerge as private organizations in response to market demand and not as state-administered entities. Finally, widely dispersed private ownership would create new constituencies in favor of a market economy. This was critical in a country with a history of successful capitalism as well as a history under socialism that had one of the highest rates of state ownership in Central Europe.

There were also clear drawbacks to this form of privatization. The wide dispersion of ownership could lead to weak corporate governance because investors generally lacked the knowledge and information necessary to provide direction and control. The voucher system was also technically difficult to implement without capital markets or financial intermediaries and without relevant legislation. Also, at a time when there were budgetary shortfalls, this method provided no government revenues.

The large-scale privatization was carried out in two waves, the first beginning in early 1992. One wave consisted of several privatization rounds. During each round a predetermined portion of enterprise shares was "sold" to the public in exchange for investment points. There was also a "zero round" in which voucher holders could delegate their points to investment privatization funds (IPFs), which were allowed by government decree to collect points from voucher holders only in round zero of the voucher privatization wave from February 17 to the end of March 1992. The IPFs could not collect points once the sale of enterprises was actually under way.

The first round of the first wave was scheduled to start in the second half of May 1992. Each round would last no longer than one month, and one wave would consist of no more than five rounds. The voucher holder could spend all of his 1,000 investment points in one privatization round or spend them gradually during several rounds. Through an iterative process, new share prices would be publicized by the Federal Ministry of Finance at the end of each round. This process would establish an equilibrium between supply and demand by the end of several rounds. The procedure for setting the prices was still not established in mid-1992, however. Proposals were published by several officials, but these were only preliminary suggestions. Also, criteria for deciding when the procedure would end had not been finally determined. Alternatives included ending the process when demand was satisfied—as indicated by a percentage of voucher points expended, by some percentage of privatized shares, or simply by a predetermined number of rounds with a pro-rata method for determining the division of shares at the end of the final round. In the latter case, a stock split would be necessary; but this was not yet allowed by the Federal Ministry of Finance even though it was also not yet forbidden by the Commercial Code. A stock split would eliminate the potential problem that could arise if the value of a highly attractive firm's shares rose above 1,000 points.

The Preliminary Experience with Large-Scale Privatization

By the final deadline for submission of first-wave privatization projects in the Czech Republic on January 20, the number of submitted projects reached 10,949 (see table 8.7 for a breakdown of submitted projects by proposed privatization method). The original Law on Large Privatization anticipated that privatization projects would *usually* be suggested by the enterprise itself. Nevertheless, only 26.3 percent of the submitted projects were proposed by firms as basic projects; and nearly 75 percent of the proposals came as competing projects. In fact, competing projects were strongly encouraged by Privatization Minister Tomas Jezek, who was the motivating force behind the decision to extend the deadline, allowing the submission of more competing proposals. For some companies, in fact, there were as many as 20 or 30 different projects from various bidders.

Supply-Side Issues. Not all of the projects proposed the use of the voucher system, and most competing projects suggested direct sale or other standard methods. The large influx of competing proposals actually changed the originally planned structure of privatization and made it more difficult to prepare, on the supply side, a sufficient number of companies for voucher privatization. Originally, the Federal Ministry of Finance preferred voucher privatization over other methods and saw the role of the Ministry of Privatization as one of ensuring that projects were properly processed. Even that role was not easy, however, because of difficulties with restitution: Each project had to produce evidence that any existing claims of original property owners had been given preference and resolved. The government also had to decide on the role of foreign investors. In order to respond to the unexpected number of competing proposals, the Ministry of Privatization had to assume more decision-making power in an extremely shorter period than had been anticipated in the Large Privatization Law. The amount of property going to voucher privatization that was finally agreed upon was 260 billion crowns' worth of assets ($9 billion). Originally, this was to include 140 billion crowns from the Czech Republic, 70 billion crowns from the Slovak Republic, and 50 million crowns of federal property. The federal contribution ended up amounting to only 12 billion crowns because most property had already been transferred to the republics, so the new contribution of each republic had to be defined. The final amount was 173 billion crowns ($6 billion) of book value of assets from the Czech Republic and 75 billion crowns ($2.8 billion) from Slovakia. This ratio between the two (2.29:1) corresponded to the ratio of voucher holders in the Czech Republic to

Table 8.7
Privatization Projects Proposed by the Final Deadline

Proposed Method of Privatization*	Number of Projects	Share of Total Projects
A: Public Auction	1,150	10.5
B: Public Tender	872	8.0
C: Direct Sale to Predetermined Buyer	4,905	44.8
D: Commercialization of SOE to Joint-Stock Company: Also a Precondition for Voucher Privatization	2,452	22.4
E: Privatization of an Already Existing State-Owned Joint-stock Company	432	4.0
F: Unpaid Transfer to Municipalities, Pension Funds, Banks, or Savings Banks	887	8.1
Voucher Privatization (out of D and E)	2,523	23.0
TOTAL NUMBER OF PROJECTS:	10,949	100.0
Basic Projects	2,884	26.3
Competing Projects	8,065	73.7

* Note that many projects proposed more than one method.

Source: Ministry for the Administration of State Property and Its Privatization.

those in the Slovak Republic. By the time of the deadline for approving projects for voucher privatization, each republic had slightly exceeded its required contribution (with a reserve in case some firms were not registered in the commercial courts in time for privatization). The Czech Republic designated 190 billion crowns' worth of property for privatization, which encompassed about 1,000 JSCs; and the Slovak side provided 85 billion crowns, which included property from over 500 JSCs. In 81 percent of the cases in Slovakia, firms allocated all of their property (except 3 percent of each enterprise, which was put aside for remuneration of restitution claims) to the voucher privatization, whereas in the Czech Republic this figure was significantly smaller.

Public Voucher Registration and Investment Funds. The outcome of the voucher privatization originally looked dim but improved as the process got under way. Perhaps people had put off buying coupon booklets until late in the eligibility period because they were not attracted by the official advertising campaign. Privately established IPFs, however, opened their advertising campaigns unexpectedly early and promised options to buy back their shares if the voucher holders would invest their coupons. This option was linked to a promise to pay back not the actual market value of the portfolio but at least ten times the registration fee. Expected book value per voucher holder at that time was close to 70,000 crowns, and 3 to 4 million people were expected to participate.

The aggressive advertising campaigns of the IPFs and the impending end of the registration period attracted large crowds to registration places. Although by January 10, only 2 million voucher booklets had been sold in both republics, in late January there were 6,918,000 registered voucher holders in the CSFR. The final number of registered voucher holders was 8.56 million citizens. This massive participation by nearly three-quarters of all eligible citizens was quite unexpected.

Clearly, the IPFs played an important role in creating demand for the vouchers. These closed-end funds, organized as JSCs, were allowed to collect voucher points from the public during the zero round and then to invest them during the first round of voucher privatization. Some of the funds were purely private, and some were established by state-owned banks or JSCs. By the end of the registration period, there were over 400 IPFs registered by commercial courts and the Ministry of Finance. Unfortunately, there was very limited regulation; the rules establishing IPFs provided only weak controls over their operations. More stringent controls—disclosure rules, diversification requirements, prevention of conflicts of interest, rules regulating operation, and others—would be included in the Law on Regulation of IPFs; but they were not applied during the sale of vouchers. The efficacy of the rules issues through ad hoc decrees was limited. Usually, the prospectus of an IPF with full disclosure of its capital stock, with a personal history of each member of the board of directors, and with complete operational charges was not widely available. In fact, only in May 1992 was it discovered that government officials who sometimes played important roles in voucher privatization procedures had been appointed to the boards of directors of many IPFs.

Problems of Large-Scale Privatization

There were many problems associated with the large-scale privatization process. On the supply side, they were mostly related to the quantity and quality of the privatization projects submitted. On the demand side, they were mostly related to the lack of regulation of IPFs and to inadequate institutional structures. First, the privatization process required the evaluation of a firm's market value, which was not easily established given past pricing systems, inadequate bench marks of value, and weak accounting systems. The firm's market value as an initial fixed-price offer might, of course, be equal to zero for a poor asset (with low expected cash flows) or might be many times greater than the book value for a good asset (especially for internationally competitive firms). In any case, to assess the market value of the firm from expected cash flows by distorted product and input prices (based on domestic individual costs and markup combined with nontransparent subsidies) was somewhat naive. Hence, case-by-case modifications of common evaluation procedures were required to indicate either potential (international) competitiveness or risk of bankruptcy. Nevertheless, the public was wary of foreign buyouts based on the book value of firms and feared that the national heritage would be sold off too cheaply.

In addition, many competing projects proposed the breakup of existing large enterprises. For the most part, this was a positive suggestion because most SOEs were too large and inefficient. The breakup of these enterprises could contribute to the creation of a private sector consisting of a larger number of small- and medium-sized firms. But unfortunately, in many cases, competing project proposals tried to divide companies that were technologically indivisible. A loophole in the privatization legislation also allowed existing management to sign long-term rental agreements, which de facto predetermined the fate of the property before privatization. Furthermore, many project proposals presented weak or poorly elaborated business plans. Moreover, during the transition period, constant changes in legislation involving the enactment of a new Commercial Code were not reflected in project proposals; and many companies needed additional time to make the necessary adjustments.

Another problem was that although the supervising branch ministries also reviewed the projects, their conclusions were sometimes at odds with those of the privatization ministries, which usually supported the existing management. The influence of the privatization ministries, however, resulted in the hierarchy and coalitions that previously ran the SOEs to remain in place for the most part.

This approach to privatization was also undermined by the fact that selection procedures and rules were not prepared in time; and there could not be a consistent, transparent means of evaluating projects. But some rules did exist. For example, in cases of two or more competing projects, such competitive forms of privatization as public auction and public tender were preferred over direct sales to predetermined buyers. Those making decisions were, however, under urgent time pressures as well as lobbying pressure from various groups with vested interests to speed up the privatization process.

Many firms to be privatized through the voucher method inherited heavy debts due to distorted price structures. This situation created adverse conditions for privatization and obstacles to the formulation of feasible business plans. As a result, the state had to clear enterprises and banks of their debts by using a 50 billion–crown bond issued by the Funds of National Property. The newly created Funds of National Property of the Czech and Slovak republics served as temporary owners of privatized property, and this strained their ability to start up and operate smoothly in the short time period before the beginning of the privatization process.

Also, laws concerning the establishment and regulation of stock markets in Prague and Bratislava (an essential element in the effective functioning of the privatization process) still had not been passed by mid-1992. The law regulating the behavior of IPFs was still under discussion by mid-1992. Given the possibly excessive option offers that had been made by the funds, many would conceivably face bankruptcy when these options matured. The average book value of assets per coupon book was almost 70,000 crowns ($2,300) when the IPFs began making their offers; but because more than twice as many coupon books were registered before the registration deadline, this figure had fallen to around 30,000 crowns ($1,100) per coupon book by mid-1992. Large-scale bankruptcies in the IPF sector could have a shock-wave effect on the whole economy.

Finally, it was still unclear by mid-1992 when dividend payments and share trading would begin. Proposed regulations that would delay dividend payments by two years could seriously harm the entrepreneurial interests of new shareholders, and those regulations delaying the ability of new shareholders to trade their marketable shares could postpone the emergence of a secondary market and hinder shareholder participation in corporate governance.

CONCLUSION

By the end of 1992, privatization in Czechoslovakia was well under way. Privatization was seen as an important part of the economic reform package and was supported both by the public and by Parliament. This was critical in ensuring that the reform process maintained its momentum. One of the most important challenges continuing to face the government was to make sure that the whole privatization process did not get mired down in details or in controversies about its problems.

Clearly, there were many problems in the implementation of the privatization process, but this had been anticipated. No process of large-scale economic change could be expected to be problem free, and many problems of privatization were, to some degree, unavoidable. What is important is that the small-scale privatization process was progressing at full speed, and that by mid-1992 the government began to give more attention to the small-business sector through the creation of several programs of support and of a Guarantee and Development Bank dedicated to small businesses.

The most important policy pursued in the large privatization process was the promotion of competitive bids that allowed the transfer of property by the voucher system as well as by direct sales, public auctions, and tenders. This policy, however, altered the process and caused many unforeseen problems that required immediate attention. Perhaps the greatest problems throughout the large-scale privatization were the lack of a firm legal framework and the uncertainty created by the frequent changes the government made in important policies.

In spite of these problems, however, the first wave of privatization was scheduled for completion by the end of 1992. In the second wave, everyone will be able to learn from the lessons of the first and thus create a more sound foundation for more efficient operation. The most important challenge remaining for Czechoslovakia in the future will be to find effective ways of restructuring and reorganizing newly privatized enterprises in order to create a properly functioning market economy.

9

The Privatization of PIVO Praha, Electronic Company

John Hannula and Kit Jackson

In January 1991 Czechoslovakia took its first serious steps toward a market economy. The lifting of price controls on 85 percent of goods sold allowed prices on retail goods to increase 25.8 percent and prices of food items to increase 31.4 percent in just one month. At the same time, the Czechoslovakian koruna was devalued in the new government's first effort to make the currency convertible. Devaluation was paralleled by a reduction in import tariffs and made Western goods more competitive on the Czechoslovakian market. Also, in the same month ex-COMECON (Council for Mutual Economic Assistance) countries began dealing on a hard-currency basis. These actions had a far-reaching effect on the Czechoslovakian economy and laid the foundation for privatizing the country's more than 4,000 state-owned enterprises (SOEs). The initial steps toward privatization began in February 1991 when auctions for small businesses were held. These businesses included pubs, restaurants, and small retail stores. But foreigners were not allowed to participate in the bidding.

Also in February, Parliament passed a law covering the privatization of large businesses. Firms had to develop their own privatization plans and submit them to the appropriate ministry by October 1, 1991. Actual privatization was not scheduled to begin until 1992 when vouchers would be sold for 1,000 korunas ($33) to any Czechoslovakian citizen interested in participating in the process. Up to 40 percent of each company's equity would be distributed to voucher holders. Unlike privatization plans in other Eastern European countries, the Czechoslovakian process allowed citizens to directly own stock in companies of their choice.

As in the business auctions, foreign investors could not participate in the voucher process. However, they could buy up to 100 percent of a firm that had bypassed the voucher system. In this way, foreign companies could be major participants in the privatization process.

COMPANY BACKGROUND

PIVO Praha, s.p. was founded in 1921 by three Czech entrepreneurs as a radio-manufacturing concern. By the early 1930s, the company had become a major competitor in the European radio market. Seimens of Germany bought PIVO from its original owners in 1935 and used the new company to supply high-tech radios to the German navy. With the defeat of Germany in 1945, ownership of PIVO transferred back to Czechoslovakia; and the company was nationalized along with many of the country's major firms. Until November 1989 all of PIVO's production, sales, supplies, and distribution were controlled by the state.

As a SOE, PIVO produced such electronic equipment as walkie-talkies, directional telephone transmitters, tape recorders, and home stereo systems for domestic and Eastern bloc markets. PIVO manufactured printed circuit boards (PCBs) for many of its own products, and only 1 to 2 percent of production went to outside customers.

After 1989, however, PIVO was hard hit by the political and economic changes occurring throughout Central and Eastern Europe. The home electronics industry was devastated. As CMEA countries liberalized their import policies, domestic producers of electronics were faced with Western products with which they simply could not compete. PIVO's tape recorder and home stereo markets evaporated. The company continued to produce these items through the first half of 1991 but simply built up significant inventories of unsalable items. At the same time, the company began to search for new products to replace these lost sales.

PIVO expanded its original role as an in-house supplier of PCBs and became a source for both domestic and foreign customers. Even though the PCB Division operated at 40 percent capacity, it attracted the attention of potential foreign investors. The division began exporting PCBs through a third party to automotive manufacturers and other end users in Germany and Austria. By meeting the specifications of these customers and by providing a low-cost product, PIVO successfully competed in the European PCB market. PIVO's biggest advantage was its low labor costs, which were one sixteenth of those of former West Germany. On an average, PIVO's workers received 20 korunas an hour, while comparable workers in Germany received approximately 20 deutsche marks per hour (1 deutsche mark = 17 korunas, 1991).

Like the PCB Division, PIVO's Tool Shop and Fabrication Division expanded its in-house responsibilities and sold injection-molded plastic parts to Western Europe. Again, PIVO outpriced its Western competition with low labor costs.

In addition, PIVO created three new divisions to recover the lost sales of its Home Electronics Division and to capitalize on the company's expertise in mechanical and electronic equipment. The new Health Technology Division planned production of an injection pump, and the new Fire Extinguisher Division received orders for 107,000 fire extinguishers in the last half of 1991. The Washing Machine Parts Division, which utilized much of the same technology used in tape recorder production, planned washing machine subassemblies for a Czech appliance manufacturer. Each of these new divisions relied heavily on PIVO's skills in manufacturing electronic and mechanical equipment.

MAJOR PRODUCT DIVISIONS

Since its founding, PIVO Praha had developed seven major product groups. These included printed circuit boards, high-frequency technology, health technology, washing machines, fire extinguishers, manufacturing tools and equipment, and home electronics.

Printed Circuit Board Division

PCB production began at PIVO in 1958. That division represented the majority of PIVO's business and employed 438 people. Most of the firm's PCB products were sold in Czechoslovakia and used in domestic autos and personal electronics (which includes television remote controls and personal computer [PC] keyboards). Because the domestic end users of these products were also having problems competing in the electronics market, PIVO's PCB Division operated at 40 percent capacity. One of PIVO's largest domestic customers canceled an order that represented 78 percent of its one-sided PCB production and 20 percent of overall PCB production. This drop in demand from traditional Eastern European markets spurred PIVO's management to aggressively seek entry into Western markets. While PCB exports to the West increased dramatically in the first half of 1991, they still represented less than 10 percent of PIVO's overall potential PCB capacity.

PIVO's PCB Division sought the Underwriters Laboratory (UL) certification for its printed circuit boards. (The requirements for this certification are considered very stringent, and PIVO is awaiting approval.) The credibility gained from the UL certification would help the company enter international markets.

High-Frequency Technology Division

The High-Frequency Technology Division at PIVO produced three major products: portable radio stations (walkie-talkies), directional telephone transmitters, and the transmitter portion of an electronic security system. It employed 220 people. Production of the radio stations, directional telephones, and transmitters was labor-intensive. The basic parts (i.e., circuits, crystals, etc.) were purchased from within Czechoslovakia and then assembled at PIVO. The company's managers admitted that their technology was 15 years old and feared that Minolta's move into the Czechoslovakian market would be their demise. Their only hope was that local governments would be their biggest customers.

Health Technology Division

The Health Technology Division began production of an injection pump on September 1, 1991. The pump allowed a medical technician to dispense liquids into an intravenous tube at a controlled rate. The development of the PIVO injection pump was the result of a joint research project with the Research Institute of Medicine and Technology in northern Bohemia. There were 400 hospitals in Czechoslovakia, and PIVO hoped to place ten units in each. The product sold for 10,000 korunas ($333), one-fifth the price of its nearest German counterpart but twice as much as a lower-quality pump manufactured by a Slovak firm in eastern Czechoslovakia.

The Health Technology Division employed 78 people, many from the old Tape Recorder Division. The manager of this division hoped to move into the production of magnetic-therapy devices. With the financial difficulties facing PIVO, the company's foreign adviser recommended cutting this division. The product was technically sound, but no true marketing research had been done. Projected sales were based solely on the number of hospitals. However, the division remained because of company politics.

Washing Machine Division

The Washing Machine Division, like the Health Technology Division, took the tape recorder production process and applied it to a new product. PIVO Praha received an exclusive contract with KAVA of Hlinsko (Czechoslovakia) to produce subassemblies for the KAVA washing machine. Production of these subassemblies was in full swing by September 1, 1991.

The managers of this division hoped to be so successful that KAVA would be forced to subcontract the production of the washing machine itself. PIVO's managers believed that the company had the capacity to produce the entire machine.

Fire Extinguisher Division

With the unification of Germany in 1990 and the East's conversion to the deutsche mark, Eastern Europe's monopoly supplier of fire extinguishers was immediately priced out of the market. PIVO saw an opportunity to fill this void and in mid-1991 began production of three types of hand-held fire extinguishers—one water extinguisher and two types of powder extinguishers. PIVO had orders for 107,000 fire extinguishers by early summer. However, financial difficulties for the purchaser forced them to cut the order to 49,000. This was a major setback for the division. By November the division had not yet reached full-capacity production and, without more orders, probably never would.

Tool Shop and Fabrication Division

The Tool Shop was originally organized as an in-house service department that provided PIVO's operating departments with parts and equipment. In addition to meeting PIVO's internal demands, it took orders from other firms in Czechoslovakia and Western Europe for plastic parts produced by injection molding. The injection molding of plastic parts did not employ high technology; and with low labor costs and efficient production techniques, PIVO became a competitor. The Tool Shop was so successful with its outside orders that other Czechoslovakian firms began to study PIVO's methods.

Home Electronics Division

Even though most of the company's home electronic products were no longer manufactured, the department continued to exist as an independent division within the organization. The division's primary product was a home security system sold on the domestic market. Sales of these systems represented a very small portion of the company's overall sales, but they did show a slight improvement.

STRATEGIC ISSUES AFFECTING PRIVATIZATION

PIVO's problems were typical of those faced by most Czechoslovakian firms, and PIVO was considered a good company compared with other Eastern European companies. But from a Western perspective, the company was a "basket case."

Management

Following the ousting of the Communists at the national level in 1989, many of the company's senior managers were voted out and replaced by younger employees. Both the director and assistant director had been at PIVO for only one year. Even though committed to privatization, both had little management experience and seemed to lack the vision and leadership skills needed to get the company through tough times.

By October 1991 it was clear that the new managing director did not have the skills or experience to help PIVO turn around. The company's foreign adviser wanted to organize a management coup to replace him. Unfortunately, the Communist legacy of "not-my-responsibility" attitudes undermined his plan.

In November, Parliament passed a law demanding that all Communists with past "undesirable" activities had to leave high-ranking business and political posts by the end of the year. Within three days, the assistant managing director resigned. However, he possessed the knowledge and connections that could have benefited the company.

Organization

Under the direction of an outside consultant, PIVO's senior management restructured the company along more traditional Western lines. The company's divisions were now organized according to product lines. While this move helped build a degree of accountability, many departments and divisions were still unsure of their roles in the new organizational structure.

In an effort to improve sales, many of the Marketing Department's responsibilities were relegated to the new product divisions. While the Marketing Department retained control of all exports, some, but not all, departments chose to manage their own domestic customers. Each division chose which particular marketing responsibilities it planned to do internally and which it would leave to the Marketing Department. This created confusion in a department that already lacked focus.

Finance

PIVO had been operating in the red for more than a year before its foreign adviser arrived. By July 1991 the company did not have the cash to make its interest payments and was forced to borrow at 34 percent to meet its short-term payments. The firm was still technically owned by the state, but the state had cut subsidies; and the company was having a hard time meeting its obligations. By October 1991 management had to borrow money just to pay wages.

Much of the problem was that PIVO's customers owed the company 110 million korunas ($3.7 million). These customers included firms in Czechoslovakia and other CMEA countries who were also having problems meeting their obligations. While PIVO had not yet written off these receivables, it would more than likely see only 20 percent of the 110 million korunas it was owed. On the other side of the coin, PIVO owed 120 million korunas ($4 million) to its suppliers. PIVO simply could not pay all of them, and some of its payables were up to 12 months old. In order to pay its most important suppliers, PIVO took out loans at 22 percent. However, the company would most likely not have to pay off the entire 120 million korunas because some of its debts would be canceled by the government as companies were allowed to go under. In November 1991 things were so bad that PIVO and other companies were forced into a barter-trade arrangement to get what they needed. The Czechoslovakian government finally recognized the problem and began a program funded with 50 billion korunas to forgive payables of companies. This offered relief, but no one knew for sure if the funds would actually make it to PIVO.

An additional problem was that a large amount of PIVO's operating capital was tied up in inventory. For example, the metal casings for its fire extinguishers had been ordered 18 months earlier and had been sitting in inventory for over 7 months while waiting for production to begin. PIVO had to order many materials up to a year in advance.

Pricing

The company continued to use a cost-plus-markup pricing structure. This was a particular problem because no coherent transfer pricing or overhead allocation system existed. Depreciation charges for equipment that was no longer being used were being allocated to the new divisions. These divisions had no real idea what their true costs were. In addition, the company did not seem to understand the concept of demand. Finished-goods inventory was overflowing with home electronics equipment that the company could not sell largely because it insisted on receiving its original cost-plus-markup price.

Originally designed as an in-house supplier of parts, tools, and machines, the Tools Department was able to deal with outside customers and export its products. Because the company had no real internal-transfer pricing system, it was more profitable for the new division to sell its products on the open market. This became a problem when fire extinguisher production was held up for three weeks because outside orders had absorbed the department's entire capacity. While the Tool Shop manager was working to maximize profit for his division, the other division managers resented having to wait for items because the Tool Shop was filling the orders for outside customers. The managing director was unable to provide any guidance on this issue.

Marketing

Because PIVO was a state-run company, its orders and production were controlled largely by the state. As a result, the company's Marketing Department did little more than process orders. Most of PIVO's goods were sold through state distributors, and the company had little idea who its end users were. This was particularly true of its export markets. For the most part, no one within the firm had the experience or skills to do basic marketing research or implement a marketing plan. More important, the company wanted to explore Western markets but did not have a sales force to do so.

Work Force

Assembly-line workers were unmotivated because the state had guaranteed employment for the last 40 years. The majority of the work force did not seem to understand the urgency of the current situation. In June 1991 there were layoffs of 260 people (12 percent of the work force). With the cash crunch that came in October, PIVO was forced to lay off 765 people (35 percent of the work force). This was frightening in a society that had never seen unemployment.

But fear was not a good motivator, and work habits did not seem to change. One real problem remained— wage increases. Inflation in the first six months of 1991 was approximately 50 percent (annually), yet workers at PIVO had received less than a 5 percent increase in their paychecks because the company was doing so poorly. Although layoffs were considered a cost-cutting measure, Czechoslovakian law required that workers be given a three months' notice before being discharged and two months' severance pay. This represented the only social safety net in place.

CONCLUSION

There were many occurrences of mismanagement and foolish business practices that concerned PIVO's foreign management adviser. For example, raw materials were being ordered even though there was a year's supply on hand; an expensive machine had been purchased for the PCB Division, but it operated at only 30 percent of capacity; and orders were misplaced and delayed to the point where the order was actually lost. Even though management was fairly competent, the company's foreign adviser and others wondered if an attempt to bankrupt the firm was under way. This had happened at other companies in Czechoslovakia so that managers could buy the firm at 5 to 10 percent of its value after bankruptcy. Although this constituted fraud, the Czechoslovakian government was too busy to police these practices. For better or worse, the managers that appeared to be attempting to force the bankruptcy were the only ones who had the skills to help PIVO in the long run. The bankruptcy would lead, of course, to more layoffs and great hardship for the workers. At the same time, if PIVO were to survive at all, a radical change had to take place.

10

Privatizing Rychtar Tools in the Czech Republic*

Jonathan Gafni and Mark Niles

Douglas McCarthy and Michael Rocca, two Americans working for the Czech consulting firm Prague International Enterprises (PIE), were called into the office of Mr. Novak one afternoon in early August 1991. Mr. Novak, a Czech professor of Western economics and finance, was the founding partner of PIE. McCarthy and Rocca had just spent the summer investigating Rychtar Tools, s.p., a state-run, hand-tool manufacturer located 150 kilometers from Prague. The managing director of Rychtar, Mr. Jizek, had hired PIE to help his company develop its privatization plan.

Every state-run company was required by the Czech and Slovak privatization ministries to develop a privatization plan. The plans were due at the end of October 1991 for all of the companies that were to be privatized in the "first wave" of privatization (due to administrative problems in the privatization ministries, the deadline for submitting privatization plans in the first wave was extended until the end of December). Rychtar was to be part of this first wave.

Upper-level management in each of 3,800 large-scale enterprises was required to submit a plan to the Ministry of Privatization for the republic in which it operated. Rychtar's privatization plan was to be submitted to the Czech Ministry of Privatization.[1] One of the goals of the Czech and Slovak privatization program was to attract foreign investment and joint ventures (JVs). The understanding between Mr. Jizek and Mr. Novak when Rychtar hired PIE was that Rychtar needed to find a foreign partner with the necessary capital as well as access to Western distribution channels in order to modernize Rychtar and provide stable markets for Rychtar's tools.

---

*The names of the company and of all individuals mentioned in the case have been changed to protect confidentiality.

McCarthy and Rocca's primary duties had been to focus on the valuation of the property and the business plan. In order to attract a Western partner for a JV with Rychtar, the two had prepared the following two-part report for Mr. Novak and PIE. An important feature of the Czech privatization program was the inclusion of "competing projects." They were accepted for two months after the "basic" or original privatization projects from upper management had been submitted. Anyone could submit a competing project. Often these interested parties were other managers who were not included in the original basic project, foreign investors, and local entrepreneurs. (Since the original projects were due at the end of December 1991, the final competing projects could be submitted through January 31, 1992.)

The basic steps of privatization from the firm's point of view included the following steps.

1.   Management of the Czech firm had to devise a plan for privatization. This plan had to include all domestic issues (e.g., financing from banks and method of privatization). Also, it was to include a list of all possible foreign investors: those considered for privatization; and those not considered, and why they were not.

2.   The plan was submitted to the company's sector ministry (i.e., an electronics firm would submit the plan to the Ministry of Industry of the Czech Republic). This ministry could make comments on the plan but had no authority to make changes.

3.   The plan went to the Ministry of Privatization for final review and publication.

4.   Once the plan was published, any interested others could make alternative proposals for the company and submit them. Two months after the first proposal was made, all existing proposals for the firm would be considered by the Ministry of Privatization. It was the responsibility of this ministry to approve or deny each proposal.

5.   If the plan was approved, the sector ministry transmitted the shares to the National Property Funds. The firm then acted on the chosen method of privatization.

Ideally, the future sale of shares in companies was to be accomplished through markets. Therefore, the timing of future sales of shares was restricted until after capital and equity markets were functioning. The stock exchange functioned in coordination with the development of large privatization.

BACKGROUND OF THE COMPANY

Rychtar was founded in 1908 by the company Tlusty Loewy in Hannulsko. The firm's first products included a wide assortment of files and rasps. In 1976 the firm switched its focus to hand tools and tighteners. By the early 1990s the firm was concentrating on the production of high-quality ratchet wrenches, socket sets, and vices.

Prior to World War II, Rychtar's business had been conducted by the firm Ajax, which had acquired Tlusty Loewy. In 1946, Ajax was taken over by Dratovny a sroubarny Bohumin (DASB), a state-owned enterprise (SOE). As a result of the nationalization of Ajax, Rychtar's business and property were nationalized as well. In 1960, DASB merged with ONTO Pecky, another toolmaking firm. Until 1990 the business of Rychtar and three other factories was conducted under the ONTO trade name. In November 1990 each of the ONTO factories was given autonomy. The Hannulsko plant took the registered name Rychtar in April 1991.

Descendants of Czech citizens who had been former owners of property nationalized since 1948 were afforded the right to seek restitution by the republic's new government. Because the portion of Rychtar's business that was Czech owned was nationalized in 1946, there were no claims for restitution concerning Rychtar's business or property. A preliminary investigation indicated that claims concerning Rychtar were unlikely to be made in the future.

Management and Employees

Rychtar employed approximately 200 people, including 120 production workers, 50 designers and toolmakers, and 30 managers and support staff. The number of workers remained fairly constant because none of ONTO's managerial staff were added to Rychtar's payroll after it was granted autonomy. Rychtar's location in Hannulsko gave the company access to a skilled labor pool that permitted the company to add a third production shift if needed. Compared with other Czech firms, the number of managers at Rychtar was very low. The top managers were young, well-educated engineers with no ties to the old regime. Hence, they were very open to Western business ideas.

Facilities and Technology

Hannulsko is located 150 kilometers from Prague along well-maintained roads. Rychtar's 9,650 square meters facility was less than 12 years old, and the company owned an additional 2,000 square meters of surrounding land suitable for expansion.

Rychtar's toolmaking and prototype shop contained some of the company's most technologically advanced milling machines, drills, presses, and lathes. Factory-based research and development allowed Rychtar to incorporate manufacturing concerns into the designs for new products. As a result, Rychtar could quickly move new products from the design phase to full-scale production.

A profile of the remaining technology used at Rychtar revealed an eclectic collection of metal working machines from the last three decades. Most of the machines were made in Czechoslovakia. The average machine in Rychtar's factory was 12.6 years old, and each was well maintained. Most new purchases were made in order to increase capacity and to take advantage of newer technologies rather than to replace worn-out machines. The following table summarizes the age of Rychtar's 199 machines.

Age of Machine	Number of Machines	Percent of Total
0–5 years	72	36.2
6–10 years	40	20.1
11–15 years	16	8.1
16–30 years	53	26.6
Over 30 years	18	9.0

The factory was roughly divided into eight areas according to the different manufacturing processes: main hall, socket pressing room, painting area, hardening shop, waste-neutralizing station, loading dock, storage area, and tool room. (This chapter only reviews the different technologies in the first five areas.)

The first and largest division was the main hall where most of the activity took place. There were two groups of machines: the automatic lathes and all the other manual tools. There were 28 automatic lathes between 2 and 34 years of age. Most were made by MAS/Kovosvit, a Czech manufacturer. Other tools in the main hall were center lathes, turret lathes, universal milling machines, grinding machines, drilling machines, roll-forming machines, and some of the factory's presses. The remaining presses, which ranged from 10 to 600 tons in size, were in the socket pressing room. In addition, the socket pressing room held a new copying lathe controlled by an Erfurt Electronic computer acquired in 1990. The painting room contained a spraying booth and a degreasing machine, both of which were six years old. The factory used latex paints that had been specially formulated to be environmentally safe. The paints were cured by heating.

Many of the factory's products were processed in the hardening shop to improve their durability. Rychtar used a three-stage hardening process. First, the products were immersed in an 850°C hardening furnace. Next, the products were placed in a 250°C tempering furnace. Finally, the products were cooled in a liquid bath. Also, some tools were chemically treated in the hardening shop before being sent for chromium-vanadium plating to ONTO Pecky, another former division of ONTO.

Rychtar recycled all scrap metal and lubricating oils used in its production processes. Using two state-of-the-art machines located in Rychtar's waste-neutralizing station, the company treated the chemicals used in the hardening shop. After neutralization, these chemicals were then shipped to approved disposal sites. As a result, Rychtar's operations had almost no negative impact on the environment.

One of Rychtar's main strengths was the quality and ability of the workers who operated its equipment. Approximately 80 percent of Rychtar's production workers had completed at least three years of vocational training.

Capacity

Prior to the economic and political changes in Czechoslovakia, accounting by Czech businesses was more concerned with labor utilization than with production costs. Furthermore, Rychtar's use of many machines in the production of more than one product limited the company's ability to measure the potential number of products that could be made by each machine. As a result, Rychtar did not measure the output capacity of its equipment in terms of units of production; instead, it measured the amount of labor used in manufacturing its products. In the absence of other substantive data, labor content was used to determine the utilization of plant capacity.

Based on both time and motion studies conducted by Rychtar, normal completion times were assigned to each operation in the production process. Based on these normal completion times and the number of products shipped by Rychtar during 1990, the total labor content of the company's 1990 output was 245,000 hours.

The maximum capacity of Rychtar in 1990 was 417,590 hours. This figure was based on the maximum number of hours that Rychtar's machines were available for production. To calculate this figure, each machine was evaluated to determine (1) if it was used directly in the production process and (2) if it could be used for more than one shift per workday. Of Rychtar's 199 machines, 121 were directly used in production; and of these 121 machines, 106 were used during more than one shift. Machines were available for 260 workdays per year.

The estimate of available machine hours also accounted for machine downtime. Rychtar's management estimated downtime for reconfiguration and maintenance of machines to be between 10.5 and 12 percent. Setup times to reconfigure Rychtar's machines in order to produce different products varied from an average of approximately four hours to reconfigure an automatic lathe to less than 30 minutes to reconfigure the computer-controlled copying lathe.

Thus, Rychtar operated at approximately 59 percent of its existing plant capacity. By adding a third shift, Rychtar could increase its available capacity by another 50 percent. In the short term, this excess capacity permitted the firm to increase production without expanding its facilities.

Product Lines

Most of Rychtar's products used chromium-vanadium-coated steel (Czech regulation n. 152 60), and all products corresponded to ISO and DIN regulations. More than half of Rychtar's production was devoted to socket sets. Rychtar produced seven different varieties of socket sets. These sets had various shaft diameters (both metric and inch calibrations), and some were equipped with a hex key (allen wrench). In addition, all socket sets came with their own metal case.

Rychtar expanded its socket sets in order to broaden its product lines. It produced torque wrenches that incorporated the different socket sizes, and it produced electricians' sets that included a standard socket set with screwdrivers and pliers designed for professional use.

Rychtar had the flexibility to make a wide variety of products and developed processes for the production of ratchet-nut tighteners, fixed-nut tighteners, bolt-on bench vices, joiner's workbench spindles and clamps, plumber's pipe vices with stands, and electrician's wire-strippers and diamond files.

As a result of this flexibility in Rychtar's production processes, the firm was able to make changes in products according to customers' specific requirements. Almost half of Rychtar's production was custom designed. One hundred percent of Rychtar's products underwent a quality inspection before leaving the factory.

One example of this flexibility and commitment to quality in production was the car jack. Rychtar won a demanding contract to supply jacks for some of the 1992 cars produced in the Skoda/Volkswagen JV. By incorporating techniques used to manufacture vices, Rychtar developed a compact, heavy-duty jack that conveniently fit inside the spare tire. The car jack demonstrated Rychtar's ability to adapt and to manufacture complex products for the Western market.

Distribution Channels

Control of Czechoslovakia's economy passed from the government to private enterprises. As this process took place, Rychtar began to sell its products through a variety of distribution channels. Approximately 80 percent of Rychtar's production was made for the domestic market. Within Czechoslovakia, Rychtar's goods were sold through two distribution networks. First, Rychtar created a consortium of four Czech manufacturers of socket wrenches and other hand tools. Pursuant to this agreement, a network of 300 sales agents was created. This sales network offered Rychtar's products to institutions, retail outlets, and individual consumers. In addition, the consortium established a network of 8 to 12 shops dedicated to their products. Independently, Rychtar cooperated with several other businesses, including Sargas and Sedlak. Plans were made for Rychtar's products to be distributed domestically through a private wholesale-retail network.

During 1990, approximately 10 to 15 percent of Rychtar's production was targeted for export to Yugoslavia, Germany, England, France, and Canada. Rychtar's exports were expected to rise significantly as high quality and low prices made Rychtar's tools competitive around the world.

Rychtar was represented in Prague by the export agency MLPH, which managed Rychtar's foreign trade affairs as well as demands for the company's products. Moreover, Rychtar used the services of the foreign trade organizations Merkuria, IMEX, and Keramika in addition to a number of other export-import firms such as Kamo, Ocean, Schuter, Stackfine, and Wesstling. The firm Czechoslovak–UK Trade Partners agreed to serve as a sales agent for Rychtar in Great Britain, Australia, and New Zealand.

Financial Data

Recent data were difficult to interpret because Czech accounting practices were designed to track inputs and employment. The values of the assets on the national balance sheets and input-output statements were listed at the original purchase price and reflected the subsidies for different inputs at the time of purchase. Also, land had no value on the previous balance sheets.

THE CURRENT DILEMMA

In midsummer 1991, McCarthy and Rocca had submitted a report to Mr. Novak in order to help him attract a foreign investor for Rychtar. When they walked into Mr. Novak's office at the university that August afternoon, he stood up to greet them.

"I'm glad that the two of you could come so quickly." Mr. Novak held up a bound copy of the report that McCarthy and Rocca had prepared. "I passed this around to a couple of people who had expressed interest in Rychtar. This morning I met with an American businessman. He has proposed a deal. The American is a Czech expatriate who emigrated to the U.S. after the 'Prague Spring.' He founded a company in Montana that also makes hand tools. Five years ago, he entered a joint venture with a Taiwanese company to produce sockets for him, and his company is doing so well that they need another partner.

"There are two problems though. First, he needs an answer in the next two days because he is returning to the States. And second, he only offered to pay $1 million for 100 percent of the company. I know that Rychtar needs this capital and that the deadline for their final privatization plan is approaching quickly, but it seems like a low offer to me. You two know our situation. What do you think we should do?"

NOTE

1. Each of the plans had to include the following information:
   - The enterprise's name and the property for privatization;
   - How the state acquired the property to be privatized;
   - Identification of the property unusable for business purposes (i.e., debts, unusable fixed assets, and stocks);
   - Valuation of the property to be privatized;
   - Manner of transferring the property to be privatized, including settlements of claims of entitled persons;
   - If a joint-stock company had been established, the distribution of stock shares and their value or type as well as information on whether or not and how investment coupons would be used;
   - If local property had been sold, the location, method of sales, pricing, and the conditions and terms of payment;
   - In some cases, the proportion of the proceeds from privatization to be handed over to the National Property Funds of the republics;
   - The manner of transfer of intellectual property rights, which must be discussed in advance with the Federal Bureau of Inventions;
   - The implementation schedule for privatization; and
   - The business plan: recommendations concerning the objectives of business activities, information on potential buyers or investors, information on the existing and anticipated market position of the enterprise, and information on the number and qualification structure of the enterprise's work force.

11

Privatization in Poland

Marek Mazur, Tomasz Dolegowski, Jerzy Suchnicki,
and Igor Mitroczuk

The processes of ownership transformation and economic reform initiated in Poland in 1989 were revolutionary, but the lack of precedent for changes of this scope and magnitude anywhere else in the world gave Poland no examples to follow in implementing its reforms. Therefore, the policies adopted during the early period of transformation from 1989 to 1992 were experiments that responded to complex and quickly evolving economic, social, and political influences.

Before World War II, Poland was a market economy. Its living standard and gross national product (GNP) were higher than those of Spain, Portugal, and the Balkan states but a little lower than those of Austria and Italy. Although the economy was dominated by the agricultural sector, industry and services were relatively well developed, especially in the western part of the country. Most industries were privately owned. The public sector also played an important role, however, because of the need for antirecessionary and national security policies in the late 1930s.

World War II had a devastating impact on both the economy and the structure of ownership in Poland. The power of the social and economic elites, who owned many of the industrial and commercial enterprises, was destroyed by the Germans during the war and by Soviet invaders and Communist authorities afterward. Furthermore, the war resulted in the loss of Poland's eastern territories and assets to the Soviet Union; but it also allowed the acquisition of western regions from Germany. The resulting effects of these changes encouraged the movement of the people into the western regions of the country.

The role of private industry was diminished by land reform and nationalization when the Communists took power. From 1948 to 1955, the Communists waged campaigns against private businesses, although they were less extreme than those in most Eastern European countries. Following reforms in 1956, policies toward private ownership became more liberal, especially in agriculture, handicrafts, and some services; however, the economy was still dominated by the public sector. Government policy toward small businesses lacked consistency, for it oscillated between tolerance and restrictions. The large but inefficient heavy industries that had been encouraged by the government emphasized the manufacturing of production inputs rather than consumption goods. Policies on economic matters were driven primarily by political and national security criteria, and economic growth depended primarily on decisions made in the Soviet Union. The Communist-era economy was characterized by the underdevelopment of services, market imbalances, high inflation, and frequent shortages of goods. Economic reforms, which were usually initiated in the aftermath of social unrest, were inconsistent and ineffective because of the distorted decisions of Communist officials, inertia in the system, and pressures from the Soviet Union.

Market-oriented reforms introduced by the last Communist government in 1988 and 1989 came too late. By then, the economy was already facing collapse. In 1988, 48 percent of the GNP was created by the manufacturing sector; about 13 percent, by the construction industry; nearly 12 percent, by agriculture; and the rest, by services. The public sector accounted for 83 percent of the GNP, and it employed 71 percent of the labor force. Although 75 percent of the land was privately held and 79 percent of the agricultural labor force worked in the private sector, the majority of farms were small and inefficient. Despite various probusiness initiatives in the mid-1980s, the government was unable to restore market balance. Radical economic reforms were possible only after the Solidarity labor union's victory in the June 1989 elections and the creation of a new government.

Thus, the Polish economy entered the transformation process in 1990 burdened by the legacy of Communist mismanagement. This made implementation of the stabilization and restructuring program proposed by Prime Minister Leszek Balcerowicz very difficult despite Poland's highly educated labor force and some relatively modern factories.

THE DEBATE ON PRIVATIZATION PROGRAMS

Although the Communist regime emphasized state ownership of economic activities, the private sector was tolerated more than in other Communist countries because of the influence of farmers, the Catholic church, and intellectuals and because of the inefficiency of state-owned factories and services. However, technological and organizational development of private enterprises and farms was not encouraged for economic and political reasons. Political opposition organizations, especially Solidarity, supported the private sector. But even among Solidarity and other opposition leaders, the idea of state ownership of industry remained quite popular; and the possibility of privatization was not considered seriously until the late 1980s. Furthermore, even those who supported the concept of returning to a capitalist market economy did not usually believe that the transformation from socialism to capitalism could happen quickly. They focused, therefore, on achieving greater efficiency in the public sector through the reform and democratization of state-owned enterprises (SOEs).

During the 1980s, Solidarity leaders and economic experts generally supported the concept of employee self-government, which, they believed, would result in less bureaucracy, improved productivity, and better labor-management relations in state enterprises. This orientation was particularly common during the early 1980s when employee self-government represented one of the few forms of independence that was tolerated by the Communist regime. Many people believed that this model would be a more effective form of management than that found in traditional state-owned socialist companies.

The increasing concern with ownership transformation in the late 1980s, however, can be attributed to a number of factors: (1) difficulties in implementing the employee self-government program due to the growing hostility of the Communist party as well as the apparent weaknesses of this solution (paralysis of decision making within companies caused by conflicts between the management self-governments and trade unions); (2) gradual liberalization of the system during the late 1980s and the growing acceptance of the private sector (especially after the proclamation of the Law on Economic Activity in 1988); (3) *perestroika* in the Soviet Union and its impact on other Communist regimes; (4) the experience with privatization in other countries and its influence on the intellectual and economic elites in Poland; (5) the inefficiency of the Communist economic and political model despite gradual reforms and liberalization (it became apparent that a combination of capitalism and communism was not a feasible solution); and (6) legal and illegal work abroad, private foreign trade, and "trade tourism" as sources of a new mentality and capital accumulation.

Supporters of radical privatization included scientists, businessmen, and political leaders from the ideological Right and Center. Even during the Communist era, one could observe "economic associations" that supported the development of small businesses. However, even at that time, opinions about privatization were very diverse. Some opposition economists still believed in employee self-government in SOEs, and supporters of private ownership had different opinions about the potential success of privatization. Some advocates of reform favored quick and radical changes, but the majority suggested a more cautious and gradual approach. The debate among opposition leaders was accelerated by the fact that Mieczyslaw Rakowski, the last Communist prime minister, initiated a process of transformation that would turn the Communist elites into capitalists through the enfranchisement of *nomenklatura*, or *nomenklatura* privatization.

The first non-Communist government headed by Tadeusz Mazowiecki decided to focus its economic reforms on promoting privatization and economic stabilization and on reducing inflation. A special office was created to prepare, coordinate, and monitor the process of ownership transformation. However, during the first stage of the reforms, the emphasis was placed on stabilization of the market and currency. It appears that privatization was included primarily because of the widespread perception that Poland was in a permanent economic crisis. The desire for political change and the need to reduce the influence of the Communist elite were among the other forces pushing for privatization. Although there were strong ideological and political motives for pursuing privatization, post-Communist government officials saw it as a means of generating revenue for the State Treasury, eliminating subsidies to inefficient state enterprises, and creating private enterprises that would be more effective than SOEs in generating jobs and tax revenues.

At first, employee self-government was considered the best tool to accomplish these goals; however, privatization quickly replaced it. The fact that the program of ownership transformation was introduced during a period of economic difficulty may have accelerated the push for privatization. It became obvious that the old system offered no effective solutions to Poland's economic problems. No one doubted that the Polish economy required deep structural transformations, but there was a recurring question about which should come first, privatization or restructuring. Many experts asserted that ownership transformations should be preceded by fundamental changes in the structure of the companies as well as of the entire economy. Enterprises had to be well prepared to undergo successful privatization. However, others believed that a major economic revival or an acceleration of the restructuring processes was not possible prior to privatization owing to the lack of several key elements: a financial infrastructure; a well-developed sector of small enterprises; capital; and experience. Eventually a general consensus emerged that the privatization and restructuring processes were intertwined.

The applicability of foreign privatization experience—especially that of the United Kingdom—to Poland's situation was widely discussed during the early transformation period. However, critics pointed to the fact that the United Kingdom, in contrast to Poland, had a long history of experience with a market economy. The German model in which banking institutions played a dominant role had also been considered; and in the establishment of the capital market, French experience was used—the Warsaw Stock Exchange (WSE) was established along the lines of the Lyon Stock Market. In contrast, approaches to privatization based on the experiences of the developing countries received somewhat less attention. Examples from the Asian and Latin American countries as well as experiences in Chile and Argentina were especially interesting to the proponents of the employee stock ownership program (ESOP). However, most attention was devoted to the European experience, including that of Spain and the Scandinavian countries; and there was little exchange of ideas among the post-Communist countries and nations on a similar development level.

Public debate over privatization during the late 1980s and early 1990s focused on several major approaches: (1) capital privatization, that is, selling SOEs to private (including foreign) investors; (2) ESOPs; (3) a Citizens Stock Ownership Program (mass privatization), that is, the distribution to all citizens of privatization vouchers that would be convertible to shares of privatized enterprises; (4) leasing, management contracts, and liquidation; and (5) reprivatization.

These alternatives were proposed in many versions and combinations. To understand why all of these alternatives were considered, it is necessary to understand the characteristics of the Polish economy during the early transition period. The economy was suffering from limited available domestic capital, a situation that required companies to attract foreign investment as well as organizational, technical, managerial, and marketing know-how. The tradition of self-government was still strong among employees, and their expectations concerning participation in ownership and decision making were high. At the same time, the government saw the need to create a strong middle class as a base for democratic reforms; but there was also widespread fear in the country of possible threats to Poland's economic and political sovereignty from the rapid infusion of foreign capital. Moreover, public opinion was influenced by negative impressions of the role played by the Communist elites, or *nomenklatura*, during the early stages of the privatization process.

POLITICAL AND SOCIAL ORGANIZATIONS' POSITIONS ON PRIVATIZATION

The government generally supported the idea of privatization even though its policies were sometimes inconsistent. Despite some differences, all Solidarity-dominated governments have been interested in privatization of the economy. The idea of privatization was also supported by President Lech Walesa, who also stressed the need for reprivatization and for privatization credits.

Although the majority of political parties supported privatization during the early transformation period, their plans varied considerably. Leftist groups and parties appeared to be somewhat reluctant to support the process; nevertheless, many of them took advantage of the *nomenklatura* privatization. Support for privatization was voiced by the Democratic Union (especially the right-oriented wing), the Forum of the Democratic Right, the Liberal Democratic Congress, the Christian Democratic party, and the majority of the Center Alliance (Porozumienie Centrum). Radical privatization was supported by a right-wing–oriented Union for Real Politics. The activists of the Liberal Democratic Congress promoted mass privatization as well as capital privatization. The Democratic Union favored capital privatization, while the Center Alliance and the Christian Democratic party supported all forms but emphasized the advantages of the ESOP plan.

The position of the right-oriented parties was more complicated. The Union for Real Politics demanded radical reprivatization. Nationalistic, conservative, and peasant parties wanted privileges for domestic investors. The Christian

National Assembly supported "family-oriented" programs of privatization. Political groups with the greatest skepticism of privatization included Party X, the Confederation of Independent Poland, some post-Communists, and right-oriented nationalists. They did not argue against the principle of privatization but rather against particular approaches to privatization. However, the role of the political parties in Poland and their social base was relatively weak.

The more powerful trade unions were divided on the issue of privatization. The opinion of post-Communist labor union members was relatively negative. Solidarity supported privatization; but members and leaders held different opinions about the best model, and the leaders usually supported ESOPs. By 1992, Solidarity leaders became increasingly critical of the privatization process due to the harmful effects associated with the scandals of *nomenklatura* privatization and the undervaluation of companies.

The Roman Catholic church, an influential institution in Poland, did not officially express an opinion about the economic changes, even though it generally appeared to support the reforms. The Church did not favor the proposals of the radical liberals, however, but rather a more moderate vision of the market economy with state intervention and ethical regulation (according to modern Catholic social teaching). It also supported cooperation of capital and labor, small business, and employee participation in ownership and decision making. From the moral and ethical point of view, the Church condemned the negative results of privatization that led to scandals, privileged access, and undervaluation of companies.

The presence of foreign capital was also a controversial issue. The majority of political and social leaders accepted the need for and presence of foreign investments despite criticisms from the nationalistic Right and the radical Left. Supporters of foreign capital argued that, without foreign aid and investment, modernization of the Polish economy was virtually impossible. Opponents were concerned, however, about the loss of sovereignty, the undervaluation of companies, the negative role of foreign consultants, and the purchase of companies by unreliable partners.

Expectations from the Privatization Process

The privatization process generated a variety of expectations. People in Poland expected a liquidation of the Communist legacy, development of entrepreneurship, elimination of market shortages, and improvements in the efficiency of state enterprises. Many intellectuals and democratic politicians hoped that privatization would contribute to the formation of a strong middle class that would provide a foundation for stability in an industrial society. They also believed that privatization should provide a link between the state and its citizens, and that it should accelerate the transition to a free-market way of thinking.

Management's expectations from privatization included freeing enterprises from excessive government control and reducing the influence of the employee self-management councils and the trade unions. Managers also hoped to have an opportunity to participate in the privatization processes. Another important issue for them was a chance to eliminate the excessive wages tax (the so-called *popiwek*). Most employees hoped for substantial increases in wages stemming from improvements in management and the elimination of the excessive wages tax. They also looked forward to participating in the privatization process through the ESOP. Many employees (especially trade union and self-government activists) hoped that the stock ownership program would allow them to regain some of the power they would lose as a result of the liquidation of self-government councils. On the other hand, employees were afraid of the possibility of layoffs and the consequences of the *nomenklatura* enfranchisement.

Consumers expected the elimination of shortages, better selection of goods, and better services. On the other hand, there were concerns about possible price increases and the elimination of useful but inefficient shops and services. And many people also feared the outcomes of privatization—for example, the unequal distribution of wealth, abuses and corruption, and layoffs.

Most people in Poland expected privatization to take a long time. .However, there were hopes for the quick privatization of small manufacturing and service establishments within the framework of the Small Privatization Program. For the large enterprises, the government decided to adopt cautious measures by allowing only strong enterprises to undergo capital privatization. Nevertheless, there was much support for accelerating ownership transformation. Over time, the belief in the necessity of taking quick and decisive measures became stronger; but there was a common agreement that the process of reform would not be completed for some time to come.

POLAND'S PRIVATIZATION PROGRAM

The first non-Communist government, led by Tadeusz Mazowiecki, initiated the privatization process and created the Ministry of Ownership Changes to monitor progress. Government initiated the Small Privatization Program and restructured the first group of large enterprises. Capital privatization was most frequently used, but the pace of transformation was relatively slow. Critics pointed to the excessive emphasis the government gave to fiscal factors and to blind acceptance of Western economic and bureaucratic models. The succeeding government, led by Jan Krzysztof Bielecki, continued the previous policy with only slight changes. Minister Janusz Lewandowski decided to accelerate the process and use a variety of privatization methods; he created the concept of mass privatization. However, opponents criticized the government's hesitation in regard to reprivatization as well as its lack of sectoral balance. The new government, headed by Jan Olszewski, put more emphasis on reprivatization. Also, it favored privatization by liquidation, sectoral and regional programs, employee participation, a more open policy toward foreign investments, and measures to reduce corruption. In addition, the fiscal aspect of privatization was de-emphasized. The government's division on the privatization issue resulted in a decision-making process that was difficult and ineffective.

Institutions Involved in Privatization

The Ministry of Ownership Changes was responsible for coordination of the privatization process in Poland. In addition to departments responsible for particular industry branches, the ministry included a Capital Market Development Department (responsible for the creation of a Polish capital market) and a Securities Commission Office that was responsible for coordinating the operations of the capital market and for maintaining control of investor-oriented privatization information (e.g., seminars and courses for individuals involved in the Polish capital market). In addition to the Ministry of Ownership Changes, other organizations were involved in the privatization process: (1) the International Capital Market Development and Ownership Changes Foundation of the Republic of Poland; (2) the Center of Privatization, whose activities involved organizing courses and seminars on the functioning of the capital market, advising the Ministry of Ownership Changes, and recommending changes in the process of privatization; and (3) foundations promoting ownership changes in Poland. By the end of 1992, there were more than 20 such foundations that both provided financial support for employees participating in the privatization process and organized courses and seminars. In addition, an Interministerial Team for the Acceleration of the Privatization Process was established on March 28, 1991, to resolve legal and financial problems impeding privatization. Also participating in the process were an antimonopoly office and a board of directors in the State-Owned Enterprises Commission that were responsible for the selection of candidates for the boards of the enterprises in which the State Treasury was one of the shareholders. The Ministers' Council was responsible for issuing licenses for the privatization of enterprises that were of particular importance for the economy, and a Foreign Investment Agency was created to control the establishment of businesses by foreign firms.

Among the most important institutions and organizations responsible for the creation, development, and control of the Polish capital market were the WSE; the Securities Commission, which was to regulate the functioning of the stock exchange and protect investors; and the National Depository of Securities. The Economic Advisers Association would transfer information; organize seminars, courses, and conferences; develop and regulate consulting firms; and make recommendations on economic issues.

In November 1990 the Securities Commission Office, established with the Ministry of Ownership Changes, was accepted as a member of the International Organization of the Securities Commissions. The tasks of the Securities Commission included approving securities for trading and then issuing appropriate licenses and permits for broker firms and dealers, regulating the capital market, developing the Polish capital market, and supplying investor information.

The WSE was created in June 1991, and a year later 14 companies were traded on the exchange. In May 1992 the total value of the shares traded was nearly 2 billion zlotys—with shares of only 3 companies, Wedel, Exbud, and Zywiec, constituting three-quarters of the market. Thus, a year after its creation, the impact of the WSE was still relatively insignificant and not expected to become stronger until the volume and variety of traded instruments increased.

Shares of certain companies were in high demand, indicating an increasing maturity of Polish investors. The number of weekly trading sessions increased from one to two. From its inception until March 1992, total trading volume was 563 billion zlotys. At the end of 1991, the WSE was accepted as a member of the International Stock Exchange Federation, which indicated that Poland was on its way to becoming a country with a well-developed capital market. Although the exchange was created under the government's auspices, the government's role is expected to diminish.

The National Securities Deposit is a computer data bank containing registration of all market securities. Each transaction is recorded so that physical transfer of shares between the seller and the buyer is not necessary.

Other institutions participating in privatization included the Polish Bank of Development and the Industry Development Agency. The bank was established to offer financial assistance to the privatization process. It was responsible for providing medium- and long-term credit through a system of banks across the country. The Industry Development Agency was responsible for the technical assistance to enterprises undergoing restructuring and privatization.

Methods of Privatization Adopted by the Government

The legal basis for the process of privatization in Poland was created in July 1991 by the enactment of the Privatization of State-Owned Enterprises Law and a number of executive regulations. The privatization process adopted in Poland was a combination of the traditional privatization methods and those created specifically for Polish conditions (e.g., the free distribution of shares to the country's citizens). Enterprises serving the public as well as those suitable for reprivatization were to be dealt with under separate laws. Since the owner was not the State Treasury, the local government was responsible for the process. The Ministry of Ownership Changes could participate with the local government's permission.

The first step in privatizing large SOEs was to commercialize them and transform them into State Treasury-owned companies. The specific approach to privatizing them would depend, to a large extent, on their size. Furthermore, specific industry branches were occasionally granted preferential treatment. For example, among the large enterprises, those active in trade and manufacturing were favored, as were small enterprises that were involved in trade, the construction industry, agriculture support industries, manufacturing, and tourist services. Prior to a sale of an enterprise, the Ministry of Ownership Changes conducted a financial analysis of the company. The analysis was undertaken to assess the company's value; to determine its needs for organizational, economic, or technical restructuring; and to assess the company's ownership status. The areas covered by the economic and financial analyses included the financial standing of the company as well as its marketing and organizational structure and its strategy. The analyses had to be conducted with at least two methods of assets valuation: discounted future cash flow; replacement value (cost of replacing the company's assets); book asset value; liquidation value; or profit multiplier (selecting similar companies trading on the stock exchange and comparing their average profit with a book value).

Beginning in 1990, the government embarked on several paths to privatization, including commercialization, public offering, trade sale, mass privatization, liquidation of SOEs, and reprivatization.

Commercialization. The Privatization of State-Owned Enterprises Law provided for the transformation of SOEs into joint-stock companies (JSCs), in which the State Treasury was the sole shareholder. To transform an enterprise into a Treasury-owned company, the management and the Workers' Council were required to submit a joint application. The application had to be approved by the appropriate government office and the employees' general assembly. The application for commercialization could be rejected due to the weak financial situation of the enterprise, its monopolistic position, or because doing so was considered to be in the national interest. The State Treasury was the sole shareholder in a commercialized enterprise. Following the transformation, the closing balance sheet of the SOE became the opening balance of the new company. All companies were required to form a board of directors. The employees were entitled to elect one-third of the board, and the Ministry of Ownership Changes selected the remaining two-thirds.

The government anticipated that the relatively healthy enterprises would be sold through capital privatization and that most of the small- and medium-sized enterprises would be bought by individual investors. Smaller, nontypical, or relatively weak enterprises would be privatized by liquidation. Within two years of commercialization, an enterprise would be privatized through one of three available techniques: individual privatization, mass privatization, or sectoral privatization. Individual privatization would take place through a public offering or a trade sale to domestic or foreign buyers.

Public Offering. Before an SOE could be sold to the public, it first had to be evaluated by a consulting firm whose report—conforming to requirements set by the Securities Commission—would become the basis for the investment prospectus. The concept of a strategic investor was particularly important in this approach to privatization; the purpose was to raise capital in order to improve the enterprise's financial situation. Shares of any enterprise privatized by this method would contribute to the development of the securities market in Poland. In 1990 the first five enterprises privatized were by this approach, as were another nine firms during 1991 and 1992.

Trade Sale. Large enterprises were sold to either individuals or groups of investors through domestic and international bidding processes. About 72 percent of the enterprises commercialized in 1991 were small- and medium-sized companies. The privatization process for these enterprises was similar to that for large enterprises. However, in privatizing smaller firms, there was more emphasis on liquidation, and the procedures were more flexible. The privatization process was facilitated by a special credit program that was established to promote the purchase of shares, payment in installments, and acceptance of the company's bonds as payment. To further facilitate the process, 14 regional offices of the Ministry of Ownership Changes were established. Shops and service outlets were privatized through this method. Although the process of transforming this sector was somewhat uncontrolled, it was very successful because of its simplicity and the small capital requirements.

Mass Privatization. Because of the lack of sufficient domestic capital to ensure that large numbers of companies would be privatized through trade sales and public offerings, the government and the Ministry of Ownership Changes decided to accelerate the process of privatization through a mass privatization program.

The mass privatization concept was finalized in June 1991. Proponents considered the economic advantages of this program to be (1) its low cost and rapid implementation compared with the capital privatization approach, (2) its ability to overcome the lack of domestic and foreign capital needed to finance privatization, and (3) its ability to find owners for commercialized enterprises and secure their access to foreign aid sources, markets, and expertise.

The National Investment Funds were to play a key role in the process. According to the mass privatization program presented by the Ministry of Ownership Changes in June 1991, the closed-end Funds were to be established in different regions of the country. They would employ people with experience in banks, private and privatized companies, and joint ventures JVs); and they would hire Western financial experts and businessmen. Such investment groups would be able to obtain loans, issue shares, and make new investments. The shares in the Funds could be purchased by both Polish and foreign buyers.

All Polish citizens above the age of 18 as of December 31, 1991, could participate in the program. Every citizen was entitled to a certificate of ownership in each of the National Investment Funds. The mass privatization program applied to 400 enterprises selected from a group of 650 in July 1991. They represented 25 percent of the total value of Poland's industrial production and 12 percent of the manufacturing labor force. The Funds would receive 60 percent of each enterprise's shares, with one Fund receiving 33 percent. The remaining 27 percent would be distributed among the other Funds. Employees were to be given 10 percent of the shares for free. The remaining 30 percent of the stock would remain with the State Treasury. Recently, the number of companies was increased to 600.

Investment Funds could sell shares of the companies to third parties. The ultimate control over the process, however, was retained by the Anti-Monopoly Office and the Ministry of Ownership Changes. The World Bank, International Financial Corporation, European Investment Bank, European Bank of Reconstruction and Development, Industry Development Agency, Polish banks, and the United Nations Development Program would assist with implementing the program.

The first version of the mass privatization program, based on the investment Funds concept, was proposed in 1988. The plan called for establishing 20 National Investment Funds, each managing shares of 20 enterprises. Most of the companies were manufacturing, construction, and transportation enterprises representing only 8 percent of Poland's total industrial output, 4 percent of its industrial employment, and 2.4 percent of all SOEs. By the end of 1991, 64 of those enterprises were turned into JSCs in which the State Treasury retained all the shares. After their creation, the Funds were responsible for the effectiveness and profitability of the companies in their portfolio. After one year, shares of the companies comprising the Funds could be traded among all the others. After a three-year period when the first results were evaluated, shares could be traded on the WSE. At that time, the ownership certificates would be given to Polish citizens. However, individuals would have to pay at least some part of the share face value. The Ministry of Ownership Changes indicated that the shares, costing between 5 and 20 percent of an average monthly salary, would not be very expensive. This version of the plan did not specify the upper limit on the number of shares that a single investor could purchase.

Plans for the establishment of the National Investment Funds were prepared by mid-1992, and the valuation of the enterprises was taking place. When all the information was gathered, it would be passed on to the management groups interested in participating in the program. In mid-1992 the group consisted of 40 leading Polish and foreign investment banks, foundations, and consulting firms, all of which were required to prepare their suggestions concerning the program. The Ministry of Ownership Changes selected the managers of the Funds based on their fees and services.

In order to decrease costs, in 1991 and 1992 the mass privatization program was combined with other privatization methods and included provisions for partial payment for shares and an increase in the number of enterprises included in the program to the originally proposed 600. The following timetable was set for mass privatization: During 1992 the first phase bidding was to be completed, National Investment Funds were to be established, and trading among different Funds was to start. During the first quarter of 1993, the Funds would announce their financial results, after which Polish citizens would receive certificates of ownership and trading in shares would begin on the WSE by the end of the year. The entire mass privatization program was expected to take ten years to complete. After two or three years it would be broadened to include at least 50 percent of all SOEs. However, by late 1992 the implementation of the program was proceeding considerably slower than expected. Since the program is still controversial, the act will probably be passed later than expected, that is, in the first half of 1993.

Liquidation of SOEs. The Law on Privatization of State-Owned Enterprises provided guidelines for the liquidation of SOEs. Liquidation could take place only after approval from the founding organization or the Workers' Council by means of one of three methods: a sale of all or part of the enterprise's assets to another private company, a transfer of assets, or the leasing of assets. The law did not set limitations with regard to the purchasing company, but the SOE's founding organization had to set the minimum price for the transaction. Leasing was intended for the liquidation of smaller enterprises and was widely used in employee takeovers of SOEs. Employees would have to pay at least 20 percent of the enterprise's value. The rate for leasing was calculated on the basis of the asset value and 75 percent of the current refinancing rate of the National Bank of Poland. Employees had an option to buy at the expiration of the lease.

Reprivatization. Reprivatization allowed the return of assets confiscated by the government from 1944 to 1962. Compensation could be made in capital bonds, return of assets, or cash compensation. The government was especially concerned that the reprivatization process be socially acceptable. Thus, reprivatization was limited to those activities that did not obstruct other privatization approaches, limit the number of beneficiaries of privatization, become a burden for a large part of society, or violate existing laws and social norms.

The Olszewski government heavily favored reprivatization. Previous owners would be granted preferential treatment in purchasing shares of privatized enterprises. Although the law applied only to previous owners whose confiscated assets were located within Poland's current borders, the claims reached 100 billion zlotys (U.S. $7 million) by mid-1992. During the first quarter of 1992, a new draft of the Reprivatization Law was prepared; and plans for the establishment of the National Reprivatization Fund were formulated. The reprivatization process would be substantially completed by the end of 1993. Since claims were expected to exceed 100 billion zlotys, some nonmonetary assets were to be transferred to the National Reprivatization Fund for the settlements.

Sectoral Privatization and Macroeconomic Policy

Privatization is one of the most important elements in the transformation to a market economy. Privatization policy should be one of the strategic issues in the government's economic reforms. However, by late 1992 the government of Poland still lacked an all-encompassing economic policy or a unified privatization strategy. A multiministry commission with representatives from the Central Office of Planning, Ministry of Trade and Industry, and Ministry of Ownership Changes was created to form such a plan. More than 30 programs developed within the framework of the sectoral privatization were the focus of the commission's work.

Experts pointed out that in order to implement privatization effectively, an institutional structure for business development had to be created, especially by developing the stock exchange, investment banking, and consulting firms. Proponents of a national policy argued that a "privatization map" was needed to establish a close relationship between privatization policy and government economic policy as well as to identify sectors that should not be privatized and would remain under government control (e.g., military industry).

The sectoral privatization program emerged because the Ministry of Ownership Changes lacked a framework within which to implement privatization plans. Thus, the sectoral privatization plan would accelerate the transformation process: It was seen as a "tool" of applied industrial policy that would create a "sector map," that is, a comprehensive strategy for privatization within a particular sector. Advocates of the sectoral privatization plan argued that it was needed to help policymakers and the public understand the relationships between privatization in different sectors and to help avoid the creation of monopolies. Only after collecting the appropriate information concerning all sectors of the economy was it possible to plan and implement industrial policy efficiently. In this context the sectoral privatization program could create synergistic effects that could help establish such a policy for the entire economy.

Sectoral privatization consisted of several steps. First, the Ministry of Ownership Changes encouraged enterprises in a particular sector to prepare for privatization. Next, the privatization plan was developed in coordination with other government agencies and a lead adviser. The adviser conducted an analysis of the sector and developed a sector strategy. During the same period, the adviser analyzed the individual companies and prepared recommendations with respect to privatization and restructuring of each company. These analyses would determine if there should be restructuring prior to privatization, what the role of foreign investors was, whether or not proceeds should go to the State Treasury, and if it was necessary to attract investment and technology for long-term development. Finally, the sectoral plan would make recommendations concerning the appropriate method of privatization, including liquidation, public offering, trade sale, mass privatization, preprivatization restructuring of individual companies or the entire sector, or a combination of various approaches. During the restructuring process, the Ministry of Ownership Changes and its advisers were expected to cooperate closely with other governmental organizations and ministries. In the future, the process of restructuring would be facilitated by concentrating all the responsibilities within one ministry.

Progress on Policy Implementation

The first public sale of shares took place in November 1990. The five companies offered for sale were the construction company Exbud, the glass factory Krosno, the clothing manufacturer Prochnik, the Silesian Cable Factory Kable, and Tonsil. Of a total of 6.5 million shares, 4.33 million were sold in the public offering; and the remaining shares were sold to employees (20 percent) and active investors. During the first two days, 11 percent of the offered shares were sold to more than 130,000 investors. The offering was oversubscribed: Exbud by 20 percent, Kable by 7 percent, and the three other companies by 2 to 7 percent. Although the offering was conducted at 200 outlets across the country, it was impossible to buy shares in some regions.

Inowroclaw Meat Processing Factory was privatized in 1990. All shares were bought by the employees of the enterprise for 5.4 billion zlotys (U.S. $0.5 million), which was equal to 20 percent of the asset value less employee discount. By January 1991, 61 SOEs were transformed into JSCs. Most of them were active in the machine and construction industries. By the end of that year, 1,194 enterprises, representing 14.5 percent of all SOEs, were transformed into JSCs.

In addition to the enterprises privatized in 1990 and early 1991, other firms that were sold in the public offering during 1991 included the furniture manufacturer Swarzedz, the textiles company Wolczanka, the Irena Steel Works, Zywiec and Okocim breweries, and the food producer Wedel. Furthermore, 18 SOEs were sold to selected Polish and foreign investors. As a result, nine more companies entered the WSE.

Some of the large companies were transformed through capital privatization. In order to qualify for this method, the SOE had to have a well-trained and qualified managerial staff, employee support, and a clear development strategy. Moreover, it had to be in an industry that had a low concentration of firms or strong competition from abroad—indicating that the enterprise was ready to compete in the free-market environment. Such companies also had to have efficiency levels above the industry average, some investment under way, no serious environmental problems, a significant proportion of output exported to developed countries, and little vertical integration of production. Other criteria included capital-intensive production (indicating the company's need for capital market financing), the existence of potential investors, clear ownership status of the enterprise, and a well-known and highly regarded product.

Some of the enterprises ineligible for capital privatization included natural monopolies and public utilities, environment-polluting enterprises, and companies with high levels of exports to the former Communist countries. Large enterprises not included in any of the above categories could privatize through public offer or a bid sale. Bankrupt large enterprises could be privatized through liquidation. Capital privatization of large enterprises helped to develop Poland's capital market and represented the greatest portion of the Treasury's income from privatization. The Ministry of Ownership Changes prepared and updated the list of enterprises offered to domestic and foreign investors. Eight to ten privatizations via public offer and 30 to 40 trade sales were planned for 1992. One of the necessary conditions for the success of the plan was the availability of financing for the privatization process.

For medium-sized enterprises—defined as organizations employing over 300 people and having sales either above 30 billion zlotys (U.S. $3.15 million) in 1989 or above 80 billion zlotys during the first half of 1990—the prerequisites for privatization were similar to those of large enterprises. In some cases an enterprise could also be sold to its employees. This approach has been especially successful in privatizing enterprises in transportation and construction industries.

Privatization of small enterprises was relatively easy. A majority stake in such enterprises was to be sold through a bid sale. Privatization through liquidation was the most commonly used method with regard to small- and medium-sized enterprises. In 1991, over 900 small enterprises were privatized. The main advantage of that technique was its low cost. In 1992, over 1,200 companies were expected to undergo privatization, perhaps through local commercial agencies that would be responsible for the sale of the privatized enterprises' assets.

By the end of 1991, 61 enterprises were transformed into JSCs; 5 large enterprises were privatized in a public offer; and 72 enterprises were privatized through liquidation. Additional enterprises were being prepared for public offer. By the end of 1991, ownership changes were under way in 1,258 enterprises, which represented about 15 percent of all SOEs.

Financial Aspects of Privatization

Proceeds from privatization of SOEs in 1991 amounted to 3,500 billion zlotys (U.S. $370 million), which represented only a small portion of the planned 15,000 billion zlotys (U.S. $1.6 billion). Additionally, 5,600 billion zlotys (U.S. $600 million) in assets were leased; and companies with a total value of 7,500 billion zlotys (U.S. $800 million) were liquidated. The new plan presented to

Parliament by the Ministry of Ownership Changes projected proceeds of 10,000 billion zlotys (U.S. $700 million) during 1992. Proceeds of U.S. $200 million were expected from the sale of enterprises in the cement and paper industries. Over U.S. $100 million dollars were expected from the sale of meat-processing enterprises; and U.S. $50 million each, from the sale of construction firms and breweries. It should be noted that the revenues were expected to come from sectoral privatization that was halted by the Ministry of Ownership Changes. It appeared that they would have been considerably higher if the cuts in the ministry's budget for the first quarter of 1992 had not been so severe. Privatization through liquidation was the most common privatization approach. Out of the total of 562 enterprises transformed into JSCs by mid-1992, 183 were active in industry, 159 in agriculture, 89 in construction, and 53 in trade.

The government's privatization program for 1991 called for the continuation of the capital technique with the participation of foreign investors. It also envisioned the conversion of Polish external debt into shares of privatized enterprises and a more active search for foreign capital. By July 1991, 100 percent of net profit and invested capital could be repatriated. There were also compensation guarantees for nationalization. Preferential income tax rates and tax holidays were available for investments exceeding 2 million European currency units. Permission for establishing joint ventures was no longer needed, except for such sectors as military, legal advice, or airport and seaport management. Although by July 1991 as many as 3,400 JVs had been created, average foreign investment was only about U.S. $140,000. From 1989 to 1991, the largest capital contributions came from Germany (U.S. $153 million) and were followed by the United States (U.S. $62.5 million). Total investment was approximately U.S. $700 million at the end of 1991.

As a result of the experience during 1990 and 1991, the government and the Ministry of Ownership Changes set several new goals for 1992. First, it sought to complete the legal framework for privatization. Second, it planned to develop a new and clearer system for selecting enterprises for privatization. Third, it began looking for ways of accelerating the process of commercialization. Plans for 1992 also envisioned the creation of new "privatization agencies" that would prepare privatization options for the Ministry of Ownership Changes. They would be JSCs controlled by the government with a minority stake by international financial institutions. At least 50 percent of the proceeds from the sale of enterprises would be channeled to the State Treasury. Agencies would charge a fixed fee for selling the enterprises. They would prepare privatization plans and carry them out under the supervision of the Ministry of Ownership Changes.

Participation of foreign capital in the privatization process was a delicate issue: important because of the lack of domestic capital and sensitive because of society's hostile perceptions of foreign participation. Permission was required to sell shares to foreign investors when their value exceeded 10 percent of the total share capital of the company and when the shares were preferential.

The Economic Council criticized the lack of a consistent policy concerning foreign investment. Some of the agreements with foreign investors had to be renegotiated. The government stressed that none of the agreements with foreign investors would be broken. However, agreements to sell Polkolor, Wedel, and Alima were labeled by the government as "not supporting Polish interests"—the meaning of which had not been defined. By late 1992, controversy still surrounded the issue of foreign consultants because some of their advice resulted in serious losses.

EVALUATION OF THE PRIVATIZATION PROCESS

Privatization is one of the basic components of economic and industrial transformation. Capital privatization, which is the most common method of transforming large organizations, has so far involved 36 companies. Seven of these enterprises underwent privatization during the first half of 1992. Commercialization of enterprises, that is, transformation into an entity owned solely by the State Treasury, took place in 348 enterprises.

Privatization through liquidation resulted in the largest number of transformed enterprises—approximately 1,288 SOEs underwent the process during the first half of 1992. Of this number, 54 percent were service-rendering companies; 22 percent were industrial enterprises; and the rest consisted of construction (nearly 13 percent), farming (8 percent), and other companies. The total value of foreign investment in recent years was $28 million in 1989; $105.2 million in 1990; $260.9 million in 1991; and $651.8 million during the first half of 1992. The companies with foreign participation were 429 in 1989; 1,645 in 1990; 4,796 in 1991; and 7,648 during the first half of 1992.

Over 20 percent of SOEs are undergoing privatization; and among these, liquidation is considerably more advanced than capital privatization. Furthermore, more than 80 percent of farming land and a majority of small service businesses have always been under private ownership. Thus, privatization is proceeding better than is generally believed. Also, the rapid process of the privatization process is reflected in the high share of the private sector in Poland's total output. Currently, almost one-quarter of industrial output (22.7 percent according to the Central Planning Office estimates), three-quarters of construction, and almost all trade can be attributed to the private sector. With the underground economy accounting for about 5 to 20 percent, the situation is clearly less dramatic than it is reported. Despite a positive trend illustrated by the above data, further analysis is needed to provide a full assessment of the privatization process.

Criteria for Assessment of Privatization

To provide an assessment of the privatization program, appropriate criteria must first be selected. For example, performance of a specific enterprise may be an overall measure in which the effectiveness is shown as the difference between the enterprise's profits prior to and after privatization. In addition to measurable financial spending, analysis of costs should also include the temporary decline in productivity caused (according to the theory of management and organization) by the transformation of both the entire economy and individual enterprises.

This measure has some drawbacks, however. First, it cannot be used to measure short-term changes because restructuring is not immediately reflected in the profits of the enterprises. Poland's general economic situation is another factor limiting the application of that measure. Since the economy is still in an initial stage of transformation, it is too early for the anticipated improvements to materialize. Therefore, to assess privatization decisions we must resort to other measures. These include (1) production increases resulting from improved labor productivity and restructuring; (2) increased sales resulting from the introduction of modern production techniques or innovations; and (3) an improvement in the quality of goods and services that strengthens the company's competitive position. In the long run, however, such general measures as profits and market share should also be applied. In a normally functioning economy, a growth in profits following the privatization of an enterprise (and usually its restructuring) should lead to a rise in its share price. But given Polish conditions, it is still difficult to find a correlation between the financial standing of an enterprise and the price of its shares.

Other basic measures of the success of privatization are the satisfaction of employees expectations and the satisfaction of society's objectives for economic reform. Employee satisfaction influences future profits by increasing workers' motivation to be more productive. From the social point of view, increased satisfaction is a value in itself; and it indicates a greater fulfillment of customers' needs. Increase in satisfaction can be achieved through higher wages, the creation of new income sources (e.g., dividends from stock), improved working conditions, and more decision-making powers.

Another method of assessing the success of the privatization process is based on the interests of the state, that is, budgetary revenues and general economic improvements stemming from privatization. Naturally, the state is inclined to increase its revenues, especially in light of the budget deficit. Nevertheless, this peculiar "privatization fiscalism" (i.e., excessive bureaucracy, excessive value assigned to privatizing enterprises, and cuts in spending for promotional programs for privatization) slows the process. On the other hand, privatization of enterprises and improvements in their performance increase budget revenues.

Consequently, despite some shortcomings, the measure of maximization of budget revenues is included in our analysis.

The impact of ownership change on economic efficiency can only be measured if it is controlled for the influence of cyclical fluctuations and deterioration of the entire economy. For example, it is difficult to expect an increase in profitability or sales in light of the growing internal market barriers—for a lack of correlation between the exchange rate and inflation level makes it impossible to compete, in terms of prices, with other countries. Since it is difficult to assess the impact of the external environment on a particular enterprise, the only reliable method of evaluating an enterprise is to compare its performance with that of other firms in the same industry. However, this method of analysis is beyond the scope of this chapter.

Evaluation of Privatization Methods

Although the number of newly established or privatized enterprises provides some indication of the success of the privatization process, it does not say much about the qualitative aspects, such as the motivation behind privatization activities, the efficiency of the process, or obstacles to privatization. Therefore, we will take a closer look at those issues by offering our assessment of various privatization methods.

The Trade Union Research Center of the Solidarity Mazovian Region carried out research on privatized enterprises. It involved 97 firms, of which 39 were privatized through the capital method, and 58 through liquidation. Decisions on the privatization of enterprises were made by various bodies such as the Ministry of Ownership Changes (Ministry of Privatization), local administrations, the "founding body" of enterprises, and their management and employees. In 77 percent of the cases, transformations through capital privatization were initiated by the enterprises' management. Privatization initiated by employees (employee councils or trade unions) was much less frequent (about 13 percent). The Ministry of Ownership Changes initiated only 2.6 percent of privatization proceedings. Privatization through liquidation was initiated by the management in about 52 percent of the cases, by employees in 22 percent, and by the ministry in less than 2 percent.

The motivations for privatization were interesting. Among the firms that chose the capital method of privatization, 38 percent admitted that their primary aim was to evade the wage-growth tax (the so-called *popiwek*). For 28 percent of the enterprises, the key reason was improvement of management; for another 23 percent, it was better development prospects; and for 23 percent, it was the improvement of the firm's weak financial status. Higher remuneration was ranked only as fifth among the most important motives (about 13 percent). Among liquidated enterprises, 30 percent of those polled claimed that better development opportunities was the most important reason; 26 percent mentioned improvement of the enterprise's financial standing; and 22 percent hoped for better pay.

Capital Privatization. Capital privatization involved a relatively small number of companies. However, because of the size of privatized enterprises, the trading of their shares on the stock exchange, and their large contributions to the state budget, it was one of the most common forms of privatization. The above-mentioned 36 firms, sold by the end of June 1992, contributed 2.4 trillion zlotys to the state budget. Shares of 13 of these companies were traded on the stock exchange. Five of these 13 enterprises, Tonsil, Krosno, Exbud, Kable, and Prochnik, were privatized in November 1990. Because of a relatively long time since their privatization, they were the only companies that could be included in the analysis. In 1991 the 5 companies had the following financial results (in millions of zlotys): Tonsil, -33,526; Prochnik, 6,329; Krosno, 807; Exbud, 150,700; and Kable, 161.

Exbud was the only company to show substantial profits during the period. Three enterprises recorded marginal profits, and 1 (Tonsil) a large loss. Thus, privatization did not lead to immediate financial gains. However, in considering these statistics it should be remembered that a precise assessment of the impact of recession on business activity was not possible and that these companies carried out restructuring programs that will not show results for several years.

Exbud was also the only enterprise among the 5 to show an increase in share price. The record high price (on March 10, 1992) was 479,000 zlotys and was due to speculative buying. Although investors' behavior was not yet very sophisticated and there was some speculative trading, the stock price reflected Exbud's good performance. Exbud's position was largely due to the strategy the company's president prepared prior to privatization. The firm restructured, sold unnecessary assets, lowered costs, and increased its marketing efforts; and at the time of privatization, it was prepared to operate in a competitive marketplace.

The plans for capital privatization included other enterprises. By the end of 1992, intensive efforts were under way to sell 348 companies owned by the State Treasury. They were grouped into 16 sectors of the national economy. Foreign investors were invited to negotiate in the sale of 72 SOEs and companies owned by the State Treasury. As a result of those negotiations, 17 firms were sold during the first half of 1992. It should be noted that several large state banks were also being privatized. Privatization of the Export Development Bank had already been completed, and its shares were to be traded on the stock exchange. Privatization of the Silesian Bank (Bank Slaski) and the Wielkoposki Credit Bank in Poznan (two out of nine commercial banks that were separated from the National Bank of Poland in 1989) was close to completion at the end of 1992.

Generally, the results of capital privatization can be summed up as follows: Capital privatization had been used primarily for large enterprises in relatively good financial condition, and the pace was quite slow. Only a dozen or so enterprises per year were privatized in this way. This form of privatization was expensive because of the need for valuation and the preparation of a privatization plan. In most companies it was difficult to determine whether or not they were ready to cope with the new contingencies involved in privatization. Moreover, more rapid privatization was impeded by capital shortages. Privatized enterprises did not receive any funds from their privatization for their own development (the Swarzedz Furniture Works (SFW) was an exception; its debts to the State Treasury estimated at 62 million zlotys were forgiven).

Capital privatization could be improved by choosing the best strategic investors through a public offering. The determining factors should be not only the price but also the investor's commitment to make necessary restructuring investments. Test sales of small numbers of shares could be made in order to set the initial price.

Stock Sales. Capital privatization was closely related to operation of the WSE where shares of privatized companies were to be traded. In late 1992, shares of 15 companies were traded; 14 of these were privatized SOEs, and the remaining one was the BIG (Business Initiative Bank) Bank, a newly established financial institution. In August 1992 the WSE's capitalization reached 2,374,105 million zlotys. Initially, trading included only shares of companies. In June 1992, trading also included state bonds. Sessions were held twice a week, and plans were being made for trading to take place three times a week.

The stock exchange had been operating for more than a year by late 1992, and some definite conclusions regarding its operations can be drawn. First, there were huge fluctuations in stock prices, very often not related to the actual condition of a company. With the exception of only the best companies (Exbud, Elektrim, Zywiec), it was still difficult to use the price/earnings ratio as an indicator of a company's attractiveness to investors. Speculative trading accounted for most of the trading activity during the stock exchange's early years, and by late 1992, the stock exchange had not yet provided capital for the development of enterprises. Institutional investors, who account for 80 to 85 percent of the market in developed market economies, are almost nonexistent in Poland. Individual investors accounted for 90 percent of Poland's capital market; yet they spent only 1 percent of their incomes on investment (as compared with more than 10 percent in advanced market economies). The lack of such intermediate institutions as brokerage firms, trusteeship funds, or investment counselors also made trading on the stock exchange more difficult, although this situation was gradually changing in late 1992 when the Pioneer Trusteeship Fund started operating on the WSE.

There were several reasons for the limited involvement of both institutional and individual investors. Privatization of large enterprises started under the slogan Learn the Strength of Your Money. But this was not a good choice, for the stock prices of privatized companies (except Exbud) immediately began to drop. This created a negative impact on the public's interest in long-term investment. Other negative factors included the scarcity of capital in investors' hands (and the general capital shortage on the market), the continuing economic crisis during 1990 and 1991, and speculative price fluctuations. Furthermore, the state did not offer incentives for investment in the stock of privatized companies. High interest on bank deposits (as much as 45 percent) also dampened interest in the stock market. Moreover, there was no taxation of incomes from bank deposits, while a 20 percent tax was imposed on dividends. The third negative factor was inadequate involvement of foreign capital in the WSE (a factor strongly influencing trade on the Hungarian Stock Exchange).

Privatization through Liquidation. Privatization through liquidation involved enterprises that were financially in poor condition (going bankrupt) as well as those in relatively good condition. The financial condition of enterprises undergoing liquidation due to bankruptcy had to be carefully analyzed. Some of them seemed to be in critical condition due to an ineffective financial system and had the potential to recover after restructuring. These companies may not have had to be liquidated. Some apparently inefficient enterprises were in better condition than their financial statements indicated and should have been assessed more carefully to determine if they could be restructured rather than liquidated. Moreover, the consequences of liquidation in many cases were not fully considered and did not always take local economic conditions into account.

Liquidation was also widely used for enterprises in relatively good financial condition, even though it was usually smaller enterprises that were privatized this way. Privatization through liquidation gained momentum in 1991. Until mid-1992 this method was used exclusively to transfer an enterprise's assets to a company operated by employees. Such a transfer usually required leasing the enterprise to employees with discounts offered to investors. Experience with this form of privatization indicated that involving employees was quite successful despite the fact that the "founding bodies" were generally passive. The prevalence of leasing assets to employees (i.e., distributing shares evenly among employees) and the absence of substantial foreign investments, however, weakened this process. The "quick-sale" method that was implemented in 1992 sought to facilitate and accelerate the process of privatization through liquidation. This method required considerably more active support by the founding bodies. Finally, experience showed that sales by tender had to be carried out as consistently as possible. In organizing a tender, companies had to obtain investment commitments from potential investors along with their pledge to maintain certain levels of employment.

Although this privatization method was used for a relatively short time, it became less popular by late 1992 because of the management's and employees' unfulfilled expectations that the government would reduce or eliminate enterprises' debts. It should also be noted that the abuse (for personal gain) of the system undermined its effectiveness. Often, privatization was carried out in enterprises that had been deliberately put into a difficult situation by the managers or employees.

Improvements in the process require that enterprises should present a business plan, a letter of intent or a contract with a foreign investor, and their rights to land in order to be considered for liquidation. Making the conditions of contract (especially the repayment of leasing installments) more attractive will accelerate the privatization process. Also, the quick-sale procedure, although attractive for domestic investors with small capital, did not show sufficiently rapid progress. Hence, the terms of sale should be made more attractive (the requirement of fixed employment level is especially troublesome). And this method should become more common and involve foreign investors as well.

Privatization through the Establishment of New Enterprises. As mentioned earlier, by late 1992 more than a quarter of the Polish industry was in private hands. The more than 1.5 million private establishments employing 2.8 million people and some 7,500 joint ventures indicated the rapid development of entrepreneurship. Considering that 80 percent of farming and a major part of small-scale services were privately owned, a more optimistic picture of the privatization process emerges. Nevertheless, privatization through the establishment of new enterprises did not proceed smoothly. At first, capital was invested primarily in sectors generating quick profits (trade and catering) and less frequently in construction and transport. Industrial sectors that required more sizable capital investments and better skills were neglected. Private entrepreneurs also entered the financial sector. About 50 to 60 small banks and several insurance companies were established. The newly created insurance company Westa started to compete with such state-owned giants as PZU or Warta. In many cases, private investors who started out in trade or services went on to take a long-term perspective and invest in manufacturing. There were, of course, also cases of failures among newly established firms (some of them due to the overall recession or simply the lack of experience and skills).

Economic recession had a negative impact on newly established enterprises. This was reflected in the collapse of many firms and in the decline in the number of start-ups. However, some blame can also be placed on government policies. The Polish Business Council, an association of entrepreneurs, frequently expressed its disapproval of the government's economic policies. The council concluded that policies and regulations regarding taxes, customs, and exchange rate were inconsistent. Frequent changes impeded economic activity. Restrictive credit and interest rate policies harmed and discouraged investment. Complete lack of protection of the Polish market in the early stages of reform resulted in large losses for Polish entrepreneurs because they were unable to compete with foreign firms. The council recommended making cheaper credits available (especially investment credits) and applying for loans from international financial institutions, including the World Bank.

Another obstacle to the growth of private enterprise was society's perception of the process. In 1991 and 1992, most Polish citizens still favored the idea of egalitarianism, which was fostered under the Communist system. Even after the reforms, profit was still a dirty word. The reports of abuses of the privatization process also weakened public support for entrepreneurship. In these circumstances, the state had to offer more support to entrepreneurs by enacting policies favorable to the expansion of private enterprise.

Sectoral Privatization. Sectoral privatization was intended to supplement industrial policies that were copied in 1991 from the experiences of some Asian countries. The analyses of 22 sectors were to provide a basis for privatization of industries in each sector. However, the quality of those analyses turned out to be quite poor. The weaknesses of the analyses were partially due to Western consultants' lack of knowledge of the Polish market and lack of competence of the Polish consulting firms acting as subcontractors. The sectoral analyses were based on the assumption that the ministry's advisers (that was the official status of the consulting firms), with their experience, reputation, and international contacts, would be the best agents for selling SOEs. It appears that only some of those hopes materialized. Too often the sectoral analyses were too general to be used in negotiations. On the other hand, foreign advisers' contacts could eventually help in finding potential buyers. This was considered to be especially important in light of the globalization of the economy and the need for strategies that took foreign competition into account.

Another argument that was advanced in favor of sectoral privatization was the need to resolve the competition among enterprises in trying to attract Western investors. This considerably weakened their bargaining position. Having an adviser who would be responsible for the entire sector might partially solve this problem. Furthermore, a sectoral approach would allow Western investors to identify the best enterprises from a particular industry.

Mass Privatization. The plan for mass privatization was completed in 1992. Some 600 of Poland's best enterprises, accounting for about 25 percent of the country's output, would eventually undergo privatization. However, the mass privatization campaign did not proceed smoothly. The method of distributing privatization vouchers was a critical point of dispute. Some critics said that free distribution of vouchers was a latent form of communism. Also, critics cited the fact that the value of the vouchers would not be specified at first and, thus, could not create the feeling of ownership in the minds of their holders. Finally, it would be difficult to appraise the market value of the enterprises and, consequently, set mutually acceptable share prices. Proposals were made to conduct a test issuance of stocks or tenders. However, because of the country's small equity market and only moderate interest in it by foreign investors, the potential for such a test was limited. Another argument against free distribution of vouchers was the loss of revenues by the state and the resulting budgetary problems. To resolve some of these problems, advocates proposed a compromise: Each adult citizen was allowed to purchase shares in investment funds for an equivalent of 10 percent of the average salary.

Critics argued that mass privatization required a secondary market for vouchers because many people expected to be able to trade shares immediately. However, a general sell-off of vouchers or shares could result in a drop in share prices, thus undermining the public's assumption that share prices would increase after they were allocated to the investment funds. Another criticism was of the potential benefits for the wealthiest people who could buy the vouchers after they were released for sale. Finally, other critics were concerned about a potential increase in consumption by the poor that could result in a resurgence in high inflation.

Mass privatization turned out to be extremely complicated. The participation of experienced Western firms like investment banks and consulting companies was generally expected to guarantee positive results. But the funds faced great difficulties. They were not typical investment funds that purchased securities, and they were not active investors with the know-how and experience needed to manage a company or industry; rather, they were something in-between. Hence, their role was unprecedented: They were bound to face the extremely difficult tasks of restructuring the enterprises, supervising their management, or even managing them. Finally, there was no procedure for public control over the operations of the investment funds. Some critics asserted that individual shareholders would only have symbolic power. Because of their large size, the funds could become institutions with substantial political influence. No one could rule out the emergence of cartels when shares of companies from one industry were concentrated in the portfolios of two or three funds. All of these concerns delayed the initiation of mass privatization until late 1992 or early 1993.

Privatization through Restructuring. The idea behind privatization through restructuring was similar to the concept underlying management buyout programs. The goal was to increase the efficiency of an enterprise's operations by hiring an administrator who could restructure it to carry out its business plan. However, several problems were associated with this privatization technique. First, this method was not well known in Poland; without an aggressive promotion campaign, there would be little public interest in it. Second, there were not many people in Poland who were qualified to manage limited-liability companies (LLCs). Finally, this approach to privatization led to undervaluing the price of an enterprise at the time of buyout. This last argument, however, was not unique to restructuring—it occurred in all approaches to privatization.

CONCLUSION

Evaluating privatization in Poland is not an easy task. Too little time has passed for a reliable assessment of the privatization process. But we can offer

Foreign Participation in Privatization

Foreign capital investment in Poland began during the late 1970s through Polonian companies (established by ethnic Poles abroad) and JVs. The economic reforms of the early 1990s encouraged new foreign capital investment, but an underlying fear of foreign capital still existed in Poland. Initially, the government was reluctant to encourage foreign investors, and some segments of the public were openly hostile. Foreign investors themselves were somewhat hesitant. Polish reforms were initiated during a difficult period, and the political situation was still unstable during the early 1990s. This was a period of severe economic disequilibrium with no clearly defined economic, monetary, and exchange rate policies. Moreover, there was only a vague understanding of privatization in Poland. All of those factors, combined with the hyperinflation of 1989, made Poland an unattractive place for investment.

Several other factors further discouraged foreign investors. These included legislation unfavorable to foreign investment; the strong position of trade unions; the egalitarian attitudes in society; a weak work ethic; bureaucratic obstacles and lengthy registration procedures; the lack of proper promotional policies; and inadequate regulations for land acquisition by foreigners. Although Poland was larger than Hungary and the Czech and Slovak Federal Republic (CSFR) combined in terms of both area and population, it had a smaller share of foreign investments than those two countries because of these obstacles. The situation started to improve only when legislation was introduced in 1991 that allowed unrestricted profit repatriation and provided other favorable conditions. The Foreign Investment Agency was transformed from a supervisory body into an organization that would be responsible for promoting investment in Poland more aggressively.

The appointment of Prime Minister Hanna Suchocka's government in 1992 further contributed to the improvement in Poland's business climate. It offered more hope for stabilization, which was so necessary for foreign investors. The revival of foreign investment was accompanied by a growing number of large investments and the participation of well-known multinational firms in the privatization process. Phillips, PepsiCo, Asea Brown Boveri (ABB), Gerber, and International Paper Company established a presence in Poland. Fiat agreed to take over 90 percent of the Small-Car Factory in Tychy, and General Motors planned to invest in the Motor Car Factory in Warsaw. Lucchini began negotiations with the Warsaw Steel Works. The value of each of these projects would exceed $100 million, which was an indication of increased interest among foreign investors in the Polish market. By the end of 1992, however, there had been no large "green-field" investment projects; and this would have to wait until the market became more stable.

The Public's and Employees' Opinions on Privatization

One criterion for evaluating the success of privatization is the satisfaction of those participating in the process, that is, employees of privatized companies and the Polish public in general. In 1991 the Silesian University conducted a study of the attitudes of those people living in Silesia toward privatization. Although privatization had been under way for more than a year, 53 to 75 percent of those polled admitted not understanding it very well; 43 percent had only a superficial understanding of what it was; 13 percent emphasized its negative features; and only 9 percent understood stock trading. The public viewed the potential benefits of privatization rather favorably. Seventy percent thought that privatization would result in better management, increased labor productivity, the elimination of unproductive workers, and wage increases. Employees of poorly performing SOEs were the most optimistic about privatization. However, about 37 percent of the employees of privatized companies saw no benefits of privatization. Some respondents believed that privatization was being carried out too quickly, and many of them feared that it would result in higher levels of unemployment. The most common negative opinion about privatization (mentioned by 30 percent of respondents) was that some groups were growing rich at the expense of others. Participation in the purchase of shares or mass privatization vouchers did not change that attitude. About 15 percent of the respondents also mentioned injustice and dishonesty, while 15 percent disapproved of the slow pace and lack of noticeable effects of privatization. Moreover, 56 percent of the employees of companies with foreign participation and 64 percent of the unemployed claimed that privatization would not result in economic revival. Nevertheless, the average rating of privatization on a scale from 1 to 5 (with 1 indicating extreme disapproval) was 3.46.

The findings of the Silesian University study should be compared with the results of an earlier survey of 1,039 Poles on the proposed mass privatization program. In this survey, 43 percent of the respondents were positive about the mass privatization program; 53 percent were not; and 4.4 percent had no opinion. This survey indicated that 25 percent of Polish society was not interested in the process and would not participate in it. Many respondents who had negative opinions said that the program would harm the Polish economy (14 percent) or that it was unrealistic (36 percent). Positive opinions were expressed about the potential macroeconomic gains from mass privatization (62 percent), but only a small percentage of those polled expected to see personal gains (16 percent).

Findings of yet another survey, conducted by Solidarity in the Mazovian Region, addressed the following question: What do the enterprises regard as the biggest hurdle in the privatization process? Firms privatized by the capital method reported five times fewer obstacles than those privatized through liquidation. Among the most frequent complaints: 43 percent were concerned about the difficulties involved in the valuation of assets and in specifying land ownership; 28 percent, about bureaucracy, formalities, and incompetence; 14 percent, about imprecise or improperly formulated regulations; and 7 percent, about financial difficulties or access to capital. Among firms privatized by the capital method, one-third did not encounter any difficulties. About 15 percent complained about imprecise regulations; 13 percent, about bureaucracy; 10 percent, about the appraisal of assets; and 10 percent, about access to credit. Of those enterprises transformed through the capital method, 5 percent reported very good financial conditions; 41 percent, good; 20 percent, acceptable; 28 percent, poor; and 5 percent, close to bankruptcy. In the second group of privatized enterprises, 5 percent of the firms described their financial condition as very good; nearly 47 percent, as good; 29 percent, as acceptable; about 9 percent, as poor; and 10 percent, as close to bankruptcy.

It is also interesting to compare changes that, according to employees, occurred after privatization. Among the changes implemented in firms that had been restructured through capital privatization the most common results were (1) organizational changes in 46 percent of the companies; (2) expansion of the scope of activities in 26 percent; (3) stimulation of sales in 10 percent; and (4) reduction of employment in 10 percent. In firms that were primarily transformed into companies owned by employees, these changes included the expansion of the scope of activities, 19 percent; organizational changes, 19 percent; stimulation of sales, 17 percent; and changes in management and work organization, 10 percent. The scope for investment activity, changes in the wage systems, and the reduction of costs were very limited in both kinds of companies.

We should note that employees had more power prior to than after privatization. However, industrial disputes have been rare, as have been strikes in privatized enterprises. Surveys showed that employee expectations were satisfied only to a limited degree, however—less than 30 percent of the employees were satisfied with the results. A comparison of the situation prior to and after privatization indicated that no significant changes occurred even though there had been some deterioration of the situation after privatization. At least to some extent, this can be explained by the change in economic conditions.

State Treasury as Beneficiary of Privatization

Whatever its other benefits, privatization did increase budget revenues, even though some critics argued that revenues from privatization could have been higher, that the appraised value of the assets of privatized enterprises were too low, that foreign consultants' fees were too high, and that the privatization process was corrupt. According to the Ministry of Privatization, the costs of privatizing the first five firms reached 39.4 billion zlotys, more than $2 million of which was paid to foreign firms for consulting services. The total value of shares that had been issued was estimated at 522 billion zlotys; and of that, the parcels earmarked for investors were valued at 443.1 billion zlotys. Thus, the total cost of privatization equaled 7.5 percent of the total value of the shares, or 8.9 percent of the proceeds from the distribution of shares.

Total revenue from privatization was about 3.5 trillion zlotys in 1991. This amount was lower than the expected total of 15 trillion zlotys. Additional revenues of 5.6 trillion zlotys came from the lease of assets and from commitments of foreign investors (contracts totaling $320 million). The costs associated with privatization during that period were estimated at 250 billion zlotys. The Ministry of Ownership Changes estimated that costs accounted for 10 to 15 percent of total revenues. However, the costs of supervising the privatization process in Poland began to increase in 1991. The ministry's work force reached 450 people, and its debts increased to 40 billion zlotys. Forecasted budget shortfalls for 1992 threatened to further slow the process of privatization.

A good deal of controversy emerged over the valuation process. Many people believed that enterprises were sold at rock-bottom prices but did not understand that despite a considerable book value, some state enterprises had no market value; and that despite their large size, the market value of state enterprises could even be negative if dismantling costs were included. Nevertheless, the issue of valuation was important, and it could not be neglected. Each of the methods used had some disadvantages.

1.   It seems that the best method of valuation was based on market value determined by negotiations between seller and buyer; however, this method was not very useful when there was only one buyer. Moreover, nonmonetary aspects of the calculation often had an impact on the final price of an enterprise. Because in the socialist economy an enterprise was not a commodity, many people found it difficult to understand that it could be traded; and the fact that there were no objective criteria for valuation made it even more difficult for people to understand how the price was set.

2.   The cash-flow method of appraisal allowed an assessment of the value of assets, market position, management skills, and employees' qualifications, that is, all the components of the company's goodwill. However, particular parameters of this method were set arbitrarily, which in the Polish situation caused a substantial distortion of results.

3.   The asset value methods were as unreliable as the others. The book value of an enterprise was an unreliable measure because it only offered information about the costs of acquiring assets in the past. Inflation caused a serious underestimation of the value of companies; and after being revised many times, the methodology began to overestimate the value of companies.

4.   The restitution method could not be used because it usually dealt with old establishments that, in many cases, could not be replaced with new ones.

5.   The liquidation method was more reasonable; it allowed for estimates that were more realistic measures of the income from the sale as well as the costs involved in dismantling and selling a company.

Of course, appraisals made with any of these methods were only estimates; the final price was set by negotiations between the buyer and seller. The seller often did not value state enterprises very highly, and the prices actually obtained from the sale of some of these enterprises seemed to be much lower than the public expected.

The participation of Western consulting companies in the process of privatization was another controversial issue. Often, their role was questioned because of their high fees, because there were no guarantees concerning the outcomes of applying their advice, and sometimes even because of their lack of qualifications. A basic problem was that consulting companies from Western countries often received contracts from their own governments through their foreign aid to Poland. This situation led to conflicts of interests because consultants often prepared appraisals of enterprises that were later sold to clients from their own countries. Also, instead of taking an active part in the preparation of plans for the restructuring of their enterprises, Polish managers were passive recipients of the documents prepared by Western consultants.

The most frequent complaints about foreign consultants were the high price of their services, their lack of cooperation with Polish consultants, and the irrelevance of their recommendations. Objections concerning high fees were often reiterated in official statements, in the press, and by managers. However, these objections resulted mainly from the lack of familiarity with how consulting companies operated. A more important issue was the relationship between the consulting firms' fees and the quality of their products. Polish enterprises needed restructuring plans, strategic business plans, and market analyses. Consulting firms prepared such studies, but implementation of their recommendations often did not produce positive results. The report prepared by Ernst & Young for Tonsil (one of the five large enterprises that had been privatized), for example, made optimistic forecasts of domestic demand for the firm's products and a positive evaluation of its export opportunities. But neither increased demand nor increased exports materialized, and the firm faced serious financial difficulties.

Often, final reports of consulting companies did not contain adequate analyses, or the analyses they provided were not useful to the enterprises. This can be attributed to two factors. First, Polish enterprises still did not know what they should expect from consultants and how to use what they got. A more serious concern was Western consultants' inability to adapt their methods to the Polish market. The procedures applied in Western countries were sometimes of little use in Poland.

The Future of Privatization in Poland

Although the process of privatization has been established in Poland, new ideas continue to emerge. When the Solidarity social movement arose in 1980, there was a common belief that the introduction of employee councils would almost automatically result in improvements within state enterprises. This was not the case, of course; and many people came to believe, by the end of 1992, that a formal change of ownership structures would not guarantee economic success in the future. In a society undergoing such rapid transformation, two political currents—progressive and conservative—were constantly competing with each other as new ideas clashed with old habits. The inertia and the old ways of thinking with regard to political, economic, and social matters delayed the transformation process in Poland. Strikes and other manifestations of popular resistance to change were a form of protest against difficulties (the primary one being unemployment) imposed by the economic reforms.

Changes in Poland and other Eastern bloc countries occurred so suddenly that the only "intellectual weapon" the leaders had for confronting the new reality was a free-market ideology. The lack of a clear picture of transformation, the failure to foresee obstacles, and the rapid pace of changes also affected the process of privatization. For a long time there was no coherent vision of the whole process. Often privatization was not perceived positively by the public. This was not only a result of the adverse consequences of economic restructuring but also a result of inadequate promotion of privatization by the government. The public's lack of understanding of the process and the charges of corruption combined to produce an indifferent or hostile attitude toward privatization policies.

Early discussions of privatization created excessive hopes for improvement. Privatization was portrayed as a quick remedy for economic problems. Initial hopes of privatizing more than 50 percent of Poland's SOEs within three years will probably not be fulfilled. By late 1992, only about 18 percent of these enterprises had been privatized; and the process remains slow—capital privatization usually required 3 to 6 months; privatizing through liquidation in 36 percent of the enterprises took 3 to 6 months; in another 36 percent, took 6 to 12 months; and in the rest, more than a year. The transformation of SOEs into JSCs owned by the State Treasury had to be done carefully. The lack of clarity about the responsibilities of the supervisory boards of privatized companies resulted in the boards often performing a destructive role; they often made conflicting decisions or delayed making decisions altogether.

There were many reasons for the slowness of the privatization process in Poland. The most important problems included inadequate plans for privatization and for valuation; inadequate promotion of privatization; abuses of the process, such as using privatization for political purposes; the shortage of qualified personnel, especially in the Ministry of Ownership Changes; lack of managerial training; and the continuing weaknesses in competition that would encourage enterprises to increase their efficiency and productivity.

Despite these problems, there were some positive results. Although privatization plans were not perfect, they provided some basis for future action. And even though the process was much slower than expected, some companies were privatized relatively quickly. Furthermore, by late 1992 stronger emphasis was being placed on the promotion of privatization both in the mass media and in the enterprises. The stock exchange, although still performing a rather insignificant role in the privatization process, was operating and continuing to develop. New legislation that could accelerate privatization was passed: the Company Pact and the Law on Restructuring of Enterprises and Banks, which is an integral part of that act. The latter provided for debt-to-equity swaps (i.e., replacing companies' indebtedness to banks with banks' shares in the debtor companies). Despite the fact that such a law could raise some new problems, it would also accelerate the privatization process. The other proposed law would allow employees to play a stronger role in the privatization process, thus motivating them to work harder.

What should be done to make privatization more effective? We have come to the following conclusions.

1. The basic issue for any enterprise is not formal ownership structure but the way in which it is managed. For this reason, Polish SOEs must take full advantage of the knowledge of foreign experts and of opportunities for management training. Of course, the issues of management and ownership are interrelated. Private owners care much more for their property than the state administration does.
2. Promotion of new management forms, restructuring, and privatization should receive top priority in government policy. In addition, promotion of Polish foreign trade should be intensified as the political and economic conditions in Poland become more stable.
3. More emphasis should be placed on stimulating active employee participation in the privatization process. This could be achieved, for example, through an offer of capital participation.
4. Companies should be able to retain part of their revenues from privatization for future restructuring. Currently, the income from privatization goes to the state budget.
5. A complete overhaul of the legal system—especially the Labor Code—is needed, for current laws often impede privatized companies' activities.
6. New laws are needed to regulate acquisition of real estate by foreign investors and to encourage foreign investment in Poland.

Ultimately, those dealing with privatization in Poland must remember that changes in ownership structures alone are insufficient to reform the Polish economy or to transform state enterprises. Competition and proper management are the key factors in the success of both ventures.

Development of the Private Sector in Poland during 1989–1990: The Early Phase of Structural Transformation

Maria Ciechocinska

Polish society made a political commitment to reconstruct private enterprise in the parliamentary elections of June 1989. Four decades of Communist rule had resulted in an almost complete destruction of the nonagricultural private sector; and such business services as banks, credit institutions, and chambers of commerce had been destroyed. The command economy had created a vast system of state subsidies, had introduced new accounting principles for calculating the profits and losses of enterprises and the output of the national economy, and had adopted a price structure that had nothing to do with world prices.

The unpopularity of the command economy could be seen as early as the mid-1950s and was manifested in the political unrest of 1956 when the intellectual movement seeking reform of the command economy was actually born. Despite recurring crises in 1970 and 1976, the actual effects of the preparation and implementation of moderate reforms turned out to be unsatisfactory in practice. Nonetheless, the Communist party introduced market mechanisms in order to salvage the country's economy and to protect its own position. As a result, in the late 1970s more ambitious reforms were introduced. These efforts increased the demand for foreign capital and led to the creation of the first joint venture companies (JVCs). However, these reforms simply created an elitist distribution of the benefits of nonagricultural market reforms in the final stage of the command economy in the 1980s because the party was trying to create the private sector in collaboration with foreign partners.[1]

The move toward a market economy in Poland in the 1980s consisted of establishing enclaves governed by different laws and taking advantage of close ties with the public sector while simultaneously obtaining foreign capital in third-country markets. With these policies came the appearance of foreign currency shops and, gradually, dealings with non-Communist countries that opened the country to democratic and market economy ideas. These reforms were strictly controlled by the government, and many Communist party members quit their jobs to start their own businesses.

Economic changes due to the development of a market economy through structural reforms are measured in this chapter by changes in the number of (1) state enterprises, (2) cooperative enterprises, (3) commercial-law partnerships,[2] and (4) small foreign businesses. This is a formal approach that is based on the form of ownership of enterprises rather than on economic criteria, and yet it reflects the significant changes that occurred in economic activity.

The reasons for using this approach were the relative ease of making comparisons between regions over various periods of time and the fact that this method is unaffected by business cycles. It also takes into account a high inflation rate that reached 351.1 percent in 1989, 685.8 percent in 1990, and 177.1 percent in the first half of 1991. Given the war on inflation and the implementation of the stabilization program, the use of financial statistics for comparisons was of limited value. Besides, the planned changes in the economy as well as the measures of suppressing inflation led to a serious recession. Therefore, it is difficult methodologically to separate the individual factors involved in the structural transformation and to measure their impacts as well. Lacking better economic indicators, changes in the number of various types of enterprises indicate the extent of development that took place in the private sector during the early 1990s despite the fact that these numbers do not provide information about the operations of those enterprises.

The statistical data were obtained from REGON (the state information system) and from the Ministry of Finance. The REGON system registers all economic units. Entries in the REGON system are made on the basis of notification or an application to a *voivodship* statistical office.[3]

MAIN DIRECTIONS OF STRUCTURAL REFORMS

Poland's political liberalization started the process of structural transformation in 1989. New economic legislation was introduced to jump start the private sector of the economy; but in practice, this activity was curbed by the lack of domestic capital, the slow inflow of foreign capital, and serious economic recession. Even so, the years of 1989 and 1990 saw a marked increase in the number of private businesses compared with the total number of enterprises: The share of commercial-law partnerships increased from 42.1 percent to 58.2 percent, while the share of state-owned enterprises (SOEs) dropped from 18.2 percent to 13.5 percent; and that of cooperatives declined from 37.4 percent to 26.7 percent.

Services

Structural changes in the economy were especially pronounced outside the manufacturing sector and mainly in services that had been severely neglected in the command economy that had emphasized manufacturing. In 1989, SOEs accounted for 5.2 percent of the total supply of services, while a year later that percentage dropped to 4.2 percent. Services had been the preserve of cooperative enterprises, but they were stripped of their cooperative status through subordination to government bureaucracies. Thus, in practice, cooperatives did not differ from SOEs except by their name and articles of association. During the early phases of structural transformation, the number of cooperative service firms compared with the total number of service companies dropped from 64.7 percent to 51.3 percent.

It should be noted that restructuring of services was markedly higher than restructuring in the national economy as a whole. This was due to the fact that privatizing services did not require large amounts of capital; it often required only an individual effort, an idea, and a small amount of credit. The Polish people's faith in the integrity of private firms and their dislike of state and cooperative companies further accelerated the changes brought about by economic reforms and the state fiscal policy.

In the first half of 1990, the structural changes led to an increased level of activity in private industry even though SOEs continued to play a major role in the Polish privatization process. However, this trend soon slowed down when the government failed to protect domestic producers. Domestic factors that had a negative impact on private industry included the rapid commercialization of municipal economies by local self-government. The withdrawal of state subsidies increased the prices of electricity, rents, water and gas charges, garbage removal, and other services. Combined with the increase in prices of raw materials, these changes forced many firms out of business.

Foreign Trade

Economic restructuring was accelerated by foreign trade developments. The collapse of socialist regimes in the Eastern bloc led to the freezing of commercial contacts between the former members of the Council for Mutual Economic Assistance (CMEA). This resulted in the severing of economic ties that had been built during the previous 40 years. SOEs and private firms that had relied on Eastern European trade faced serious difficulties. Previously, selling to other Communist bloc countries had been easy because administrative and political decisions limited competition. Therefore, there had been no pressure on the producers to modernize their products and processes.

However, switching to other markets turned out to be highly complicated. Because of the opening of its borders, the abolition of import duties, and the full liberalization of trade, Poland encountered difficulties with strict import quotas and prohibitive tariffs imposed by the European Community (EC) countries. However, Polish consumers chose foreign-made goods over domestic ones, primarily due to attractive packaging.

CHANGES IN THE STRUCTURE OF ECONOMIC ACTIVITIES DURING THE EARLY TRANSFORMATION

The transformation of Poland's economic environment resulted in the restructuring and creation of several different forms of business activity. Many SOEs were privatized or became Treasury-owned joint-stock companies (JSCs). In addition, numerous JVCs, commercial-law companies, and small private businesses were established.

Privatization and Problems of SOEs

The command economy had created a system of large, vertically integrated enterprises. This structure seriously limited the technological flexibility of individual factories and prevented rapid adjustment to change in demand. This, in turn, led to low productivity and underutilization of capacity.

Poland then embarked on massive privatization without any prior experience, with few specialists in such operations, and without sufficient funds. The country faced the danger of populist claims that Poland was becoming a disoriented society with irresponsible politicians. In particular, during the first stages of privatization, the authorities did not make allowance for the inertia of the SOEs or for the psychological barriers, the technological and organizational gaps, and the huge costs involved. The government had not provided for diverse options for privatization until the summer of 1992. As a result, these proposals did not meet with popular support; and the government's privatization plans underwent numerous revisions and were changed primarily by political bargaining. Also, the media, which had widely advertised the sale of the first five SOEs, created an idealistic vision of an instant solution to all the problems experienced by the state industrial sector; and there was no legislation regulating the implementation of the reforms.

Given the inadequate state control over the early stage of privatization, some people made windfall profits overnight, while others did not know how much they were losing. As a result, not only the management of individual enterprises but also the Solidarity trade union were at a loss, not knowing how to extract back pay from the new foreign owners. At the same time, there was no clear policy on the return of the property nationalized by the Communists. The government was accused of dealing in stolen property as it refused to respect the rights of former owners. The lack of definitive action combined with conflicting declarations made by politicians during election campaigns further slowed the reforms. Obviously, the process of privatization conducted by government agencies lacked clear guidelines, and this resulted in frequent charges of financial manipulation and corruption.

Privatization of SOEs

One of the easiest and most effective steps in industrial restructuring was the breaking up of large enterprises into separate units on the basis of their technological processes. The resulting smaller enterprises had a greater chance of adapting to the new economic environment. As a result, in 1990 the number of state economic organizations increased from 7,300 to 8,500, (i.e., by 15.2 percent) (see table 12.1). This growth can be attributed to the organizational restructuring that was gradually being extended to all areas of the Polish economy. By the middle of 1992, the process of restructuring had reached all the way down to such state municipal enterprises as urban transport, water and sewage, power, town cleaning, and waste-disposal services.

These changes were a direct result of the transfer of municipal property to *gminas* (local governments). One old enterprise could be replaced by several economic entities, and SOEs could be changed in such a way as to guarantee that they could efficiently operate in a market economy. To this end, the enterprises needed a clearly defined owner.

As a result of the new fiscal policies (especially new tax rates and the payment of interest on refinancing credit), SOEs felt pressured to undergo restructuring in order to identify and eliminate inefficient firms. Restructuring was expected to result in a series of bankruptcies in the beginning of 1990. However, these expectations turned out to be wishful thinking. The government was forced to relax its tough policies owing to a rapid increase in unemployment, social tensions, and the overall lack of resources at the authorities' disposal.

Despite some improvements shown by the statistics, the new market mechanisms and monetary policies were not effective in restructuring the economy. The growth in the number of SOEs due to the breaking up of existing firms was a result of the effort to survive and simultaneously adapt to a market economy.

Despite the proposal of numerous ideas, for over two years the country lacked a clear strategy for restructuring SOEs. The scale of the undertaking and the difficulties associated with it exceeded both the government's and the foreign experts' expectations. British, Belgian, and other countries' experiences proved to be of little use; for in no country that had privatized its state enterprises did

Table 12.1
Number of Economic Units by State Enterprises and Commercial-Law Partnerships, 1989-91

Periods	State Enterprises				Commercial-Law Partnerships										
					Treasury				Joint Ventures			Private		
		Type A	Type B	Type C		Type A	Type B	Type D		Type A	Type E		Type A	Type B
12/3/89	7,337	2,440	1,542	1,384	208	23	54	55	429	240	229	11,693	2,769	2,640
3/31/90	7,647	2,604	1,555	1,433	227	26	51	58	681	363	139	16,589	4,082	3,455
6/30/90	7,908	2,731	1,574	1,474	232	29	59	61	926	493	164	21,542	5,160	4,195
9/30/90	8,345	2,830	1,590	1,509	237	33	56	62	1,306	700	200	26,275	5,914	4,779
12/31/90	8,453	2,860	1,595	1,543	248	41	57	63	1,645	853	258	29,650	6,416	5,171
3/31/91	8,578	2,890	1,580	1,588	282	73	57	64	2,290	1,164	331	34,642	7,168	6,053
6/31/91	8,591	3,000	1,512	1,686	283	92	54	57	2,840	1,431	296	38,516	7,698	7,164

Type A = Industry   Type B = Construction   Type C = Agriculture   Type D = Trade   Type E = Other Branches of Material Production

Source: Compiled by author.

the operation embrace the whole national economy. Besides, in those countries, privatization had been facilitated by the presence of a capital market, commercial banks, and insurance companies.

Another important source of private capital was the establishment of private companies on the premises of the old SOEs. Many of these companies made use of state subsidies to become competitive in external markets. Despite the drawbacks, this process contributed to capital formation and learning.

The move to the private sector guaranteed high incomes to the managers of SOEs. Many of those firms fell in the class of *nomenklatura* companies owned by members of the Communist party elite. These companies grabbed state property by making artificially low appraisals of the value of the SOEs' assets. Access to such profits was restricted to a rather narrow circle of inner management and former activists of the Communist party. Their access to power, information, and contacts made it easier for them to take shares in the new companies. Despite its unethical nature, this process contributed to the acceleration of the structural reforms.

Labor Unions

One of the goals of privatization was to solve the management dilemma in enterprises. One legacy of the Solidarity's political struggle was the strong influence of Workers' Councils (a self-management body) and trade unions. In the late 1980s it was not uncommon in Poland to have three different unions with three different political agendas participating in the decision-making process in a single enterprise. The self-management bodies and the union councils tied the hands of the management. However, management often sided with workers in disputes with government ministries. As a result, the issue of economic performance was simply neglected. The arbitrary nature of the early phase of structural transformations coupled with hyperinflation made it difficult to formulate objective assessments of enterprise performance. In practice, nobody was in charge because everybody was involved in decision making; and any decision could be subject to negotiations. In reality, SOEs operated without an owner, and any decision that put the interests of the enterprise before the interests of the workers stood little chance of being implemented. Consequently, any attempts to implement changes misfired. Prospective foreign investors lost interest once they realized the magnitude of the problems. The Workers' Councils, the unions, and management were referred to as the three corners of the Bermuda Triangle. The few enterprises that managed to adapt to the conditions of structural transformation and to go through the ownership reform on their own initiative were exceptions.

Cooperatives

In the late 1980s a debate was in progress about the government policy toward cooperatives. There was widespread criticism of the strategy of breaking up huge cooperative organizations. The critics suggested that it would have been better to revive cooperative ideals and the social movement on which they were based. The cooperatives, holding until recently a monopoly position, were clearly losing ground to commercial-law partnerships (the latter rose from 29.8 percent to 42.7 percent in just a year) (see table 12.1). Data indicate that cooperative enterprises in a market economy must be thoroughly overhauled if the cooperative movement has any chance to survive at all.

On the whole, cooperatives were faced with problems similar to those of the SOEs; and the only difference was the cooperatives' smaller size and areas of activity. Also, the growth rate during the period in question was similar to that of SOEs, even though there were twice as many cooperatives (see table 12.1). The restructuring of the cooperatives involved breaking up large cooperatives into smaller ones and reducing the size of the administrative staff. Owing to the depreciation of the zloty, the value of members' shares was reduced to symbolic levels at a time when government subsidies and cheap credit had disappeared. Only the cooperatives' assets represented any significant value. For these reasons, many critics argued that the government should attempt to rebuild cooperatives; however, the new economic realities called for different strategies and new skills.

Foreign-Owned Firms and Joint Ventures

Foreign-owned firms first appeared in Poland in the 1970s and were called "Polonian" companies because they were established by ethnic Poles living abroad. They played an important role at that time because they represented models of efficient enterprises. They offered better pay, better organization of work, and modern technology. They also achieved quality standards acceptable to foreign buyers. These companies helped the average Pole overcome a feeling of isolation from the rest of the world. They proved that a Pole could be successful in business and that there were reasons for doing so.

In a sense, the activity of Polonian enterprises created a good climate for the emergence of a market economy. At the same time, Poland's political and economic opening to the world, which came in the wake of abandoning the self-sufficient concept of the 1960s, prepared the way for future changes in the political system. Ideologically, it was easier to tolerate foreign capital coming from Poles who lived overseas than from foreigners because foreign capital was perceived as investment by Poles. Polonian companies cleared the way for other firms and for other fundamental reforms.

In this context, the relatively slow growth of the number of foreign firms, which are no longer called Polonian companies, should be attributed to the unstable economy and deep recession that characterized the period of transition from a command to a market economy. In May 1991, Poland's industrial production was almost 18 percent lower than in 1990; 8.9 percent lower than in January 1991; and 36 percent lower than in 1989.

On the other hand, the recession did not slow down the development of JVCs. In 1990 there were four times as many as in 1989. At the end of June 1991, the number was more than six times higher than in 1989. One explanation of their rate of growth was, of course, the small number of such firms in 1989. Nevertheless, the growth rate justifies the prediction that JVCs played an important role in the privatization of ownership in Poland. Such firms, while taking advantage of the already existing assets and skills in Poland, accelerated the transfer of technology, opened up access to foreign markets, and facilitated the influx of foreign capital.

Treasury-Owned or Commercial-Law Companies

In examining the changes in the number of commercial-law partnerships, one should note the existence of the so-called socialized companies. They included Treasury-owned JSCs and JVCs. The growth of the number of Treasury-owned companies, which also happened to be commercial-law partnerships, was extremely slow. Since ownership by the Treasury was designed as a transitional stage in the privatization of SOEs, a faster pace of change was expected. During the first quarter of 1991, 120 firms were transformed into Treasury-owned companies. Many SOEs filed requests for commercialization, but that did not meet with an enthusiastic response from the Ministry of Ownership Changes because commercialization had initially been devised only as a transition to privatization for enterprises that could not be sold immediately.

In the summer of 1991, privatization through bankruptcy became a real threat to Polish industry. Therefore, commercialization was used to facilitate and accelerate the process of change. However, many SOEs applied for the transformation into a company wholly owned by the Treasury only when they faced bankruptcy or when they were no longer suitable candidates for privatization through the sale of shares. The benefits of commercialization included lower taxation and occasional reduction or write-offs of debts. Financial benefits were, therefore, considerable. However, the legislators did not expect that so many enterprises would prolong their privatization by selling and leasing out their assets, limiting output, laying off workers, and taking out loans. Only then would they apply for commercialization. Therefore, there was a real danger that these forms of transformations would be blocked.

Newly Created Commercial-Law Companies

During the 40 years of Communist rule, there was little room for entrepreneurial activity. Entrepreneurs walked a fine line between legal and unlawful activities. The need to develop the nonagricultural and private sector required new legal regulations. The urgency was so great that the pre-World War II Commercial Code that had controlled the registration process of limited liability companies (LLCs) was reestablished. However, it was not adequate for the existing conditions. Under the old Communist code, LLCs and commercial-law partnerships could be created; and the growth of such companies was facilitated by outdated prewar provisions regarding the amount of start-up capital. The sum of 15 zlotys was so low that no one had any problems coming up with it. It was only in April 1990 that the law was amended, and the amount was raised to 10 million zlotys. This investment represented a barrier for many people.

The law required the registration of various types of commercial-law partnerships, namely, SOEs and JVCs as well as State Treasury and private firms. In addition, it required the registration of social organizations, religious organizations, and small foreign businesses.

As a result, the number of newly registered LLCs rose at a frantic pace. The lack of appropriate legal provisions and financial guarantees, however, allowed companies to accumulate capital very quickly. This often amounted to the robbery of state assets due to various legal loopholes and to the lack of appropriate controls characteristic of a market economy. The demise of the tradition of honest trading only made matters worse.

The dynamic development of private commercial-law partnerships can be regarded as a barometer of economic restructuring. Their rapid growth demonstrates the fragility of structural transformations in Poland. The development of trade was the most spectacular and the easiest to achieve. Consequently, shortages of goods, a common occurrence under the command system, were eliminated. This was a measure of success of Poland's peaceful revolution.

Owing to severe food shortages, the government authorized private imports of food by owners of foreign exchange accounts in the closing years of the command economy. This important move freed the mechanisms of capital formation and enlivened the spirit of enterprise while promoting the development of domestic businesses. People imported such foods as tea, coffee, or wine that were distributed through the state retail network. This activity, nicknamed "suitcase imports," led to an abundance of goods at a time when domestic production was declining. At the same time, wholesale operations that specialized in selling to Polish traders sprang up in West Berlin, Vienna, Hamburg, and Frankfurt.

The boom in private imports lasted for only eight months from June 1989 to February 1990. However, this was long enough to allow the emergence of a professional group of traders and trading companies and the accumulation of the first fortunes running into the millions of dollars. The Treasury also benefited from the stamp revenues from such trading.

The development of private trade was reflected in the shop windows of Polish towns. During the command economy, state retail enterprises had liquidated many small shops and replaced them with large stores that enjoyed a monopoly position. By 1990 these large shops were already being divided into smaller ones owned by various firms. Particularly in the older parts of towns, shops were reopening on premises that had originally been used for shops but had been turned to other uses.

The unfavorable trends that had affected commercial-law partnerships to a greater extent than had originally been anticipated reflected the general situation of Poland's industry. Economists came to see that the successful structural transformation of a country with considerable economic potential, extensive raw materials, and a population of 38 million could not rest on the development of trade alone.

Private Small Businesses

Private small businesses deserve separate treatment. To embark on this form of economic activity, an entrepreneur had to register with a local Fiscal Office. The increase in the number of registrations became an indicator of the progress of structural transformation. In the early years of the transformation, there was an immediate and spontaneous eruption of activity launched by individuals. These entrepreneurs usually had much enthusiasm but little capital (often borrowed) and no commercial premises (office or store space or buildings).

The opening of the economy was a sufficient stimulus for hundreds of thousands of people to start working for themselves, implement their own ideas, and take advantage of available opportunities. Entrepreneurship was encouraged by local governments and the Solidarity labor union. A network of counseling stations and various institutions supporting local and regional economic initiatives was set up with the use of foreign expertise and financial support. In addition to money, some countries sent volunteers. These volunteers helped accelerate the pace of reforms by providing training and assistance.

The combined effect of these spontaneous and organized activities was that 1.2 million small businesses were registered by the end of the first quarter of 1991; these businesses employed approximately 2 million people. Despite the very small size of most of these businesses, this form of activity was important from a public-relations point of view. It promoted, with some exaggeration, an alternative to the huge, heavily bureaucratized SOEs.

Private small businesses in Poland were breeding grounds for a new social class, and the development of their businesses was a vehicle for socioeconomic restructuring. However, this is a very oversimplified, idealized representation of occurring changes. In reality, this process of small-enterprise development was quite complicated and did not always succeed. There were many failed attempts to transform into entrepreneurs people who had been laid off by SOEs. But even the best methods of training and the best specialists could not help much when the spirit of business, the will to act, the right atmosphere, and the appropriate support institutions were lacking. Only then was it acknowledged that the transformation was a process that required sacrifice of at least one, and possibly two, generations.

According to statistics, the number of businesses operated by individuals in 1990 was 39.6 percent higher than at the end of 1989. The bulk of the newly registered businesses were engaged in trade. At the same time, some private firms, especially handicrafts, were liquidated. Another reason for the failure of businesses was the drop in demand caused by the impoverishment of a large part of the society. The difficult financial situation forced many households to reduce consumption and forgo the use of services.

Not all of the existing and new businesses were efficient enough to survive, but many that failed were replaced by better ones. This was a new phenomenon in Poland because there had been practically no bankruptcies and very little economic mobility. Small private businesses effectively accelerated the restructuring of the entire economy and of individual industries and bred a new class of businessmen and entrepreneurs.

REGIONAL VARIATION IN THE DEVELOPMENT OF BUSINESS ACTIVITY

Analysis of Poland's economic restructuring points to regional differences in the development of business activity.[4] Thus, the growth rate of commercial-law partnerships and small private businesses can be partially explained by each region's geographic location, economic development, and industry structure.

Commercial-Law Partnerships

The growth of commercial-law partnerships is one of the most important signs of a transition to a market economy. An analysis of spatial distribution shows differences in the rate of their development in individual regions.

The index used here standardizes the data on the growth of commercial-law partnerships by region. From the methodological point of view, the index is open to criticism because the average size of both a state enterprise and a newly established commercial-law partnership is incomparable. Such elementary economic indicators as the value of assets or level of employment vary widely.

Nonetheless, during the initial phase of the transformation, the emphasis of studies of privatization was on the quantitative growth of new economic units. By analogy to the growth of crystals, they could be referred to as nuclei of privatization. For all its deficiencies, the proposed indicator could be useful for this kind of analysis.

Analyses have shown that the speed at which commercial-law partnerships are being formed is proportional to the overall economic potential of a region. The rate of growth was the highest in the big urban centers and in heavily in-dustrialized areas. Those areas had over 2.3 partnerships per state enterprise in 1989 and over 4.5 in 1990. It should be noted that these regions had a relatively large number of state enterprises; and, thus, the high level of the indicators attested to a large number of new commercial-law partnerships that emerged during the early transition period.

Under the command economy, the regions around big cities and metropolitan areas were the most intensely developed and, despite restrictions, had the largest number of private firms. Political and economic changes in 1989 made it possible for those people to start operating legally and to expand the scope of their activities. This may account for the rapid growth of the number of companies in these areas. The index of the quantitative change doubled in almost every region despite the simultaneous growth of the number of state enterprises, which was a result of the breaking up of larger units.

The growth of the number of commercial-law partnerships in 1990 was approximately proportional to that in 1989. This led to the growth of disparities between regions and increased the polarization of economic growth. No major shifts were observed in the ranking of the regions. This attested to the strong link between the development of new firms and the existing state of the economy.

Some commercial-law partnerships illegally took over part of the assets of the state enterprises from which they emerged. The public was especially sensitive to the so-called *nomenklatura* partnerships formed by members of the former Communist establishment. Indeed, quite a few companies lived parasitically inside or on the fringes of the state sector and funneled assets into the private sector. During the initial period, there were no adequate regulations on this practice. As a result of years of indoctrination, a large part of Polish society tended to regard any manifestation of private economic activity as profiteering.

Small Businesses

The analysis of regional variations in the development of small businesses operated by individuals was based on the percentage increase in the number of such firms from 1989 to 1990. The pace of growth of small businesses depended on the type of region and the region's overall economic potential. The index used here shows the net of newly created and liquidated businesses. Thus, the index is somewhat lower than the actual number of new businesses. If only new businesses are considered, the resulting list closely reflects the generally known ranking of Poland's regions in terms of economic development: Katowice *voivodship* accounted for 10.3 percent of new firms; Warsaw, for 8.5 percent; Poznan, for 5.4 percent; Lodz, for 5.0 percent; and Gdansk, for 4.0 percent. The same *voivodships* accounted for the largest proportion of liquidated businesses. The order was somewhat different with regard to the number of firms suspending operations: Warsaw *voivodship* was followed by Katowice, Cracow, Lodz, Wroclaw, and Szczecin.

The fastest growth of the number of new small businesses occurred in 1990 in Legnica (64 percent). It was followed by Katowice (62 percent), Lublin (59 percent), Wroclaw (58 percent), and Szczecin (50 percent). On the basis of this information, one can say that the growth of the number of such firms was accelerated by the existence of large SOEs engaged in the extraction of raw materials. The highest growth was concentrated in western and central Poland, while the lowest growth was recorded along the eastern border. This is an empirical confirmation of the thesis that the development of small businesses is facilitated by the attainment of a certain level of regional economic development. A good illustration of this hypothesis is provided by considering the handicrafts alone, which, if the circumstances are right, can be a springboard for the development of production on a larger scale.

In general, medium and high indices of the growth of small businesses were recorded in areas with low population density and a low level of economic activity, regardless of geographical location. The lowest growth was recorded in Zielona Gora, which lies along the western border, in Pila and Konin, and in the *voivodships* situated along the northeastern and eastern border.

Thus, there is an indication of either the saturation of most regions with handicraft activities or the presence of barriers to growth. During the period in question, growth was very slow. In some areas the number of handicraft firms actually declined. Even in regions with moderate growth, the situation was not much better, especially when it is considered that those regions included Katowice, Warsaw, Poznan, Czestochowa, Leszno, or Torun *voivodships*. This should be interpreted as an indication of the unused potential of handicrafts. Their activity was suppressed by some of the negative aspects of the government's monetary policies. Furthermore, the utilization of this potential was prevented by the recession in the industry (e.g., lack of orders and severing of cooperation ties), a drop in the standard of living, and the flooding of the market with imports.

As mentioned above, many of the handicraft businesses that had survived the command economy were liquidated in the wake of the sudden introduction of draconian market economy rules. The liquidation of such businesses, many of which had a tradition going back many decades, was a dramatic outcome of their failure to adapt to changing conditions. In these circumstances the question arose frequently whether it was really impossible to find other solutions or if it was necessary to employ a different strategy for transforming the economic system. These were not rhetorical questions, for a similar situation occurred in the private farming sector as well.

Among the regions with the highest growth, the number of handicraft businesses rose by approximately 12 percent. The corresponding figure for trading companies showed a 540 percent increase during 12 months. The regions with the highest growth lie along the border with Germany. The western border was opened immediately after the Berlin Wall was torn down. Despite subsequent temporary restrictions, the cooperation of border regions and local traffic were defined here faster than in any other border region. The treaty of friendship and cooperation with Germany was signed in June 1991. These moves led to a growth of private trade on a scale unknown until then. Poland became an attractive shopping venue, especially for food.

The eastern regions were also an area of animated trade. However, in the absence of international treaties and political and economic stability in the Soviet Union, Lithuania, Byelorussia, and the Ukraine, the predominant form of trade was that practiced by "tourists" and bore a closer resemblance to smuggling than to a legal activity. It can be assumed that the eastern border has also become an important area of regional development in Poland despite difficulties stemming from an unclear political situation. As normalization makes headway, one should expect a growth in the number of registered small firms that had previously operated in the black market.

The lowest rate of growth in the number of small businesses engaged in trade (a fourfold growth compared with 1989) occurred in a horizontal belt in central Poland beginning at Wloclawek and Plock and stretching to the border with Byelorussia. These regions were characterized by low-grade soil and the lowest productivity in farming. They were also characterized by industries' catering to the needs of farmers (e.g., the nitric fertilizer factory in Wloclawek and the combine harvester plant in Plock) and by the dominance of state industrial enterprises specializing in production for the Soviet market.

The collapse of the monopoly of rural trade led to the opening of new sales outlets, typically in farmers' homes. New beer bars were often situated under huge umbrellas or in makeshift premises like hastily adapted toolsheds along major roads. Customers (with modest means) could buy all kinds of goods, provided they were not deterred by the anonymity of the producers of the food and unsanitary conditions.

One can conclude that Poland has already passed the first stage of growth of small businesses. For the next stage to follow, it is necessary to introduce policy corrections and to provide regional development programs.

CONCLUSION

This chapter deals with many subjects at once because it examines structural transformations at an initial phase when it is especially difficult to make unequivocal judgments. The Polish information system has not sufficiently adjusted to describing the new reality. Nevertheless, an attempt was made to embrace a wide range of changes and their determinants on the basis of the available statistics in order to pinpoint the endogenous and exogenous factors.

This chapter also points to a number of phenomena characteristic of structural transformations. It can be said that there is a positive correlation between the development of the private sector and the economic potential of a given region. This is a result of the tendency to concentrate economic activity. However, the kind of activity preferred during a given period by the private sector—in this case, trade—is also important.

The interest in trading was particularly marked among small businesses. Given the recession and the much smaller capital requirements, this is perfectly understandable. Nevertheless, this trend attests to the weakness of restructuring processes in Poland as it guarantees the petrification of state ownership and production, which are already weakened by the recession and the government's privatization policy. Inevitably, the problems associated with restructuring of SOEs (their commercialization and gradual ownership reforms) are becoming central to the success of structural transformations. The possibility of spontaneous transformations on the basis of market forces alone has proved to be illusory.

The impressive growth of small business has an impact on the economy. However, this impact should not be overrated because of the small scale of the operations (they employ 1.6 persons on the average) and the predominance of trade. On the other hand, the scale and ubiquity of small businesses play a great role in overcoming psychological barriers and paving the road for the privatization process.

The creation of an institutional network for the private sector may have outpaced the capacity of people to adjust. For two generations, people forgot how to be independent, resourceful, and enterprising. This caused immense losses that will be hard to repair. The transition from the philosophy of passive to active participation in economic activities requires a change of habits, new ways of reacting, and the development of a new ethos. Therefore, it is not surprising that so many people felt lost, or even deceived, as they experienced the shocks of the transformation. The Poles, similar to other Central European cultures, demanded change and hoped for the advent of an era of prosperity. They found it hard to accept that it is first necessary to lay foundations for a civic society and then rebuild everything that had been destroyed during 45 years of rule subordinated to a utopian doctrine.

On the other hand, commercial-law partnerships and especially the dynamically growing JVCs are an important element of the market economy in Poland. The latter exert an invigorating influence on local and regional economies and make it possible to use available physical and human resources. Commercial-law partnerships, not all of which enjoy a good reputation with the public, create the opportunity for efficient accumulation of the capital necessary for the development of an effective private economy. The challenge ahead is to find a sensible equilibrium between industrial and trading activity.

NOTES

1. Maria Ciechocinska, "Determinants of the Restructuring of Poland's Economy in the 1980s," in E. Ciciotti, N. Alderman, and A. Thwaites, eds., *Technological Change in a Spatial Context: Theory, Empirical Evidence, and Policy* (Berlin: Springer, 1990), pp. 339–355.

2. A *commercial-law partnership* is a Treasury-owned joint-stock company. Commercialization represents a first in the privatization process.

3. A *voivodship* is an administrative region. Poland is divided into 49 *voivodships*.

4. Maria Ciechocinska, ed., *Restructuring and Spatial Strategy* (Warsaw, Poland: Institute of Geography and Spatial Organization, 1991).

13

Private Enterprise Development and the Economic and Political Restructuring of the Cracow Region in Poland

Malgorzata Bednarczyk, Janusz Jaworski, Janusz Kot, and Kazimierz Zielinski

Poland was one of the first countries in Eastern Europe to initiate an ambitious program of economic reforms to create a market-oriented system after the fall of the Communist regime in 1989. The reforms called for eliminating those policies that had created an unbalanced economic structure, for ending the domination of the economy by state-owned heavy industries, and for dismantling the artificial barriers among geographical regions in Poland. The impacts of these reforms, the complexities in implementing them, and their initial success in fostering private enterprise are no better illustrated than in the Cracow region of southeastern Poland.

Cracow, with 750,000 inhabitants, is the third-largest Polish city and the capital of the Cracow *voivodship* (administrative unit), a region with nearly 1.2 million residents. Historically, it was a strong center of economic, scientific, and cultural activities; but the policy of rapid industrialization introduced by the Communist government in Poland after World War II shaped the economic structure of the region from 1945 to 1989. The aim of this socialist policy was to increase the production levels of existing industrial plants and to stimulate the development of nonindustrial regions by constructing new plants. A large number of industrial facilities were built during this phase of accelerated industrialization.

The construction and expansion of the Sendzimir Steel Works played a particularly important role in the Cracow region. Other large production facilities were constructed in Cracow, namely, the Aluminum Works in Skawina, the Telecommunication Assembly Works, the Concrete and Ferro-Concrete Works, the Clothing Enterprises, the Drilling Tools Factory, and the Measurement Equipment Works. The industrialization process was further accelerated by the expansion of such previously existing industrial plants as the Cracow Cable Factory, the Tobacco Enterprise, the Szadkowski Machinery Works, the Rubber Works, the Pharmaceutical Enterprise, the Wawel Sugar and Sweet

Factory, and the meat processing plants. As a result of this accelerated industrialization policy, the Cracow regional economy developed rapidly during the 1960s and 1970s.

The reform policies of 1990 that were enacted to move Poland's economy toward a market system and its government toward democracy had to be implemented, ultimately, in various cities and regions of the country. This chapter examines the economic and political factors affecting the implementation of reform policies in one urbanized region, Cracow. It explores the following questions: What were the main features of Cracow's regional economy during the Communist era? What were its strengths and weaknesses as it entered a period of transformation after 1989? What were the regional impacts of economic reforms after the fall of the Communist regime in the early 1990s? What role is private enterprise playing in the emerging market economy of the Cracow region?

THE EVOLUTION OF CRACOW'S ECONOMIC STRUCTURE

Cracow served as the capital of Poland from about A.D. 1000 to about A.D. 1600. During that time, Cracow was a "center of gravity" for an area covering most of current Poland, the Ukraine, Byelorussia, Lithuania, Latvia, and Estonia. These countries composed the Polish-Lithuanian Commonwealth and accounted for about 10 percent of the territory and population of sixteenth-century Europe. As a result, Polish is still spoken, or at least understood, in many areas of the Ukraine, Byelorussia, and Lithuania. The beginnings of the system of local government in Cracow date back to the Middle Ages. Its structure and legal framework were fashioned after the German system.[1] Medieval cities generally enjoyed extensive powers and rights. Cracow, being the capital of the country, was especially prosperous and powerful.

As early as the fourteenth century, universities were established in Cracow, Prague, and Budapest. As a result, Cracow's cultural influence spread to the territories of current Czechoslovakia and Hungary. These three capital cities represented important centers of political, economic, cultural, and scientific life; and they maintained close contacts in those domains. For most of the fifteenth and part of the sixteenth centuries, the Polish-Lithuanian Commonwealth, the Czech Kingdom, and the Hungarian Kingdom were all ruled by the Jagiellonian dynasty.

Cracow's development was slowed by a series of devastating wars that started in the middle of the sixteenth century and lasted for about 70 years. What followed was a 50-year period of stagnation. Some attempts were made at political reform at the end of the eighteenth century when the powers of the Cracow local government were broadened dramatically. However, those attempts failed to prevent the partitioning of Poland. Cracow became one of the provincial towns of the Austrian Empire. From the end of the eighteenth century to the end of World War I, Cracow and the southern region of Poland were part of the Austro-Hungarian Empire. That period was marked by growing political, economic, and cultural ties between Cracow and other large cities of that empire: Lvov, Prague, Budapest, and especially, Vienna.

The modern system of self-government emerged in Cracow during the 1860s. It followed the defeat of Austria in the war against Prussia and resulted in the restructuring of the political system in the Austro-Hungarian Empire. Cracow's new progressive system of local government was instrumental in restoring the city's economic prosperity.[2]

Between the two world wars, Cracow's experiences mirrored those of the rest of Poland. In 1918, Poland was formed from areas formerly under Russian, German, and Austrian rule; and the first several years of the country's independence were marked by efforts to create a single legal and financial system. After a short period of relative stability in the late 1920s, Cracow experienced a recession during the early 1930s. From 1936 until the outbreak of World War II in 1939, it experienced a period of prosperity that was reflected, for example, in rapid growth of high-quality housing. Many laws, which had been introduced during the Austrian rule, remained in force until 1933. New laws passed by Parliament in 1933 limited the powers of the local governments.[3]

Regional Economic and Political Development under the Communist Regime

Cracow remained under German occupation from September 1939 until January 1945 when the city government resumed its activities under the Communist system.[4] The law providing for local government in Poland was changed again in 1950 and virtually eliminated the system of local government by replacing it with a system of "national councils."[5] National councils only superficially resembled local governments because their powers were quite limited. The elections for national council seats were not free; all candidates had to be approved in advance by a special Communist-dominated organization; and the presidium of the national council, although appointed formally by the council, had to be approved by the central government under the guidance of the Communist party. This mechanism followed the principle of a "democratic centralism," and it was used to provide the Communists with a monopoly of power. Local governments could not own property and did not have their own finances; their budgets were simply part of the national government's budget.

Under the system of central planning, local authorities had virtually no economic powers. The day-to-day decisions of the local governments' executives were influenced heavily by the local Communist party committee. The councils were unable to appoint and effectively control their local executives, and mayors and governors were not accountable to the councils. The domination of the Communist party was almost complete. That system survived until the collapse of communism in Poland in 1989 and 1990.

Economic Development under Communist Rule

The post-World War II economic policies of the Communist regime created an economic structure in the Cracow region that was dominated by large state-owned heavy industries that preempted decisions on investment, employment, fixed assets, infrastructure, and services. Industrialization in the Cracow region was more intensive than in any other region of Poland. The annual rate of growth of Cracow's industrial employment averaged 11 percent between 1950 and 1956, compared with the national rate of 6 percent.[6] By 1990, industry accounted for 37 percent of the region's employment as compared with 29 percent for Poland. Industrial fixed assets accounted for 34.5 percent of the total, with the national average being 24.5 percent. Between 1986 and 1990, industry accounted for 33.2 percent of the total investment in Cracow. Development of the Cracow region's economy after World War II was driven by increased industrial production and employment and was achieved primarily by expanding the size of factories. The role of technological improvement in regional economic growth was negligible.[7] The post-World War II employment growth in industry stemmed from mass population migration from villages to towns. In the Cracow region, more than 200,000 people migrated from rural to urban areas.[8] At the beginning of the postwar industrialization process, the agricultural areas of the region were overpopulated. During the interwar period, the region's agricultural labor surplus was estimated at 200,000 to 400,000 people.[9] The density of rural population in 1950 was 112 people per 100 hectares of agricultural land, compared with 57 people per 100 hectares in Poland as a whole.

Among Poland's largest cities, Cracow had the highest proportion of migrants from rural areas. For instance, in 1976 this percentage was 65 percent, compared with 59 percent in Lodz, 49 percent in Poznan, 48 percent in Wroclaw, and 42 percent in Warsaw.[10] Because of rapid migration, some of Cracow's newest districts suffered from a lack of spatial planning. Large areas of land were left unused, and many enterprises occupied more land than necessary.[11] Land-management zones were created for agricultural areas in the northern part of the region, for industrial areas in the western and central part, and for mountain areas in the southern part. From 1960 the zoning regulations were generally respected due to the efforts of the Cracow *voivodship* authorities and the rejection of several proposed projects (e.g., the large industrial facility Slomniki) that failed to meet the zoning requirements.[12]

Postwar industrialization policy emphasized the concentration and expansion of specific types of plants in different regions. In Cracow this resulted in an industry sector that was specialized in metallurgical activities and that was insufficiently diversified. Raw materials industries, such as iron and aluminum metallurgy, dominated the economic base. The metallurgical industry accounted for about 40 percent of the Cracow region's industrial output. The acceleration of industrialization in Cracow was achieved primarily by the expansion of the Sendzimir Steel Works. This enterprise absorbed the majority of the industrial investments allocated to Cracow: 70 percent in 1950; 63.4 percent in 1960; 65 percent in 1970; 28.8 percent in 1980; and 41.7 percent in 1990.[13] From 1950 to 1965, industrial employment in Cracow increased by 60,000 people, with the Sendzimir Steel Works accounting for 40 percent of it. The secondary investment resulting from the construction of that facility led to the creation of several thousand additional jobs. The Sendzimir Steel Works, with its 30,000 employees, was the largest metallurgical plant in Poland. It produced 25 percent of the country's steel, 40 percent of pipes, all of the automobile body sheets, and all of the transformer sheets. During the 1980s and 1990s, Sendzimir Steel Works accounted for less of the national industrial output than during the 1970s because of the construction of the Katowice Steel Works. Nevertheless, Sendzimir remained Poland's largest producer of iron and steel and dominated the industrial base of the Cracow region. It was the only plant employing more than 5,000 people. Only a few small plants existed in the region, and most of them were state owned. Only 30 percent of the plants in the region employed fewer than 50 people.

The expansions of the Sendzimir Steel Works followed fluctuations in the levels of industrial investment in the Cracow region. From 1961 to 1965, the second stage of the plant's construction was possible because of the heavy investment allocated to Cracow's industrial sector. The level of investment in infrastructure was low during that period. During the 1970s and 1980s the metallurgical industry became less important as investment shifted to different sectors.

The Polish model of development overestimated the advantages of a large size for enterprises, however, by assuming the existence of unlimited external economies.[14] As a result, the entire Cracow region suffered from severe pollution. The rapid growth of heavy industry was generally cited as the main source of the problem, and Cracow became one of Poland's 27 most ecologically threatened areas.[15] This disregard for infrastructure and environment was particularly evident at the Sendzimir Steel Works and Skawina's Aluminum Works. Sendzimir increased its production capacity by 400 percent to 6.7 million tons of steel, and Skawina doubled its output to 50,000 tons of aluminum. Sendzimir's plans for further expansion envisioned the production of as much as 9 to 12 million tons of steel.[16] Other industrial enterprises, such as the Cement Works or Cracow's Ferro-Concrete Works, were established to provide construction materials for the local market—particularly for the construction of the Sendzimir Steel Works and Cracow's Nowa Huta district. However, these enterprises became nationwide suppliers. As a result, raw materials were sent to distant markets, and the finished goods had to be shipped back.

Because of the concentration of investment in the metallurgical industry, the Cracow region's economy lacked diversification. And even though the region was considered one of the most industrialized in Poland, its infrastructure and service sector were underdeveloped. According to J. Kruczla and K. Kisielewski, "Usually, industry has not participated in the expenditures for the expansion and construction of communal facilities. This burden falls almost exclusively on the territorial plan."[17]   Furthermore, the main difficulty "of the voivodship's economy involves disparities between the rate of industrial development and the growth of other sectors of economy, housing and communal systems, and especially services."[18]   Others noted that the "dynamic development of industry has fulfilled the role of the main town-forming factor in the postwar period. . . . However, the process of industrialization has, at the same time, adversely influenced living conditions and the environment."[19]   As in the rest of the country, these disparities influenced the structure and functioning of Cracow's economy for a long time.[20]

Also, the largest industrial plants were not effectively integrated with other plants in the region. For example, the Sendzimir Steel Works lacked ties with the region's other enterprises. During the 1970s a large proportion of its output was sold to enterprises outside of Cracow, and about 12 percent was exported. Only 2 percent of its output was sold to buyers located in the Cracow area, and they were mostly construction firms. This included not only raw and other basic materials (iron ore, coal, flux, scrap metal) but also conservation and restoration services.   The leading buyer among local enterprises was the Metal Packing "Opakomet" Factory. Other buyers included the Skawina Aluminum Works, construction materials enterprises, and the chemical industry. The Sendzimir Steel Works purchased only nonessential materials in the Cracow region. Analysis of the linkages between the Skawina Aluminum Works and the industry in the Cracow area led to the same conclusion: This enterprise's only link with local industry was with the local power plant.[21]   The large size of these enterprises and the requirements of a command economy were the main reasons for the development of such an unintegrated regional economic structure.[22]

In contrast to industry, agriculture was better integrated into the Cracow market; however, many agricultural products came from outside the region. Only 30 percent of the fruits and livestock sold locally were produced in the region. The structure of agricultural production was quite similar throughout Poland.

The main feature of Cracow's economy was the domination of state-owned enterprises (SOEs). Industrialization required a high labor input; and although the increase in industrial employment was a positive development, this increase was partially achieved at the expense of small private businesses such as services and handicrafts. Between 1948 and 1955 Cracow experienced a rapid decline from 11,900 to 4,400 people employed in the small-business and handicrafts sector. Later, in spite of unfavorable political, economic, and social conditions faced by entrepreneurs, the number of private firms gradually increased. At the beginning of the 1980s, there were approximately 5,000 private manufacturing businesses that employed a total of only 12,500 people. Ten years later there were about 40,000 private firms, 800 domestic private commercial-law companies, and 22 joint ventures. But the regional economy still depended on state-owned activities for 81 percent of the industrial employment.[23] Agriculture was an exception—the private sector accounted for 92 percent of its output. In 1990, about 90.7 percent of agricultural land was privately owned. The farms were small; 90 percent of the 80,000 existing farms had less than five hectares of land. This indicated the antiquated state of agricultural technology and low labor productivity.

ECONOMIC TRANSFORMATION AND THE STRUCTURE OF CRACOW'S REGIONAL ECONOMY

After the fall of the Communist regime in 1989, the Cracow *voivodship*, as well as the entire country, had to undergo a drastic economic transformation. The changes included growth of private enterprise, privatization, transfer of communal property from the state to the *gminas* (communes), and an influx of foreign investors. Many private businesses managed to survive Communist rule, and most of them belonged to such organizations as the Chamber of Handicrafts or the Congregation of Merchants. In the new economic system some of these businesses flourished, doubling or tripling the size of their operations in 1990 and 1991. The new laws, which allowed former owners to reclaim their property, led to the resurrection of some old businesses. Property that belonged to the *gminas* before 1950 was returned to them.

The most complicated aspect of the transformation involved privatization of SOEs. This process could take one of three forms: (1) transformation of a SOE into a company solely owned by the State Treasury—a transitional stage that had to be followed by full privatization within two years; (2) the sale of a portion of the enterprise's stock; or (3) the unrestricted sale of the entire enterprise.

The rapid pace of economic reforms in Poland and the lack of reliable statistical data make it difficult to draw strong conclusions about the consequences of these policy changes. However, it is clear that during the early 1990s the structure of Cracow's economy was undergoing major changes with regard to its ownership structure. For example, the number of private companies in the Cracow *voivodship* increased by 18.4 percent during the first six months of 1991.

These changes were especially pronounced with respect to small businesses (employing usually no more than one or two people, including the owner). The number of small commercial and service businesses in the Cracow *voivodship* grew at a rapid pace, about 1.5 times higher than the national rate. Only in transportation did the number of small businesses decrease, largely because there was a surplus of taxis. Table 13.1 provides a good illustration of a free market at work. Rapid transformation in the structure of small businesses resulted from changes in supply and demand in various segments of the market. Under the planned economy, consumers' needs had gone unfulfilled; but the reforms of 1990 made possible the introduction of a free-market economy and allowed a sorely needed process of adjustment.

Table 13.1
The Share (percentage) of the Private Sector in Economic Activity in the Cracow Region

| | Share of the Sector | | | |
| | Public | | Private | |
	Oct. 1991	Nov. 1991	Oct. 1991	Nov. 1991
1. Employment	76	75	24	25
2. Share of Total Sales:	86	85	14	15
Value Including Trade	33	31	67	69
3. Structure of the Sales				
Value:				
• Industry	73	72	47	47
• Construction	12	13	19	15
• Transport	3	2	1	1
• Trade	2	2	19	21
4. Average Monthly Wage*	103	101	92	123

* Average monthly wage in the six economic sectors of Poland = 100.

Source: Local Statistics Office, Cracow, 1991.

Political and Administrative Reforms

Poland is divided into 49 *voivodships*, each composed of a number of *gminas* (communes). The Bill on Local Government of March 8, 1990, and the Local Government Duties and Powers Act of May 17, 1990, provided the legal basis for the system of local government across Poland.[24] The *gmina*, defined as a self-governing community, became the basic territorial, political, and administrative unit of the country. From the legal point of view, Cracow itself is a *gmina*; and as such, it has the right to pass local laws. Similar to other urban *gminas*, Cracow has the right to establish auxiliary units called *dzielnice* (districts). The process of organizing these districts in Cracow was slow due to people's lack of interest in running for the seats and in voting.

The Cracow *gmina* has responsibilities for a wide range of local services: spatial organization; environmental protection; roads; streets; bridges; squares; traffic organization; local public transport; water supply; collection and treatment of sewage; environmental, health, and sanitary facilities; municipal refuse dumps; waste recycling; energy and heat supply; health services; welfare; education; culture; public libraries; recreational grounds; sports facilities; marketplaces; shopping malls; parks; cemeteries; public order; fire prevention; and maintenance of public premises, facilities, and buildings.

Full control over some of these functions is still being transferred by the state to the local governments. For example, in mid-1992 the state still controlled primary education and most of the important roads in Cracow. The rationale behind keeping these matters under state control was that the newly elected councils were not yet ready to assume their management. The general legal principle guiding the new laws was that all powers not legally reserved for any other administrative body belong to *gminas*. Powers belonging to other bodies could be delegated to *gminas*, but only with the latters' consent.

Referendums were authorized for decisions such as recalling elected officials or determining local taxes. In Cracow, the city council of 75 deputies is elected every four years. Early elections can be held if the council is recalled in a referendum that is requested by at least 20 percent of the voters and with a turnout of at least 50 percent. The city council appoints the board, which consists of Cracow's mayor, three deputy mayors, and three other members. Four of the members must be elected members of the city council. There are also two nonvoting members of the board—a secretary and a treasurer. The mayor heads city hall, which is organized into departments. These departments perform all administrative tasks in their respective areas of responsibility. The board and city hall constitute the executive branch of local government, and the city council is its legislative organ.[25] The city council is composed of commissions. The structure of these commissions is similar to the departmental structure of city hall. City hall employs more than 1,000 officials.

Until 1990 the *voivodships* were governed by local branches of the central government. In Cracow the highest official was the city's mayor, who simultaneously served as the governor of the Cracow *voivodship*. He was appointed by the central government and was accountable to both the government and the local committee of the Communist party. Under the new system each *voivodship* has a representative of the central government and is headed by an appointed governor and his office (*urzad wojewodzki*). In Cracow the governor's office employs over 300 officials who serve the 1.2 million people living in the *voivodship*.

This dual system of government, with an appointed central government representative ruling over an entire *voivodship* and the elected local government ruling over each *gmina*, requires a balance between national and local interests. Generally, the governor is responsible for dealing with regional problems, while the commune councils and their mayors have powers limited strictly to local matters. Under special circumstances the governor can intervene in the *gmina*'s matters and can even suspend its council. But because some rights and duties of the central government's representative can be transferred to the local governments, this may result in a changing balance of power between these two levels of government and may become a source of future conflicts. This duality of the system of local government can also lead to a growth of bureaucracy and frictions between city hall and the governor's office.

Aside from these legal changes, the Solidarity labor union remains the most important political force in Cracow. Its territorial structure does not follow the administrative division of the country, for the regional board of the union covers not only the entire Cracow *voivodship* but also the neighboring *voivodships* of Tarnow and Nowy Sacz. Its influence also reaches to some parts of the Bielsko-Biala *voivodship*.

Despite Solidarity's strength and after the fall of the Communist government, the political situation in Poland became very fragmented. In February 1992 the most powerful parties included the Democratic Union, the Center Alliance, the Confederation of Independent Poland, and the Liberal Democratic Congress. The Cracow Civic Committee, which served as the main organizer of the elections in June 1989 and which in May 1990 won 73 out of 75 seats in the city council, seemed to be in total disarray and played an insignificant role in the political and economic reforms in Cracow. Another major political force in Cracow was represented by the associations of businessmen. The Cracow Industrial Society, known as the center of dynamic business activity, became involved in training and acted as a chamber of commerce. Two other organizations—the Chamber of Handicrafts, associating several thousand small businesses, and the Congregation of Merchants (established in 1410) with about 2,000 members—have also taken an active role in supporting the economic transformation of Cracow.

OPPORTUNITIES AND THREATS IN THE RESTRUCTURING OF THE ECONOMY OF THE CRACOW REGION

By late 1990 it became clear to many observers that to achieve the necessary structural changes in Cracow's economy, enormous efforts had to be made by local authorities and local citizens to regain the capacity to invest. As in other regions of the country, investment decisions in Cracow under the command system had little to do with production and consumption needs.[26] After World War II the rapid process of industrialization required enormous sacrifices from the population. The government's goal of investing heavily in industrial production was at odds with the population's consumption aspirations.[27] The government's intention of creating a positive investment climate was initially accepted by the Polish people, but in the early 1980s, their willingness to continue sacrificing to achieve these goals weakened rapidly in the face of economic hardships. Consequently, the government simply abandoned its investment plans. The resulting lack of investment led to a gradual depreciation of fixed assets. At the end of the 1980s, capital consumption in the Cracow region exceeded 45 percent, while the national average was about 38 percent; and the region's depreciation of industrial assets was 56 percent, compared with 48 percent nationwide.

The antiinvestment attitude prevailed during the 1980s, and by 1990 it was clear that recovering investment capacity would take a long time.[28] Therefore, Cracow had to utilize its regional advantages, restart the investment processes, and create a proinvestment social climate. Despite some serious structural problems, the Cracow region had a number of strengths in the early 1990s that helped to accelerate its economic transformation. Some of these factors included Cracow's historical importance, new economic developments through privatization, new business laws, and a new tax system. The region was still an academic and cultural center, and its population was characterized by a high level of education. The 50,000 students enrolled in 13 universities represented one-eighth of all the students in Poland. More than 17 percent of Cracow's labor force had a college degree; and unemployment, at about 5 percent, was not a serious problem in the region. However, some small towns on the outskirts of the region lacked economic diversification and faced a threat of unemployment; and some of Cracow's large enterprises (e.g., the Sendzimir Steel Works) threatened to become a source of unemployment due to economic restructuring.

The Cracow *voivodship* with its 3,254 square kilometers (1.4 percent of Poland's territory) was geographically the second-smallest *voivodship* in the country. It contained relatively more farmland and much less forest and inland waters than the rest of Poland, and the highly urbanized province also had a large share of land used for buildings and roads. But there were some areas of particular natural value (about 12 percent of the *voivodship*) that were under special legal protection and could be used for tourism and recreation. One of the region's most serious problems, however, was that compared with the rest of Poland the Cracow *voivodship*'s natural environment was severely polluted. Cracow ranked third in terms of emission of air pollutants with a level seven times higher than the national average.

With a population of 1.2 million (3.2 percent of Poland's population), the Cracow *voivodship* ranked fifth in the nation. About 70 percent of the *voivodship*'s population lived in urban areas (the national average is 62 percent), and about 59 percent were of productive age (18 to 64 for men, and 18 to 59 for women).

Total employment in the Cracow province in 1990 was 544,900 (3.3 percent of Poland's total employment). Compared with other highly urbanized and densely populated *voivodships* (Warsaw, Lodz, Katowice, Poznan, and Wroclaw), a high proportion of Cracow's labor force was active in agriculture, due largely to the small size of farms and the overpopulation of rural areas. Consequently, migration from the rural to urban areas was expected to continue creating a strong need for employment opportunities in services and commerce.

One strong advantage of Cracow was the quality of the work force, at least in terms of its level of education. With 14 percent of the work force holding college degrees, Cracow ranked second in Poland (nationwide about 11 percent). A substantial share of workers with university degrees could be found in construction, science and technology, culture and arts, and education, although the percentages in industry, administration, and law were significantly lower than in Poland. The unemployment rate in the Cracow region at the end of 1991 was 5.1 percent, only half of Poland's rate.

The total book value of the fixed capital in the Cracow *voivodship* at the end of 1990 was estimated at about 99.5 trillion zlotys, or about $U.S. 10 billion (about $8,080 per capita). This represented less than 3 percent of Poland's asset value. Almost 80 percent of the fixed capital was publicly owned (mostly state owned). The depreciation of this capital was estimated at 36 percent, indicating that in the Cracow *voivodship* it was on average older than in the rest of Poland. The share of the productive fixed capital in the region was lower, and the share of nonproductive capital was higher than in Poland as a whole.

The total sales of Polish industry in 1990 amounted to 577.3 trillion zlotys, and 3.7 percent of it was in the Cracow region. Poland's labor productivity in 1990, measured by the value of production per worker, equaled 157 million zlotys, while the value of the fixed capital per worker was equal to 261 million zlotys. On average, industrial labor productivity in the Cracow region was about 30 percent above the national average. This can be partially explained by the fact that the amount of fixed capital per worker in the Cracow region was nearly 22 percent higher than the national average. However, because the depreciation of fixed capital in the province was much higher than in the rest of Poland, the productivity of the region's industrial work force exceeded the national average.

Foodstuffs and minerals industries were the most efficient sectors in terms of both labor and capital productivity. Labor productivity was particularly high in the energy-related industries, while fixed capital productivity was relatively high in textiles, leather, electromechanical, and chemical industries.

Approximately 93 percent of the Cracow region's farmland was held privately. This was primarily due to the fact that the large, state-owned farms were created mostly in Poland's northern and western provinces. The southern part of the country maintained large numbers of small, private farms.

The transportation system in the Cracow *voivodship* was relatively well developed. The Balice Airport, located about 10 kilometers from Cracow, offered direct flights to several cities in and outside Europe. A new airport was being planned halfway between Cracow and Katowice (about 35 kilometers from each). The region had 264 kilometers of railroads and 5,200 kilometers of public roads. Electricity was available throughout the region; water and sewage systems were well developed in the urban areas but not as well in the rural areas.

Implementation of Transformation Programs

Because of these advantages, economic reforms in the Cracow region could be implemented quickly, as indicated by the progress achieved in ownership changes and in the participation of foreign capital in 1990 and 1991. The rate of creation of new firms in the Cracow region was one of the highest in Poland. At the end of the third quarter of 1991, the region had about 2,400 new commercial-law companies. However, the privatization of state enterprises could not be accomplished overnight. Ninety-two firms were transformed into Treasury-owned companies by the end of 1991. That step represented only the first stage in privatization and should not be considered a complete transformation but rather an organizational change without any real capital restructuring. Joint-venture companies (JVCs) exhibited the most rapid growth. In December 1991 there were approximately 190 JVCs, mainly trade and manufacturing companies.[29] During that period most of the JVCs in the Cracow region involved Germans (approximately 30 percent) and Americans (approximately 20 percent). Other joint-venture partners included Austria, France, and Italy.

During the third quarter of 1991, the number of private firms in the region increased by 30 percent to 52,000. The rate of growth was 72 percent higher in 1991 than in 1990. Most of these firms were involved in trade. One of the main reasons for their rapid growth was the favorable tax law for private trade firms. In addition to the trade firms, there was a surge in the number of service firms in such industries as consulting and computers. That increase resulted from the high level of flexibility exhibited by the small companies. For example, a firm called Akita International, which was established in 1984, followed the typical developmental cycle of a small business. It started out as a very small handicrafts factory with a capital of 60,000 zlotys (approximately $100).[30] In

1991, sales reached 11.7 billion zlotys ($1.5 million dollars), of which 20 percent came from exports.

In spite of the rapid growth of private firms, the public sector still dominated economic activities in the region in 1992 and still employed about 75 percent of the labor force. Private companies and the SOEs accounted for 15 and 25 percent of the total revenue, respectively. These proportions were reversed only in the trade sector. Private trade firms accounted for 70 percent of total sales.

Thus, the restructuring of the Cracow region's economy began not so much through privatization of SOEs as through the development of small businesses and trade firms, thereby diversifying the regional economy. The proportion of large SOEs (those with over 100 employees) declined from over 50 percent in 1980 to 24 percent in 1991. A 1991 survey of private businesses found that 89 percent of the firms employed fewer than 5 people; 9 percent employed 6 to 20 people; and only 2 percent employed over 20. There was a relationship between the size of the firms and the industries in which they operated. In agriculture, 92 percent of the firms employed fewer than 5 people. Of the firms that employed between 6 and 20 people, 30 percent were in construction; 21 percent, in manufacturing; and 20 percent, in the restaurant industry.

The transition from a command economy to a market economy in the Cracow region, however, was made more difficult by several serious problems: the inefficient allocation of funds during the restructuring process; the negative impact of pollution on agriculture; the declining tax revenues due to the collapse of SOEs (during the first half of 1991, tax revenues equaled only 35 percent of the expected amount); the reduction in SOEs' capital investment; high capital utilization in SOEs; and the relative financial insignificance of private firms (in 1991, SOEs accounted for 96 percent of the current assets).

However, restructuring the economy in the Cracow region was supported by the central and local governments, local lobbies, bank credits, and external foreign loans. Local government supported the development of private enterprise because tax revenues from that sector accounted for 50 percent of its 1991 income. Only 5 percent of the tax revenues came from state enterprises. But because of its tight budget, the local government's backing consisted mainly of promoting the region.

The Cracow government formed a number of foreign JVCs to combat the city's problems.[31] For example, JVCs with the European Board, the Danish Aid Agency, the World Bank, and several foreign firms were established to undertake construction projects in the city. To improve technical infrastructure in the fields of energy conservation, a local firm was transformed into a Treasury-owned company and immediately began seeking active partners. Local authorities decided that all new investments in telecommunications financed by a credit from the World Bank had to be in foreign equipment.[32] The local government and local lobbies helped the agricultural industry by facilitating contacts with partners in other regions and abroad (e.g., the Ukraine).[33]

Restructuring the Cracow region's economy was closely linked with restructuring SOEs but depended on support from the private sector. The success of the privatization of SOEs depended heavily on external financial support. Credit in Poland was expensive—annual interest rates ranged from 44 to 60 percent. Thus, credit from foreign financial institutions was more attractive (see table 13.2). Loans from the European Community were used especially for developing small businesses and JVCs but also for the privatization of SOEs. The PHARE Program provided funds for the protection of the environment and the development of the tourist, food, agricultural, and energy industries. In addition, the Polish-American Enterprise Fund (PAEF) was particularly active; as of September 1991 its investment commitments totaled $105.3 million for 25 major projects and for 518 small-business loans (of $35,000 or less) throughout Poland.[34] In the Cracow region, PAEF owned 25 percent of Akita International (investment of $375,000) and 50 percent of Qumak International (investment of $350,000). PAEF also invested in the Cracow banking and finance system. Its $2 million investment in the First Polish-American Bank represented a 46 percent stake.

CONCLUSION

In general, as a result of economic and political reforms that were enacted early in 1990, the Cracow region began to regain its position as a strong center of economic activity, especially in the southeastern part of Poland. By mid-1992 the process of economic transformation in the Cracow *voivodship* was on average faster than in the rest of the country, especially in the development of small businesses. The political and administrative reforms were successful, at least in creating an atmosphere that was favorable for new economic activities. The Cracow region's labor and capital productivity and the value of fixed capital per worker were much higher than in the rest of the country. The combination of a relatively well developed technical infrastructure and highly skilled labor force provided the region with a stronger potential for economic growth. It remains to be seen whether or not Cracow and its region will continue this rate of growth and whether or not they are successful in attracting foreign capital. Some multinational companies have already established their presence in Cracow (e.g., Levi's, Benetton, Salamander, Adiddas, and Puma), and this success indicates that continued foreign investment and local entrepreneurship will largely determine the success of Poland's integration into the world economy.

Table 13.2
The Foreign Credit Links of the Polish Economy

Credit Value	Use of Credit	Borrower	Amount Already Given
$260 Million	Investment in Industry	Polish National Bank	$81.4 Million
$100 Million	Investment in Food and Agricultural Industry	Polish National Bank	$33 Million
$100 Million	Investment in Private Agriculture	Polish Government	0
$18 Million	Management, Protection of the Environment	Polish Government	$18 Million
$145 Million	Transport: Modernization of the Railways and Infrastructure	Polish Government/ Railways	$145 Million
$4.75 Million	Use of Street-Surface Modernization	Ministry of Transport	$4.75 Million
$250 Million	Development of Production of Energy Media	Polish Energy Media Agenture	$250 Million
$300 Million	Program of Structural Economic Adaptation	Ministry of Finance	$300 Million
$120 Million	Development of Telecommunications and Satellite Communication Network	Polish Post and Telegraph Agenture	0
$100 Million	Restructuring of Employment	Polish Government	0
$200 Million	Development of Banking System and Technical Bank Equipment	Ministry of Finance	0
$280 Million	Support of Privatization Program and Restructuring of the Social Economy	Polish Government	0

Note: Seven banks take part in this credit network. Of these seven banks, there are three that are also active in Cracow: Bank Handlowy InC., Bank Rozwoju Eksportu InC., and Bank Przemyslowo-Handlowy.

Source: *Gazeta Bankowa* 49, 1991.

NOTES

1. Adam Ginsbert-Gebert, "Samorzad terytorialny i jego gospodarka," in *Fundacja rozwoju demokracji lokalnej* (Warszawa: 1990).

2. The contribution of the city government of Cracow to the political, economic, spatial, and cultural development of the city is described in J. Purchla, "Pozaekonomiczne czynniki rozwoju Krakowa w okresie autonomii galicyjskiej," *Zeszyty naukowe akademii ekonomicznej w Krakowie*, vol. 96 (Krakow: Special Series, 1990).

3. Published in the official governmental bulletin *Dziennik Ustaw* no. 35/-1933/294.

4. The Polish Army withdrew from Cracow without trying to defend the city against attacking German troops to prevent the destruction of the old architecture and art collections.

5. Published in *Dziennik Ustaw* no. 18/1950/147.

6. J. Gajda, *Steel Works in the Development of Industry and the City of Krakow* (Krakow: AE, 1981).

7. J. Gajda, ed., *Programowanie rozwoju produkcji przemyslowej* (Warszawa: PWE, 1987).

8. W. Czarkowska and M. Dobrowolska, "Wezlowe problemy demograficzne regionu," in J. Czarkowski, ed., *Rozwoj ekonomiczny regionu krakowskiego w dwudziestoleciu Polski Ludowej* (Krakow: PAN, 1965).

9. Ibid.

10. W. Rakowski, *Uprzemyslowienie a proces urbanizacji* (Warszawa: PWE, 1980).

11. B. Luchter, *Ocena sposobu uzytkowania ziemi w miescie Krakowie* (Krakow: AE, 1992).

12. K. Zielinski, *Terytorialna struktura aglomeracji krakowskiej* (Krakow: AE, 1992).

13. A. Haranczyk, *Procesy inwestycyjne w rozwoju gospodarki Krakowa w latach 1950-1990* (Krakow: AE, 1992).

14. S. M. Komorowski, "Przestrzenna organizacja gospodarki polskiej," *Proba analizy krytycznej* (Warszawa: PAN, 1982).

15. K. Gorka, "Changes in the Environmental Policy of Poland," *Economic and Legal Instruments of Environmental Policy in the Market Economy* (Krakow: EAERE, 1991).

16. S. Suchonski, "Podstawowe kryteria ksztaltowania terytorialnych kompleksow przemyslowych w przemysle hutnictwa zelaza," *Problemy Ekonomiczne*, vol. 4 (1976).

17. J. Kruczla and K. Kisielewski, *Zagadnienia rozwoju miast w wojewodztwie krakowskim*, vol. 1 (Mysl Gospodarcza: 1958).

18. *Zagadnienia perspektywicznego rozwoju wojewodztwa krakowskiego w latach 1961–1975* (Krakow: WKPG, 1961).

19. "Wezlowe problemy rozwoju miasta Krakowa w okresie perspekty-wicznym," *Studium Miejskiej Komisji Planowania Gospodarczego* (Krakow: 1972).

20. B. Boniecki, "Miasto Krakow w roku 1962," *Problemy Ekonomiczne* (1963).

21. B. Kortus, "Krakow jako osrodek przemyslowy," in *Rozwoj i struktura wielkiego miasta* (Krakow: UJ, 1968).

22. J. Gilmour, "External Economies of Scale, Interindustrial Linkages and Decision Making in Manufacturing," in F. Hamilton, ed., *Spatial Perspectives on Industrial Organization and Decision Making* (London: Wiley, 1974).

23. M. Bednarczyk, "Rozwoj prywatnej przedsiebiorczosci w woj. krakow-skim," in J. Targalski, T. Mroczkowski, and A. Masny, *Studium przedsie-biorczosci* (Krakow: AE, 1991).

24. These two bills were published in *Dziennik Ustaw* no. 16/1990/95; and no. 34/1990/198, respectively.

25. Some of the areas of the city council's authority include passage of the *gmina*'s statutes, appointment of the mayor and the board, approving the *gmina*'s budget, local land-use plans, local economic programs, purchasing or leasing of the *gmina*'s property, issuing bonds, borrowing money, creating and dissolving joint-stock companies, and creating and restructuring enterprises.

26. A. Kuklinski, "Gospodarka przestrzenna Polski," in *Diagnoza i rekonstruk-cja* (Wroclaw: Ossolineum, 1984).

27. J. Pajestka, *Polski kryzys lat 1980–81* (Warszawa: KiW, 1981).

28. Kuklinski, "Gospodarka."

29. *Informacja statystyczna o sytuacji gospodarczej w woj. krakowskim* (Krakow: WUS, 1992).

30. T. Mroczkowski and J. Targalski, "Case Study and Case Commentary THE AKITA INTERNATIONAL CO., LTD.," in *Entrepreneurship in Poland, CSFR, Hungary and Yugoslavia* (Berlin: 1991).

31. *Kierunki strategii i rozwoju miasta Krakowa* (Krakow: Zarzad Miasta, 1991).

32. Ibid.

33. S. Owsiak and K. Surowka, *Prognozy ostrzegawcze w sferze spoleczno-ekonomicznej dla duzego regionu krakowskiego* (Mogilany: 1991).

34. Polish-American Enterprise Fund, *1991 Annual Report.*

14

Privatization of Prochnik—A Case Study

Tomasz Dolegowski and Jerzy Suchnicki

Prochnik was established as a state-owned enterprise (SOE) in Lodz in February 1945. Initially, the company produced clothing for the army. During the 45 years of its existence, Prochnik has occupied a dominant position in the Polish market as a producer of men's garments, especially men's coats and jackets.

In 1949 the company began to expand its range of products and its sales outlets. In 1959 Prochnik won its first export order from the Soviet Union; this was followed by orders from former West Germany, France, the United Kingdom, and the United States. During the 1960s and 1970s the company grew by acquiring new production facilities in Poddebice, Rawa Mazowiecka, Uniejow, and Lodz. In 1987 Prochnik initiated a program of technological modernization and general reorganization. In 1990 the enterprise was included on the list of SOEs to be privatized. On September 27, 1990, as a first step of privatization, Prochnik was transformed into a State Treasury–owned company, and the privatization process was completed in February 1991.

ORGANIZATIONAL STRUCTURE

The company was composed of three bodies: the Board, the Supervisory Council, and the General Assembly of Shareholders. The Board consisted of a chairman and two vice chairmen. The Supervisory Council consisted of at least five persons elected by the General Assembly for a five-year term.

Important personnel changes occurred in February 1992. Previous management (the Board) consisted of three persons: Longin Barski (chairman) and Boguslawa Kielan and Wlodzimierz Zajdel (vice chairmen). The Board was chaired by Wojciech Kolignan, a Lodz Polytechnic University engineering graduate. Having worked as both a foreman and production manager, he was an experienced employee of Prochnik. His experiences also included a position as production manager at Telimina, another textile company in Lodz. Vice Chairman Boguslaw Kielan, who joined the Board in 1990, was a chartered accountant. His educational background included a master of economics as well as training in computer science. Vice Chairman Krzysztof Trzewikowski worked as an accountant at a Lodz chemical company; his experience included a job as a sales manager. He was responsible for domestic sales and marketing.

The company's main offices and one of its factories were located in Lodz, the second-largest town in Poland and a center of the textile industry. Two smaller factories were located in Rawa Mazowiecka and Poddebice.

The organizational structure was centralized and functional (see figures 14.1 and 14.2). The four functional areas were accounting and finance, supply and sales, production, and technology. Despite changes in the early 1990s, the organizational structure remained rather traditional. The company was especially weak in the areas of marketing and human resources management.

SITUATION BEFORE PRIVATIZATION

For many years Prochnik had been one of the leading manufacturers of men and women's clothing in Poland. At the time of privatization, the company had an annual production of about 700,000 units, for sale both domestically and abroad. During the 1960s and 1970s the company increased its production by acquiring new facilities in Poddebice, Rawa Mazowiecka, Lodz, and Uniejow and by constructing a new factory in Lodz. In the late 1980s a program of technological modernization and reorganization of the production process was initiated.

The company had two main product lines: men's overcoats and jackets and women's overcoats. The most important products were men's overcoats. Until the second half of 1990, Prochnik also produced a variety of other products, mainly underwear. At that time, the company decided to discontinue those production lines.

Domestic Market

At the time of privatization, domestic sales represented 31 percent of the value and 59 percent of the volume of the total sales. Prochnik's brand name and high quality were well known. During the first half of 1990, Prochnik's share of the Polish market for men's winter overcoats and men's summer overcoats was 25 percent and 38 percent, respectively. Prochnik's share of the market for men's short jackets was much smaller. In women's garments, Prochnik had a 12 percent share of the market for winter overcoats and small shares of the markets for summer and short overcoats. The main Polish competitors included Lewar-

Figure 14.1
Organizational Structure before Privatization

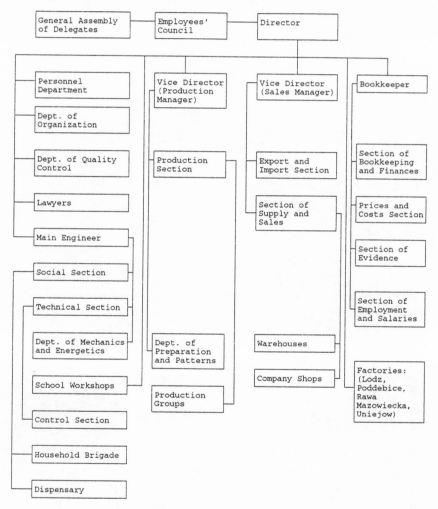

Source: Interview at the Prochnik Office, 1991.

Figure 14.2
Actual Organizational Structure of Prochnik

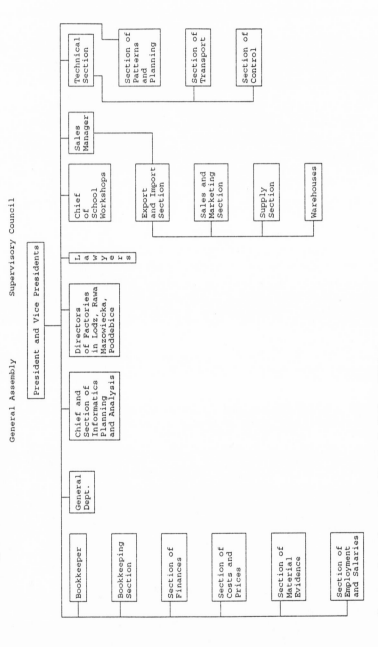

Source: Interview at the Prochnik Office, 1991.

towski, Rafio, Kalpo, Goflan, Cora, Delia, Modena, and Emfor. The main raw materials used by the enterprise were cotton, wool, and viscose fabrics. The most important suppliers included Andropol, Fasty, Norbelana, Mazowia, Dolwis, Nowar, and Silwana.

Exports

During the first half of 1990, exports accounted for 41 percent of total sales by volume and 69 percent by value (see table 14.1). The main buyers of Prochnik's products abroad included Gruner, Weber, and Continental Casmere in the United States; Brinkmann, Gebhardt, Flick, and Salko in Germany; Morwill in Canada; Vestebeno in Italy; Bulte in Belgium; Trent, Rose, and Nowrose in Great Britain; Balling, Regent, and Fotex in Denmark; Halonen, Seppala, and Kesko in Finland; Y. Bourges in France; and C&A in Holland, Germany, and Great Britain. Sales did not depend on one dominant buyer. Prior to privatization, exports to the other Eastern European countries played a significant role. The merchandise was exported through the Foreign Trade Association's Confexim and a group of local dealers with ties to foreign markets. During the late 1980s, Prochnik developed its own distribution network on the foreign markets. Thirty-one percent of Prochnik's exports were made through its own distribution channels at the beginning of 1990, and the remainder were arranged by Confexim.

Employment

Prior to privatization, Prochnik employed 2,479 people, of which 313 were in administration, 1,601 were in production, and 565 were in other areas. Compared with other textile factories in Lodz, the labor force was highly skilled due to Prochnik's relatively advanced technology. As a result of those skills plus low salaries in the public sector, many employees received attractive job offers from private industry. This was one of the reasons for quick privatization. Relations between the management and employees were relatively good, and serious conflicts and strikes had been avoided.

Capital, Real Estate, and Machinery

According to the balance sheet and income statements of September 30, 1990, Prochnik's capital totaled 68.3 billion zlotys; liabilities were 16 billion zlotys; and the cash balance was 8.4 billion zlotys (see tables 14.2 and 14.3). The land

Table 14.1
Turnover (by value and volume) in the First Half of 1990

	Value (million zlotys)	%	Volume (pieces)	%
Men's Winter Overcoats	2,900	5	19,571	4
Men's Summer Overcoats	29,156	54	132,099	30
Short Jackets	4,905	9	31,526	7
Women's Overcoats	4,428	8	26,217	6
Women's Costumes	2,111	4	16,796	4
Others (Mainly Underwear)	10,448	19	222,042	49
Total:	53,948	100	448,251	100
Of Which Is Domestic	16,743	31	265,825	59.3
Of Which Is Export	37,205	69	182,426	40.7

Note: The rate of exchange of the dollar against the zloty was about 9,500 zlotys in early 1990.

Source: *Privatization Prospectus*, Prochnik, p. 11.

and buildings, previously property of the State Treasury, were transferred to Prochnik for free. Prior to privatization, the company held 18 hectares of land in Lodz, Poddebice, Uniejow, Rawa Mazowiecka, and Janikowo. Most of the machines were modern, and the average age was about five years. They had been purchased abroad, primarily in Germany.

PROCESS OF PRIVATIZATION

On October 1, 1990, Prochnik was transformed into a joint-stock company owned by the State Treasury. By the end of October, consulting firms had prepared an investment prospectus for Prochnik; and on November 30, 1990, Polish banks started selling its shares. Prochnik was one of the companies to be privatized according to the "capital" procedure. The value of capital was estimated at 30 billion zlotys and divided into 1.5 million shares, each valued at 20,000 zlotys. However, the sale price of each share was set at 50,000 zlotys, and the excess funds were allocated to reserve capital. As of September 30, 1990, Prochnik's capital equaled 68.3 billion zlotys. Capital evaluation was carried out by Morgan Grenfell and Co., Ltd. and Poland's Doradztwo Gospodarcze (Economic Counseling, Ltd.). Out of the 1.5 million shares, 1.2 million were offered for public sale, and the remaining shares were reserved for Prochnik's employees. Employees could purchase shares on preferential terms

Table 14.2
Balance Sheet of the Prochnik Company for 1987–90
(in millions of zlotys)

	1990 (nine months of)	1989	1988	1987
Assets				
Fixed Assets				
Buildings & Equipment	27.9	25.2	1.8	1.8
Investments	5.9	1.5	277.0	48.0
Advancements for Investments	0.0	0.0	0.0	3.0
Capital Investments	70.0	70.0	24.0	5.0
Total Fixed Assets	33.8	26.8	2.2	1.8
Current Assets				
Inventories	46.1	18.2	3.6	1.8
Accounts Receivable	12.5	13.0	1.6	991.0
Cash	8.4	7.1	199.0	126.0
Other	0.0	0.0	0.0	13.0
Total Current Assets	67.0	38.3	5.4	2.9
Total Assets	100.8	65.1	7.5	4.8
Liabilities				
Initial & Accumulated				
Capital	1.8	1.9	1.9	1.9
Revaluation	23.9	23.9	747.0	747.0
Profits: From the Past	18.6	1.5	852.0	11.0
Profits: Current	23.9	22.3	1.2	1.0
Total Initial & Accumulated	68.3	49.5	4.7	3.7
Long-Term Liabilities	10.0	10.0	20.0	20.0
Current Liabilities	32.4	15.5	2.8	1.0
Accrued Expenses	57.0	18.0	3.0	2.0
Total Liabilities	100.8	65.1	7.5	4.8

Source: *Privatization Prospectus*, Prochnik, p. 24.

Table 14.3
Income Statements of the Prochnik Company for 1987–90
(in millions of zlotys)

	1990 (nine months of)	1989	1988	1987
Sales	103.9	34.4	11.3	7.1
Costs	71.9	27.2	9.7	6.1
Operating Profit	32.0	9.2	1.7	1.0
Additional Sale	21.0	46.0	36.0	0.0
Financial Income	4.8	14.4	31.0	7.0
Tax Returns	5.5	920.0	469.0	365.0
Exceptional Profits	1.7	6.1	48.0	34.0
Exceptional Losses	2.3	518.0	64.0	26.0
Profit before Taxation	41.7	30.2	2.2	1.4
Taxes Paid from Profit	17.8	7.9	989.0	362.0
Profit after Taxation	23.9	22.3	1.2	1.0

Source: *Privatization Prospectus*, Prochnik, p. 25.

at only 50 percent of the sale price. Polish investors submitted applications for the purchase of shares at the branches and agencies of Bank Polska Kasa Opieki SA (Warsaw), Bank Gdanski (Gdansk), and Wielkopolski Bank Kredytowy (Poznan). Foreign investors could apply only at the headquarters of Bank Polska Kasa Opieki SA (Warsaw). Applications were accepted between November 30, 1990, and December 21, 1990. The minimum number of shares for which investors could apply was five; there was no maximum limit. Investors could pay for the shares with cash (in Polish currency) or convertible Treasury bonds. Owners of the shares were eligible for dividends from the date of the registration of the company. The dividend amount was decided by the General Assembly during its regular meetings held within four months of the end of an accounting period.

Employees could afford to buy stock with the Treasury bonds they received as a profit bonus. Payment with government bonds entitled buyers to a 20 percent discount. Employees who worked for the company for over one year could obtain up to 80 shares in this way; those employed for a shorter period could purchase up to 40. However, many employees chose not to buy at all or to buy only a small number of shares. One of the reasons was that the Treasury bonds allowed employees to purchase only a total of 900,000 zlotys' worth of stock. Yet the value of 80 shares was 2 million, an amount that was relatively high for an average worker. During the second stage of privatization, a more liberal program of share distribution among employees was introduced—again, it was only partially successful. Finally, after further liberalization of the sale process, the issue was oversubscribed. Despite allegations that the stock was purchased mainly by management, the outcome of the share distribution among employees was considered a success.

Hopes Concerning Privatization

Initially, everyone was interested in privatizing Prochnik: The government expected additional revenue, while the management hoped for more autonomy. The employees were looking forward to higher wages, better management, and a greater participation in the ownership and decision-making process. There were also hopes for the inflow of new capital and for the introduction of new technologies and marketing techniques. At the same time, there were fears of job loss, of foreign competition, and of a high dependence on foreign suppliers.

RESULTS OF PRIVATIZATION

In the absence of a major shareholder, the ownership structure was quite diversified. The largest shareholders included Insurance Company Westa (about 17 percent), employees and management (about 20 percent), and several banks and British and Scandinavian investment groups. Changes in the owner- ship structure were expected due to the secondary market activities.

Product

During 1991 no major changes in the product line were introduced, but some changes did occur. One of the changes involved an increase in output in women's garments. There was a trend toward an increase in the product quality and modernization of the manufacturing process. Previously, about 80 percent of Prochnik's output was made from Polish raw materials and patterns; however, this number decreased to only 40 percent.

Consumers

Prochnik sold its products both in Poland and abroad. Its products were marketed among consumers in the middle- to upper-income brackets. The company exported 62 percent of the value of its output. The main importers included Germany (25 percent), Great Britain (15 percent), Holland, France, and Finland. After a sharp decline of exports to the former Soviet Union, Prochnik managed to establish new trade in Russia, the Ukraine, and the Baltic countries. The trade was primarily conducted in the form of barter.

Current Situation

As a result of privatization, the tax on excess wages was eliminated. Similarly, the division of power among the management, employee self-government, and the trade unions no longer existed. Privatization occurred during a difficult period of time and was characterized by antiinflationary policies, economic recession, low demand for products, collapse of trade with the former Soviet Union, and a changing legal environment. Polish exports also experienced problems due to the excessively high exchange rate of the Polish currency against the U.S. dollar.

Marketing

Prochnik lacked a well-developed marketing strategy. Although product quality was high, distribution and advertising had been neglected. Marketing analyses indicated that Prochnik should create its own distribution network (e.g., company shops and warehouses) and do more advertising.

Labor Force

Cuts in the number of part-time employees reduced the size of the work force to 2,243 people. Approximately two-thirds of the employees were women. About 85 percent of the employees were classified as "blue-collar" workers, and 1,523 were directly involved in production. Following privatization, wages and salaries increased by about 50 percent. Since the pay level was competitive with that of other companies, the loss of employees to other textile firms was significantly reduced. However, the high-skill level of Prochnik's work force still resulted in the loss of some workers. Monthly pay ranged from 1.7 million to 3 million zlotys (approximately $120 to $215), which was close to the national average and slightly above the Lodz region's level.

Although the organization had been restructured, Prochnik still lacked a modern human resources department. However, management acknowledged a need for such a department. To accelerate the adjustments to the realities of the free market, the company arranged courses for employees in marketing, market economy, and negotiations. The influence of labor unions was minimal. Of the union members, two-thirds belonged to the Independent Union of Prochnik Employees, while one-third joined Solidarity.

Economic Performance after Privatization

Prochnik's output declined slightly during 1991, primarily due to the collapse of trade with the former Soviet Union (see table 14.4). Prochnik hoped to rebuild those ties, mostly through barter. The company increased its sales both in Poland and abroad. As a result of cost-cutting measures, investment spending was reduced. However, management believed that additional investment in machinery and equipment was necessary. The last devaluation of the zloty (in 1992, U.S. $1 = approximately 14,000 zlotys) helped the company by making its exports less expensive. The management was concerned, however, that a further devaluation of the zloty would increase the costs of the imported equipment and raw materials.

From October 1, 1990, to December 31, 1991, total revenues amounted to 228 billion zlotys, with 146 billion zlotys of export sales. Net income during the period was 10.8 billion zlotys (7,202 zlotys per share). During January and February of 1992, revenues were 32 billion zlotys; and the net income was 2.6 billion zlotys. As of June 1992 the number of shares was 1.5 million(750,000 were offered to the public). On March 26, 1992, the market value of the stock was 51.7 billion zlotys. The highest stock price was registered on April 16, 1991 (56,000 zlotys), while the lowest occurred on June 11, 1992 (18,500 zlotys). The stock price fluctuated around 30,000 zlotys, with a large decline in May and June 1992. However, the stock regained some of the losses after June 11, 1992. The P/E ratio of about 3.4 was relatively high when compared with the national average of 2.1. The stock price on July 6, 1992, was 24,000 zlotys.

EVALUATION OF PRIVATIZATION IN PROCHNIK

Opinions about privatization varied. Prochnik's employees, for example, were asked what they expected from privatization; the degree to which their expectations were fulfilled; their opinion about the situation before privatization in terms of the organization of work, prospects for the future, relations between management and workers, and job security and benefits; and their opinion about the situation after privatization. They responded as follows:

1. All respondents expected higher wages; 77 percent thought they would gain better working conditions; 84 percent expected more preferences in buying shares; 58 percent hoped for greater participation in decision making; and 93 percent looked for better benefits.

Table 14.4
Information about Prochnik's Activity in the Last Decade

	1980	1985	1988	1989	1990	1991
Output (Volume)	—	911,584	887,375	843,328	684,919	604,422
Output (Value in Million Zloties)	1,984	4,391	11,344	36,444	156,992	175,353
• For Domestic Market	901	2,505	5,782	18,623	34,136	68,551
• Export to the West	701	1,659	5,009	16,630	94,268	103,775
• Export to the Eastern Countries	382	227	543	1,171	28,171	1,640
Investments (Million Zlotys)	7	62	277	1,526	12,253	8,234
Liabilities (Million Zlotys)	62	25	2,821	15,508	17,350	32,367
Profitability (% Net Profit: Sales)	—	7	11	61	18	4
% Profit: Costs	0.1	8	13	82	24	4
Employment (End of Year)	3609	2851	2,922	2,732	2,344	2,2430
Salaries (Found in Million Zlotys)	235	677	1,858	6,252	25,709	48,969
Taxes (Million Zlotys)	—	215	989	7,902	21,551	4,063

Note: The rate of exchange of zlotys against the dollar changed very much during the last decade due to inflation: from about 100 zlotys in the late 1970s, to about 1,000 in the mid-1980s (black market), to 9,500 in 1990, and 11,150 in 1991. Now the rate of exchange is about 14,000 zlotys per dollar.

Source: Interview at Prochnik Company, 1991.

2.   Rating the fulfillment of their expectations on a scale of 0 to 10, the workers clearly were disappointed. The ratings were as follows: wage growth, 1.2; improvement of working conditions, 2.1; buying the shares, 2.3; participation in decision making, 1.7; and better benefits, 3.6.

3.   Also rating the situation before privatization on a scale of 0 to 10, they ranked organization of work, 2.9; prospects for the future, 2.9; relations between management and employees, 3.7; and job security and benefits, 3.2.

4.   Assessing the situation after privatization on a scale from 0 to 10, they evaluated organization of work, 3.2; prospects for the future, 2.3; relations between management and employees, 3.1; and job security and benefits, 1.9.

Privatization led to some positive developments: abolition of the excess wage tax, simpler management structure, and the reduction of excessive union powers. The highest level of satisfaction with conditions was shown by the managers rather than by the workers, by the men rather than by the women, and by those with a longer tenure at Prochnik.

However, there were also some disappointments such as deteriorating work force morale. The employees were dissatisfied with the decrease in their influence, with the methods of the ownership transformation, and with the confusion surrounding the privatization process (e.g., many employees could not understand the difference between share's par value and offer price). The management complaints dealt with the instability of the legal environment, with the high costs of credit, and with the fact that the company did not receive any of the revenues from the sale of stock (the State Treasury retained all of the revenues). This last concern was often mentioned as the major weakness of Poland's privatization process.

In light of the mixed nature of the economic indicators, it was too early to fully assess the impact of privatization on Prochnik. Also, enthusiasm for the transformation appeared to be greater among managers than among workers. However, as time passed, more people expressed dissatisfaction with the results of the privatization.

15

Privatization of the Swarzedz Furniture Works

Jerzy Suchnicki

The Swarzedz Furniture Works (SFW), with markets in Poland and abroad, produces furniture lines ranging from the inexpensive to upscale, high-quality pieces. Swarzedz was formed in 1952 from two nationalized furniture firms. In 1965, Swarzedz initiated a process of centralization and acquisition of new facilities that was completed in 1980. Currently, Swarzedz consists of eight manufacturing plants located about 100 kilometers from its headquarters. The age and technology of the enterprise's assets vary widely. The most modern and largest of the plants, located in Mosina, started operations in 1989. In 1990 the enterprise owned or managed real estate of more than 834,000 square meters.

The company occupies a strong position on the Polish market. The furniture from Swarzedz is regarded as a luxury product; and until the end of the 1980s, demand outstripped the supply in Poland. The bulk of the output was exported, mostly to former West Germany (in 1990 it accounted for approximately 60 percent of total exports) and Sweden (imported by IKEA Company—in 1990 it accounted for approximately 36 percent of total exports).

In the past, exports were arranged by the foreign trade enterprise PAGED. The nature of cooperation between PAGED and Swarzedz changed over time. During most of the post-World War II period, the state had a monopoly on foreign trade. Exports and imports of entire industries were handled through intermediaries nominated by the state, with companies like Swarzedz having no influence on those decisions. The liberalization of trade regulations in 1986 allowed companies to conduct foreign trade without intermediaries. Since October 1990, PAGED and Swarzedz have cooperated under a bilateral agreement that could be terminated on six months' notice.

In 1985 Swarzedz (via PAGED) signed a contract with Sweden's IKEA for a lease of equipment to the Mosina facility. Payments were to be made in the form of a discount on the furniture manufactured by this machinery; the production process was to be controlled by IKEA. Prices could be renegotiated annually while the contract remained in force until 1993. After the expiration of the contract, the equipment was to be taken over by Swarzedz at a nominal price. In 1991 a dispute over prices resulted in tensions between the two parties.

Swarzedz also enjoyed a strong market position with regard to purchasing raw materials. Until 1990, low price and availability of domestic raw materials helped the company increase both the output and profit. However, these opportunities were eliminated shortly before privatization as the domestic prices caught up with world prices.

PERFORMANCE PRIOR TO PRIVATIZATION

Since 1988 Swarzedz's financial situation has undergone tremendous changes (see table 15.1). In 1989 the ratio of net profit to sales exceeded 50 percent. In 1990, despite a gross profit equal to 10 percent of total sales, the company experienced a loss of more than 7.5 billion zlotys.[1] A comparison of those two years shows a change in the external conditions of the enterprise's operation. The 1989 profits stemmed partially from inflation and devaluation of the zloty. Moreover, the company received subsidies for exports to the former Soviet Union, and the negative real interest rate reduced the debt burden. The first half of 1990 brought a number of new developments. On the one hand, the devaluation of the zloty in January 1990 resulted in increased profits from exports. On the other hand, a large increase in the interest rates raised the company's costs. In addition to obtaining a sizable level of investment credits, the firm had to increase its working capital by obtaining short-term bank credit. An almost 20-fold increase in these short-term loans and an interest rate of over 45 percent per month had a further negative impact on performance. The second part of the year was even worse: Domestic demand declined, while exports suffered due to a substantial increase in costs and an artificially high exchange rate. Furthermore, Swarzedz, as a state-owned enterprise (SOE), was subject to additional taxation of its net profits. In 1990 its tax payments amounted to 12.2 billion zlotys. In November and December alone, the company also paid 11.7 billion zlotys in taxes on excessive wages.

Financial statements reflect the deterioration of the company's situation (see table 15.2). During the period under consideration, the firm's liquidity deteriorated. Between 1989 and 1990, cash reserves remained virtually unchanged—at the same time, current assets more than tripled, mainly due to the growth of inventories. Raw materials represented the largest portion of current assets of over 50 billion zlotys. However, the decline in demand is illustrated by the 18-fold increase in the value of finished goods in the inventories. The increase in the accounts receivable paralleled the rate of inflation. Simultaneously, accounts payable grew at a faster pace, thus becoming a source of relatively cheap financing. At the end of 1990, the company's current liabil-

Table 15.1

Performance of the SFW in 1988–90 (millions of zlotys)

	December 31, 1988	December 31, 1989	December 31, 1990
Sales	13,637	41,449	297,010
Selling Costs:			
Material Costs	6,388	15,876	151,050
Wage Costs	2,555	10,972	53,949
Depreciation Costs	195	307	5,928
Other Costs	2,428	3,004	55,595
Gross Profit	2,071	11,290	30,558
Other Incomes	316	10,534	5,339
Excess Profits	614	5,008	5,770
Excess Losses	75	471	13,863
Profit before Taxes	1,970	24,224	12,442
Turnover Tax	527	2,817	7,750
Excessive Wage Growth Tax, etc.	0	0	12,269
Net Profit	1,443	21,407	(7,577)

Source: SFW's Issuance Prospectus, United States, 1991.

ities exceeded the value of its current assets by 15.8 billion zlotys. The ratio of current assets to current liabilities, an indicator of liquidity, fluctuated widely. In 1989 and 1988 it was 77.6 and 45.2 percent, respectively; but in 1990 it fell to 22.6 percent, its lowest level in years. Fixed assets represented the largest item on the assets side, and they showed the highest rate of growth. This, however, was not a result of investment projects (whose value totaled only 12 billion zlotys) but of two revisions of the value of the assets in 1990 that increased book value by 238.5 billion zlotys. In addition, the value of the assets was adjusted for inflation, which reached an annual rate of almost 250 percent by 1990. These adjustments resulted in an additional loss of 49.8 billion zlotys. All of these numbers were included in Swarzedz's stock offering prospectus and, thus, were available to potential investors.

PROCESS OF PRIVATIZATION

In July 1990 the government enacted the law on privatization requiring SOEs either to be privatized or liquidated by the Ministry of Ownership Changes. The

Table 15.2
Annual Balance Sheet of the SFW in 1988–90

	December 31, 1988	December 31, 1989	December 31, 1990
Assets			
Working Assets Total	4,930	31,414	102,951
Of Which: Is Cash	191	4,056	4,720
Demandable Payments	1,466	8,256	21,653
Inventories	3,117	18,225	76,121
Capital Assets Total	7,884	15,550	265,816
Of Which Is Fixed Capital	7,551	14,404	264,717
Total Assets	12,814	46,964	368,767
	December 31, 1988	December 31, 1989	December 31, 1990
Liabilities and Shares			
Current Liabilities			
Bank Credits and Other Liabilities	1,365	4,055	59,000
Vis-à-Vis Suppliers	1,023	7,458	28,472
Others	1,849	5,479	31,336
Current Liabilities Total	4,237	16,992	118,808
Long-term Liabilities			
Credits	2,395	3,863	1,731
Shares			
Share Capital	1,941	1,941	50,000
Other Shareholders' Assets	4,241	24,168	198,228
Total Liabilities	12,814	46,964	368,767

Source: SFW's Issuance Prospectus, United States, 1991.

choice depended on the enterprise's preference and an assessment of its economic situation. The new Treasury-owned entity took over all liabilities of the transformed enterprise and any claims on its property.

On October 31, 1990, Swarzedz was transformed into a joint-stock company. The Treasury became the sole owner of 2 million shares, while the Ministry of

Ownership Changes proceeded with the privatization of the firm with the assistance of (1) the International Finance Corporation, based in Washington, D.C., as the ministry's financial adviser; (2) Professor Stanislaw Soltysinski as the ministry's legal adviser; (3) Doradca consulting company from Gdansk as financial adviser to Swarzedz; (4) KPMG's Frankfurt office as Swarzedz's charted accountant; (5) Poznan branch of Bank Gdanski as the company's bank; (6) Bank Staropolski SA from Poznan as the bank coordinating the sale of shares to large investors; and (7) Bank Polska Kasa Opieki (PKO) SA as the leading bank in the sale of shares.

The book share price was set at 25,000 zlotys, and the offering price at 50,000 zlotys. Out of 2 million shares owned by the Treasury, 1.4 million were to be sold through a public offer. Some 400,000 shares were earmarked for sale to the enterprise's employees at half price; 6,250 shares were granted to PKO SA and other banks participating in the offering as a compensation for their services; 18,750 shares were deposited with the Warsaw Stock Exchange; and 75,000 shares were given to the International Finance Corporation as compensation for its services. The State Treasury kept 100,000 shares as a reserve for settling any property restitution claims. In addition, the number of shares to be sold was increased by 500,000, thus increasing to 1.9 million the number of shares that were put on the market. The revenues from the sale of 1.4 million shares were to be collected by the Treasury, while those from sales of the remaining additional 500,000 shares were to be added to the company's reserve capital. The sale of all shares composing the public offering was guaranteed by four banks.

Shares could be purchased by domestic investors without any limits. Foreign investors could buy up to 10 percent of the company's entire capital; any purchases above that limit required the approval of the Foreign Investment Agency. One million shares were earmarked for investors who would buy more than 10,000 shares. This type of purchase was to cover at least 500,000 shares. The Ministry of Ownership Changes reserved the right to modify the allocation of shares even with the sale already under way.

The prospectus presented potential investors with the information concerning the company's operations. The anticipated problems facing the company included:

- The uncertainty about future exchange rates and inflation, and their impact on exports;
- Lack of a sufficiently developed financial management system;
- Increasing wages;
- Loss of the domestic distribution network;
- Loss of the former Soviet market;
- Possibility of restitution claims by former owners; and
- Contract with IKEA that forces Swarzedz to export at relatively low prices.

2The future success of the company would depend on:

- The ability to maintain relatively inexpensive, experienced, and highly skilled labor force;
- Completion of the already launched organizational reorganization;
- Greater emphasis on marketing;
- The Ministry of Ownership Changes' taking over the company's liabilities on short-term credits and overdue tax payments totaling 66.4 billion zlotys;
- Continued supply of inexpensive timber;
- Proximity of major selling outlets;
- Use of underutilized capacities, especially in the modern plant in Mosina; and
- Maintaining reputation as a high-quality producer.

Swarzedz's reputation for high-quality production appeared to be the primary factor in the success of the stock sale. All of the shares allotted to small investors were sold on the first day. However, despite the reduced price, only 40 percent of the shares earmarked for employees were sold by March 1992. All employees were entitled to buy 105 shares at 25,000 zlotys each. Moreover, the company offered financial assistance for the purchase of shares; depending on the length of employment, employees received 30, 45, or 60 free shares.

PERFORMANCE AFTER PRIVATIZATION

During 1991 the company suffered a loss of 39.2 billion zlotys on sales of 435.7 billion as the problems encountered in 1990 continued. The difficulties were mostly caused by external factors such as high costs of raw materials and a combination of the high inflation rate and a lack of appropriate adjustment in the exchange rate of the zloty. However, some improvement in the company's situation could be observed. The introduction of the gradual devaluation of the zloty and personnel changes in the company's management contributed to the profitable fourth quarter of 1991, with the profit equal to 0.5 percent of the total sales. This positive trend continued into 1992.

Strategy Prior to and after Privatization

It is difficult to determine precisely when the transformation of Swarzedz began. Technical and financial restructuring started before the stock offering. The changes were aimed at increasing output and at lowering costs through more efficient operations. The company created a sales and marketing department. Furthermore, the company was reorganized into profit centers. At the same time, a new management information system was introduced, together with a new a new management information system was introduced, together with a new pattern of material flow among plants. This was to modernize the manufacturing system and to provide a better feel for the market. The ultimate objective was to export to a more upscale market segment and to consolidate the company's position on the domestic market. These steps would allow an increase in prices.

Owing to uncertainties about the exchange rate, Swarzedz's management decided to concentrate on the domestic market. During the early and mid-1980s, the domestic market accounted for 60 percent of sales. In 1989, domestic sales accounted for about 47 percent of total sales; in 1990 and 1991 they were 31 and 64 percent, respectively. These data are interesting when compared with the output during the previous years. Although 1990 was exceptionally unfavorable due to a sharp decline in sales, the increase in finished goods inventories did not occur in 1991 as virtually the entire stock was sold. Nevertheless, the management continued to search for further improvements. A new distribution network was planned in order to increase market share; an aggressive advertising and sales campaign was launched on radio and television; and plans called for gaining direct access to retail stores abroad. Furthermore, the company planned to expand by acquiring new plants and suppliers. To reduce the financial costs, the company developed a close cooperation with several banks, which all became company shareholders.

The most painful changes involved the restructuring of the work force, which resulted in layoffs and an increase in the number of employees directly involved in the production process. At the end of 1990, 3,240 people were employed at Swarzedz: Approximately 17 percent were in management and administration, 18 percent were indirectly involved in the production process, and the remaining 65 percent were production workers. By March 1992 the size of the labor force was reduced to 2,850 people. The organizational structure was simplified, and some managerial positions were eliminated. Further reductions in employment of at least 10 percent were expected, and the plan called for approximately 75 percent of the employees to be directly involved in the production process.

Employee Assessment of Privatization

A survey of a sample of employees to learn their opinions about the changes occurring in the company suggests that privatization was expected to be a panacea for all possible problems (see Figure 15.1). This opinion was characteristic of the youngest, oldest, and least-educated employees. It should be noted that those groups partially overlap. For instance, among the employees 50 and older, only one person had a high school diploma. They all expected more decision-making powers as a result of privatization. Also, all respondents believed that privatization would lead to wage increases and improvement in the

Figure 15.1
SFW Survey

EXPECTATION FROM PRIVATIZATION

  1. Expect a rise in wage (salary)
  2. Expect more influence on decisions
  3. Expect better work conditions
  4. Expect an increase in social benefits
  5. Expect an acquisition of preference shares

EXTENT TO WHICH EXPECTATIONS WERE FULFILLED

  6. Rise in wage (salary)
  7. More influence in decision making
  8. Better work conditions
  9. Increase in social benefits
  10. Acquisition of preference shares

ASSESSMENT OF SITUATION PRIOR TO PRIVATIZATION

  11. Organization of labor
  12. Management-employee relations
  13. Development prospects
  14. Job security

ASSESSMENT OF SITUATION AFTER PRIVATIZATION

  15. Organization of labor
  16. Management/employee relations
  17. Development prospects
  18. Job security

---

working conditions. About 75 percent of the employees expected an increase in benefits, but none of the college graduates anticipated an improvement in that area.

The assessment of the extent to which these expectations had been fulfilled reveals a high level of dissatisfaction among those polled (see table 15.3). Employees with a university education were most satisfied with wage changes—the average score for this subgroup on a scale from 0 to 10 was 6.7, while the overall average was 1.5. Male workers were significantly more satisfied with changes than women. With regard to wages, the most critical evaluations were offered by the youngest and the oldest workers. Overall, managers perceived the situation after the privatization more positively than the workers (see table 15.4). Management-employee relations, compared with other issues,

Table 15.3
Assessment of Expectations

Question Number	Employees	Educational Level			
		University	Secondary	Vocational	Primary
	Total Percent	Rated in Percent			
1.	100	—	—	—	—
2.	81	71	71	84	83
3.	100	—	—	—	—
4.	73	0	71	87.5	86
5.	87	71	86	86	100
		Rated on a Scale of 0 to 10			
6.	1.5	6.7	0.4	1.3	0.5
7.	1.1	4.0	0.8	0.7	0.3
8.	1.5	4.9	1.0	1.2	0.0
9.	1.4	5.7	0.0	0.9	0.3
10.	7.1	7.4	8.2	7.0	8.3
11.	4.1	4.0	3.8	3.6	5.0
12.	5.5	5.9	4.6	5.7	4.5
13.	3.7	4.4	3.0	3.0	3.3
14.	6.1	6.7	6.1	6.1	3.3
15.	3.2	5.1	2.6	2.6	3.3
16.	3.7	5.4	3.7	3.7	4.6
17.	2.7	4.6	2.4	2.4	2.5
18.	2.6	4.4	3.2	3.2	0.5

Source: Compiled by author.

Table 15.4
Management-Employee Assessment of Privatization

Question Number	Production Employees	Executives and Top Managers
	Percent	
1.	100	100
2.	80	82
3.	100	100
4.	85	22
5.	89	78
	Ratio on a Scale of 0 to 10	
6.	0.9	5.3
7.	0.6	3.1
8.	0.8	3.9
9.	0.6	4.4
10.	7.1	6.7
11.	4.3	4.0
12.	5.7	5.7
13.	3.7	4.3
14.	6.2	6.3
15.	3.0	4.2
16.	3.6	4.9
17.	2.7	3.6
18.	2.4	3.4

Source: Compiled by author.

received a relatively high rating; and the average scores for managers and workers were virtually identical at 5.7.

According to the company's chief executive officer, Swarzedz did not make any major improvements during the time when it operated as a State Treasury–owned joint-stock company. The management became more effective and flexible once full privatization was completed. Since then, the company's objective has been the optimal utilization of assets and maximization of profit. New sales and financing techniques for customers have been introduced, advertising campaigns have been launched, and decision making has been decentralized. For instance, retailers were given a free hand in offering sale discounts when necessary.

Cooperation with foreign advisers did not live up to its expectations, however, and did not result in new foreign contacts. Furthermore, Western advisers exhibited a lack of understanding of the Polish market. Thus, the company has become more cautious with respect to this type of cooperation. The management was satisfied with its banks and with the competition that has developed among banks since the liberalization of the banking laws. Relationships with wholesalers, which disappeared with the collapse of the state network, caused some concern, but new relationships were being formed.

The management believed that the state should not interfere in individual enterprises. Unfortunately, the matters for which the state should have been responsible suffered from a lack of attention. According to the management, while the previous economy was subject to political interference, current economic policy is virtually nonexistent. This has resulted, for example, in the collapse of SOEs. Furthermore, the management complained about difficulties due to fluctuations in the exchange rate of the zloty: During the early 1990s, Swarzedz lost foreign markets because its exports became unprofitable.

Despite numerous difficulties, the management anticipated further expansion because it believed that the company's situation was better than that of its competitors. Furthermore, the privatization process allowed the company to make decisions that were not possible under the old system.

The Company's Stock

Stock exchange quotations in March 1992 indicated that the share price never matched the issue price and that the highest stock price was recorded on the first day of trading. To management's disappointment, recent restructuring had only a slight impact on the stock price, which increased to less than 30,000 zlotys—only several thousand higher than the record low price of 25,500 zlotys. There had been a noticeable lack of balance between supply and demand; trading of the stock had to be suspended several times in 1991. During early 1992, trading became more stable, but it still showed a declining trend. The market value of Swarzedz in February 1992 was 71.2 billion zlotys, with the book value equal to 330.66 billion zlotys. Warta was the biggest shareholder, with 13.8 percent of the shares. Under Polish regulations, shareholders with a stake of less than 10 percent may remain anonymous.

CONCLUSION

In assessing Swarzedz's privatization, one should first consider whether the company was ready for privatization at this time. The unstable economic environment, the contract with IKEA, the possibility of restitution claims, and a high debt level placed the company in a difficult situation from the very beginning. Although a major reorganization was initiated by the company several months before the equity offering, the effects of these changes cannot be immediately observed.

Employee morale deteriorated as a result of privatization. Expectations of changes were unrealistically optimistic and were doomed to lead to disillusionment. Workers tended to blame the company's difficulties on the management rather than on external factors. Many workers failed to understand that the difficult measures taken by Swarzedz were essential for the survival of the company.

With respect to the manufacturing process, employees found it difficult to adjust to a more flexible system needed to make frequent changes in product specifications. Prior to privatization, production runs were long because the management could disregard consumers' preferences and market demand. In mid-1992 the stock price was not expected to increase much in the future. The company could not pay a dividend until it made up the 1991 losses (40 billion zlotys). Thus, the interest in the stock should continue to be lackluster.

Over the long term, Swarzedz appeared to be on the right track. Its experience, modern machinery, and unutilized capacity provided a strong grounding for growth. The imminent construction boom in Poland and a strong demand for furniture in Germany would offer some opportunities. As the entire Polish economy recovered, the company's situation could improve despite the high price of its products since the demand for Swarzedz's furniture was sensitive to fluctuations of the economy.

NOTE

1. The exchange rate of the zloty against the U.S. dollar was 316 zlotys on December 31, 1987; 503 zlotys on December 31, 1988; 6,500 zlotys on December 31, 1989; and 9,500 zlotys on December 31, 1990.

Selected Bibliography

BOOKS, ARTICLES, AND REPORTS

Bajt, A. "Trideset godina privrednog rasta." *Ekonomist* 38, no. 1 (1984), pp. 1–20.

Bednarczyk, M. "Rozwoj prywatnej przedsiebiorczosci w woj. krakow-skim." In J. Targalski, T. Mroczkowski, and A. Masny, eds., *Studium przedsie-biorczosci*. Krakow: AE, 1991.

Bobinski, Christopher. "Poland: Much Lost Time Has to Be Made Up." *Financial Times* (July 3, 1992, Special Supplement), p. 4.

Bokros, Lajos. "Spontaneous Privatization—Hungary." Ljubljana, Slovenia. Paper prepared for delivery at the Second Central & Eastern European Privatization Network Annual Conference: Privatization in Central/Eastern Europe, November 29–30, 1991.

Brown, Byron. "Transforming Postcommunist Labor Markets: The Polish Case." *RFE/RL Research Report* 1, no. 32 (August 14, 1992), pp. 50–56.

Center for International Private Enterprise and the Futures Group. "Poland Case Study." *Economic Reform Today* 1, no. 1 (1991), pp. 9–15.

Chand, S. K., and H. R. Lorie. "Fiscal Policy." In V. Tanzi, ed., *Fiscal Policies in Economies in Transition*. Washington, D.C.: International Monetary Fund, 1992.

Ciechocinska, Maria. "Determinants of the Restructuring of Poland's Economy in the 1980s." In E. Ciciotti, N. Alderman, and A. Thwaites, eds., *Technological Change in a Spatial Context: Theory, Empirical Evidence, and Policy*. Berlin: Springer, 1990.

———, ed. *Restructuring and Spatial Strategy*. Warsaw, Poland: Institute of Geography and Spatial Organization, 1991.

Colitt, Leslie. "Czech Parliament Told of Gloomy Economic Picture." *Financial Times* (March 28, 1991), p. 4.

Colitt, Leslie, and Anthony Robinson. "Heavy Going Slows the Pace of Race to Reform Czechoslovakia's Economy." *Financial Times* (March 26, 1991), p. 2.

Crane, Keith. "Property Rights Reform: Hungarian Country Study." In Hans Blommestein and Michael Marrese, eds., *Transformation of Planned Economies*. Paris: OECD, 1991.

Csepi, Lajos, Gustav Bager, and Erzsebet Lukacs. "Privatization in Hungary—1991." In Marko Simoneti and Andreja Bohm, eds., *Privatization in Central and Eastern Europe 1991*. Ljubljana, Slovenia: Central and Eastern European Privatization Network, 1992.

Csikós-Nagy, Béla. "Privatization in a Post-Communist Society—The Case of Hungary." *Hungarian Business Herald* 4 (1991), p. 37.

Czarkowska, W., and M. Dobrowolska. "Wezlowe problemy demograficzne regionu." In J. Czarkowski, ed., *Rozwoj ekonomiczny regionu krakow-skiego w dwudziest-oleciu Polski Ludowej*. Krakow: PAN, 1965.

Czesany, Slovoj. "Stabilizing Aspects of the Economic Reforms and the Macroeconomic Developments in Hungary, Poland, the USSR and Czechoslovakia." In S. P. Prasad and R. B. Peterson, eds., *Advances in International Comparative Management*. Vol. 7. Greenwich, CT: JAI Press Inc., 1992.

Denton, Nicholas. "Privatization: Race against Time." *Financial Times* (October 30, 1991), p. vii.

———. "From Infancy to Mid-Life Crisis." *Financial Times* (July 3, 1992, Special Supplement), p. 4.

Essaides, George. "Prospects for Profits: Czechoslovakia through 1993." *Business International* (February 25, 1991), pp. 68–69.

Fischer, Michael S. "New Laws in Eastern Europe Set Terms for Restitution." *Business International* 38, no. 31 (August 5, 1991), pp. 261–262, 268.

Flaes, F. Angela. "GM in Hungary: Expanding the EE Production Base." *Business Eastern Europe* 20, nos. 27–91 (July 8, 1991), pp. 211–212.

Frydman, Roman, and Adrzej Rapaczynski. "Markets and Institutions in Large Scale Privatization: An Approach to Economic and Social Transformation in Eastern Europe." In V. Corbo, F. Coricelli, and J. Bossak, eds., *Reforming Central and Eastern European Economies*. Washington, D.C.: World Bank, 1991.

Gajda, J. *Steel Works in the Development of Industry and the City of Krakow*. Krakow: AE, 1981.

———, ed. *Programowanie rozwoju produkcji przemyslowej*. Warszawa: PWE, 1987.

Gilmour, J. "External Economies of Scale, Interindustrial Linkages and Decision Making in Manufacturing." In F. Hamilton, ed., *Spatial Perspectives on Industrial Organization and Decision Making*. London: Wiley, 1974.

Ginsbert-Gebert, Adam. "Samorzad terytorialny i jego gospodarka." In *Fundacja rozwoju demokracji lokalnej.* Warszawa: 1990.

Gobec, Vinko. "7,612 Firms—Half of Them Operative." *Slovenian Business Report.* Vol. 4. Ljubljana, Slovenia: CIOS Business Incubator, December 1991.

Gorka, K. "Changes in the Environmental Policy of Poland." *Economic and Legal Instruments of Environmental Policy in the Market Economy.* Krakow: EAERE, 1991.

Haranczyk, A. *Procesy inwestycyjne w rozwoju gospodarki Krakowa w latach 1950–1990.* Krakow: AE, 1992.

Havel, Jiri, and Eugen Kukla. "Privatization and Investment Funds in Czechoslovakia." *RFE/RL Research Report* 1, no. 17 (April 1992), pp. 37–41.

Humphrey, Gary. "Privatisers Get Back on Track." *Euromoney* (March 1991), p. 48.

Inotai, András. "Foreign Direct Investments in Reforming CMEA Countries: Facts, Lessons and Perspectives." In Michael W. Klein and Paul J. J. Welfens, eds., *Multinationals in the New Europe and Global Trade.* Berlin-Heidelberg: Springer Verlag, 1992.

International Finance Corporation. *Small Scale Privatization in Russia: The Nizhny Novgorod Model—Guiding Principles.* Washington, D.C.: IFC, 1992.

Janacek, Kamil. "Survey of Major Trends in 1991." *RFE/RL Research Report* 1, no. 12 (March 20, 1992), pp. 31–32.

Jedrzejczak, Gregory T., and Henryk Sterniczuk. "Privatization in Poland— 1991." In Marko Simoneti and Andreja Bohm, eds., *Privatization in Central and Eastern Europe, 1991.* Ljubljana, Slovenia: Central and Eastern European Privatization Network, 1992.

Johnson, Russell. "Hungary: New Investment Frontier." *Business America* 112, no. 2 (October 7, 1991), pp. 2–7.

Katz, A. "The Adaptability and Feasibility of Market Socialism: Lessons from Yugoslavia." Mimeographed. Pittsburgh: University of Pittsburgh, 1987.

Klacova, Eva, and Charles Jelinek-Francis. "Privatization in Czechoslovakia— 1991: Legislative Requirements and Their Results." In Marko Simoneti and Andreja Bohm, eds., *Privatization in Central and Eastern Europe 1991.* Ljubljana, Slovenia: Central and Eastern European Privatization Network, 1992.

Klaus, Vaclav. "A Perspective on Economic Transition in Czechoslovakia and Eastern Europe." In S. Fischer, D. deTray, and S. Shah, eds., *Proceedings of the World Bank Annual Conference on Development Economics 1990.* Washington, D.C.: World Bank, 1990.

Kobylka, Jari. "Polish Mass Privatization Could Be Disappointing." *Business Eastern Europe* 20, nos. 33–91 (August 19, 1991), p. 259.

———. "Privatization Process Slows in Czechoslovakia." *Business Eastern*

Europe 20, nos. 47–91 (November 25, 1991), pp. 421–422.

———. "The Hard Realities of Doing Business in the CSFR." *Business Eastern Europe* 21, nos. 32–92 (August 10, 1992), pp. 385–386.

Komorowski, S. M. "Przestrzenna organizacja gospodarki polskiej." In *Proba analizy krytycznej.* Warszawa: PAN, 1982.

Korže, Uroš. "Decentralized Privatization Strategy: Pitfalls and Benefits—Slovenia." In Marko Simoneti and Andreja Bohm, eds., *Privatization in Central and Eastern Europe 1991.* Ljubljana, Slovenia: Central and Eastern European Privatization Network, 1992.

Korže, Uroš, and Marko Simoneti. "Privatization in Yugoslavia." Ljubljana, Yugoslavia: World Bank and United Nations Development Programme. Paper prepared for delivery at the Conference on Privatization in Eastern Europe, November 1990.

Kovács, András. "A vegyesvállalatok fele a kereskedelemben mûkddik" [Half of joint ventures are operating in trade]. *Magyar Hirlap* (January 31, 1992), p. 10.

Kruczla, J., and K. Kisielewski. *Zagadnien rozwoju miast w wojewodztwie krakowskim.* Vol. 1. Mysl Gospodarcza: 1958.

Kurcz, Adrienne. "Egisztencia-hitel: Alapvetô a banki részvétel" [E-credit facility: banking participation is a basic issue]. *Figyelö* (April 2, 1992), p. 11.

Langenecker, Juliane, and Bela Papp. "EE Human Resources: East-West Perspectives." *Business Eastern Europe* 21, nos. 32–92 (August 10, 1992), pp. 387–388.

Luchter, B. *Ocena sposobu uzytkowania ziemi w miescie Krakowie.* Krakow: AE, 1992.

Madzar, Ljubomir. "Privatization in Yugoslavia 1991: Programs, Obstacles and Results." In Marko Simoneti and Andreja Bohm, eds., *Privatization in Central and Eastern Europe 1991.* Ljubljana, Slovenia: Central and Eastern European Privatization Network, 1992.

Martin, Peter. "The 1991 Budget: Hard Times Ahead." *Report on Eastern Europe* 2, no. 9 (March 1, 1991), pp. 12–16.

Math-Cohn, Deli. "First Wave of Large-Scale Czechoslovak Privatization." *Business Eastern Europe* 20, nos. 30–91 (July 29, 1991), pp. 233–234.

Matolcsy, György. "Years of Our Reconvalescence: The Hungarian Privatization: Trends, Facts, and Experiences of Privatization." Budapest: 1991.

McDermott, Gerald A., and Michal Mejstrik. "The Role of Small Firms in Industrial Development and Transformation in Czechoslovakia." Prague: Charles University Center for Economic Research and Graduate Education, Working Paper, 1991.

Mejstrik, Michal, and James Burger. "Privatization in Practice: Czechoslovakia's Experience." Prague: Charles University Center for Economic Research and Graduate Education, 1991.

Mencinger, J. "The Yugoslav Economic Systems and Their Efficiency." *Economic Analysis* 19, no. 1 (1986), pp. 31–43.

Mroczkowski, T., and J. Targalski. "Case Study and Case Commentary THE AKITA INTERNATIONAL CO., LTD." In *Entrepreneurship in Poland, CSFR, Hungary and Yugoslavia*. Berlin: 1991.

Mulej, Robert. "Company Boom in the City." *Slovenian Business Report*. Vol. 4. Ljubljana, Slovenia: CIOS Business Incubator, December 1991.

———. *Employment, Unemployment and the Measures of the Active Policy of Employment in Ljubljana Region for 1991*. Ljubljana, Slovenia: Republic of Slovenia Ministry of Work, Bureau of Employment, 1992.

———. "Employment, Unemployment, Retirement . . ." Ljubljana, Slovenia: Regional Chamber of Economy Ljubljana, Special Analysis, 1992.

Muti, Mario. "Privatization of Socialist Economies: General Issues and the Polish Case." In Hans Blommestein and Michael Marrese, eds., *Transformation of Planned Economies*. Paris: OECD, 1991.

Nuskey, Sharon. "Eastern Europe's Private Affair." *Across the Board* (October 1992), p. 58.

Organization for Economic Cooperation and Development. *Economic Surveys: Hungary 1991*. Paris: OECD, 1991.

———. *Reforming the Economies of Central and Eastern Europe*. Paris: OECD, 1992.

Owsiak, S., and K. Surowka. *Prognozy ostrzegawcze w sferze spoleczo-ekonomicz-nej dla duzego regionu krakowskiego*. Mogilany: 1991.

Papp, Bela, and Joseph Hollos. "Hungary: Ansaldo Salvages Bankrupt Ganz Electric." *Business Eastern Europe* 20, nos. 33–91 (August 19, 1991), p. 260.

Pehe, Jiri. "Czechoslovakia: The Agenda for 1991." *Report on Eastern Europe* 2, no. 3 (January 18, 1991), pp. 11–16.

———. "Building a State Based on the Rule of Law." *Report on Eastern Europe* 2, no. 9 (March 1, 1991), pp. 7–11.

Penn and Shoen Associates Inc. *Democracy, Economic Reform and Western Assistance in Czechoslovakia, Hungary and Poland: A Comparative Public Opinion Survey*. New York: Freedom House and the American Jewish Committee, 1991.

Petkoski, Djorjija. "Conference Report." In Marko Simoneti and Andreja Bohm, eds., *Privatization in Central and Eastern Europe 1991*. Ljubljana, Slovenia: Central and Eastern European Privatization Network, 1992.

Pirek, Zdenko. "Czechoslovakia's Needs in Training in Market Economics and in Business Management." Washington, D.C.: White House Conference on "Economics in Transition: Management Training and Market Economics Education in Central and Eastern Europe," Paper prepared for delivery, February 26–27, 1991.

Purchla, J. "Pozaekonomiczne czynniki rozwoju Krakowa w okresie autonomii galicyjskiej." *Zeszyty naukowe akademii ekonomicznej w Krakowie*. Vol. 96. Krakow: Special Series, 1990.

Rakowski, W. *Uprzemyslowienie a proces urbanizacji*. Warszawa: PWE, 1980.

Regional Chamber of Economy. *Assessment of the Economic Performance of the Ljubljana Region for 1992*. Ljubljana, Slovenia: Regional Chamber of Economy Ljubljana, 1992.

Rondinelli, Dennis A. "Developing Private Enterprise in the Czech and Slovak Federal Republic: The Challenge of Economic Reform." *Columbia Journal of World Business* 26, no. 3 (1991), pp. 27–36.

Rondinelli, Dennis A., Jerry VanSant, and Scott Daugherty. "Management and Technical Assistance Needs of Small Businesses in Czechoslovakia." Washington, D.C.: Central European Small Business Enterprise Development Commission, 1991.

Ruzicka, Milan. "Czechoslovakia Hopes to Be Energy Crossroads." *Journal of Commerce* (March 26, 1991), p. 8B.

Schares, Gail E. "Czechoslovakia: Reluctant Reform." *Business Week* (April 15, 1991, Special Report), p. 55.

Simai, Mihály. "Foreign Direct Investments in the Hungarian Economy—1990." Budapest: Institute for World Economics of the Hungarian Academy of Sciences, Manuscript, 1990.

Slay, Ben. "Roundtable on the Hungarian Economy." *RFE/RL Research Report* 1, no. 29 (July 17, 1992), p. 44–52.

State Property Agency. "Information on the Privatization of State-Owned Enterprises 1990." Budapest: SPA, Information Office, 1990.

Suchonski, S. "Podstawowe kryteria ksztaltowania terytorialnych kompleksow przemyslowych w przemysle hutnictwa zelaza." *Problemy Ekonomiczne* 4 (1976).

Sullivan, John D. "Barriers to Private Sector Growth: Prospects for Enterprise Development." *Economic Reform Today* (Fall 1991), pp. 23–24.

Thumm, Ullrich R. W. "World Bank Adjustment Lending in Central and Eastern Europe." In V. Corbo, F. Coricelli, and J. Bossak, eds., *Reforming Central and Eastern European Economies*, Washington, D.C.: World Bank, 1991.

United Nations. *World Investment Report 1992*, ST/CTC/130. New York: United Nations, 1992.

Vanous, Jan. "Recent Czechoslovak Economic Performance." *PlanEcon Report* 7, nos. 40–41 (November 8, 1991), pp. 1–44.

Venta, Zinka. "Strategies of Public Services Development." In Niko Toš, ed., *Public Services in Ljubljana—Strategies for Their Further Development*. Ljubljana, Slovenia: University of Ljubljana, Faculty of Social Sciences, 1991.

Ward, Lucy. "The Long Road to Restitution." *Prognosis* (April 1991), p. 12.

Wolchik, Sharon L. "Czechoslovakia's Velvet Revolution." *Current History* 89, no. 551 (December 1990), pp. 413–416, 435–436.

Zielinski, K. *Terytorialna struktura aglomeracji krakowskiej*. Krakow: AE, 1992.

UNSIGNED MATERIALS

"$3.5 Billion of Foreign Capital Seen in First Phase of Czech Privatization." *BNA's Eastern Europe Reporter* 2, no. 8 (April 13, 1992), pp. 280–281.

"Accounting: New Law Adopts EC Standards." *BNA's Eastern Europe Reporter* 2, no. 1 (January 6, 1992), p. 10.

"Addidas in Hungary: A Long-Term Commitment Beats Fancy Footwork." *Business International* 38, no. 32 (August 12, 1991), p. 271.

"Bids to Reclaim Property Increasing: Total Bill Could Reach $23 Billion." *BNA's Eastern Europe Reporter* 1, no. 3 (November 25, 1991), p. 113.

"East European Statistics: Looking for Clues." *Economist* (August 10, 1991), pp. 58–59.

"Egységes hitelgarancia-intézmény várható a privatizáció támogatására" [A unified deposit guarantee-institution is to be established in order to promote privatization]. *Magyar Hirlap* (April 9, 1992), p. 10.

"Government Reports Accelerated Privatization Process in 1992." *BNA's Eastern Europe Reporter* 2, no. 7 (March 30, 1992), p. 243.

"Government Trying to Save Troubled Ursus Tractor Plant." *BNA's Eastern Europe Reporter* 1, no. 1 (October 28, 1991), pp. 13–14.

"Hungary: In the Vanguard of Reform." *Euromoney* (March 1991, Supplement), p. 48.

"Joint Ventures, Acquisitions and Privatization in Eastern Europe and the USSR." *Economist Intelligence Unit/Business International*: Report No 2105 (February 1991).

"Nation Seen Facing More Hurdles, Making Additional Progress in 1992." *BNA's Eastern Europe Reporter* 2, no. 2 (January 20, 1992), pp. 46–48.

"New Law Allows Foreign Branches, Sets Rules for New Banks, Subsidiaries." *BNA's Eastern Europe Reporter* 2, no. 5 (March 2, 1992), pp. 164–166.

"New Law Will Allow Cooperatives to Become Private Enterprises." *BNA's Eastern Europe Reporter* 2, no. 2 (January 20, 1992), p. 46.

"New Privatization Program Launched to Break Up 'Hollow' Parent Companies." *BNA's Eastern Europe Reporter* 2, no. 8 (April 13, 1992), pp. 286–287.

"Officials Look to Private Sector to Pull Country Out of Recession." *BNA's Eastern Europe Reporter* 2, no. 1 (January 6, 1992), pp. 29–30.

"Private Sector Grew Sharply in 1991 Despite Recession Government Says." *BNA's Eastern Europe Reporter* 2, no. 7 (March 30, 1992), p. 243.

"Privatizációs tények" [Facts about privatization]. *Figyelö* (January 16, 1992), p. 39.

"Privatization Get Tough with Tenders." *Euromoney* (March 1991), p. 46.
"Sell-Off of State Companies Proceeding Slowly, Data Show." *BNA's Eastern Europe Reporter* 1, no. 1 (October 28, 1991), p. 13.

Index

About the Contributors

MALGORZATA BEDNARCZYK teaches and does research on private enterprise and strategic management at the Cracow Academy of Economics. She serves as a consultant and adviser on privatization of state-owned enterprises and has co-authored three books and published more than 22 papers and reports.

JAMES BURGER is a researcher at the Center for Research and Graduate Education (CERGE) at Charles University in Prague, the Czech Republic. He is also associate editor of *The Privatization Newsletter of Czechoslovakia.*

MARIA CIECHOCINSKA is professor of geography at the Institute of Geography and Spatial Organization of the Polish Academy of Sciences. She has published widely in the fields of East European regional sociology, economics, and planning. During 1991 she was a Citibank International Fellow at the Kenan Institute of Private Enterprise at the University of North Carolina.

GYORGY CSAKI is an expert on international financial and monetary affairs, international capital flows, and international economics. After 13 years of teaching at the University of Budapest, he has been working since 1989 as senior research fellow at the Institute for World Economics (IWE) of the Hungarian Academy of Sciences. Dr. Csaki has published two books and about 30 articles in the field of international economics, and he has served for years as the editor of English-language publications at the IWE. He is in charge of several joint research projects with American and Western European academic institutions on privatization and financial sector reforms in Central Europe.

TOMASZ DOLEGOWSKI is completing a Ph.D. dissertation at the Warsaw School of Economics where he is on the staff of the Department of International Transportation and Logistics in the Foreign Trade Faculty. He has previously worked for transport and forwarding companies and the Solidarity Central Election Committee.

JONATHAN GAFNI is a senior analyst specializing in business, investment, and regulatory issues with the EOP Group—a natural resource, science, and international trade consulting firm based in Washington, D.C. He has also worked with Equity Expansion International\Prague by providing Czechoslovak enterprises with advice on privatization and investment matters.

PAVEL GANTAR is on the faculty of Faculty of Social Sciences at the University of Ljubljana in Slovenia. He teaches and does research on the sociological aspects of spatial development, the sociology of urban planning, and sociological theory; he has published widely on these topics.

JOHN HANNULA is a consultant with Coopers & Librand International Management Consulting Group in Arlington, Virginia. He has worked as a privatization consultant for Equity Expansion International\Prague by analyzing manufacturing enterprises interested in privatization.

KIT JACKSON is an analyst with Dean Witter Reynolds Inc. research department.

JANUSZ JAWORSKI is director of the International Center for Enterprise Development and teaches quantitative methods in economics and management at the Cracow Academy of Economics. He has served as a Fulbright scholar at the University of California, Berkeley, and as head of the Department of Science and Technology at the Cracow City Hall.

UROŠ KORŽE is managing director of the Development Fund of Slovenia. He has worked in marketing and corporate finance in the United States and Slovenia and was a consultant to and later vice president of IMO, a manufacturing and contracting conglomerate.

JANUSZ KOT is a consultant to local government in Cracow specializing in privatization, real estate management, and the economics and organization of investment. He serves as senior assistant in the Department of Real Estate at the Cracow Academy of Economics.

MAREK MAZUR is on the faculty of the Warsaw School of Economics' Foreign Trade Department as well as of the Central School of Public Administration in Warsaw. He is chairman of the board of the Powszechny Bank Kredytowy in Warsaw and has served as an adviser to Poland's minister of finance since 1991.

MICHAL MEJSTRIK is acting director of the Centre for Research and Graduate Education (CERGE) at Charles University in Prague, the Czech Republic. He is also a professor of economics at Charles University, where he formerly worked at the Institute of Economic Sciences. He has served as an adviser to the Ministry of Privatization of the Czech Republic, is editor-in-chief of *The Privatization Newsletter of Czechoslovakia*, and has lectured and written on all aspects of economic reform in the Czech and Slovak republics.

JOZE MENCINGER is on the faculty of Economics and Social Sciences of the Ljubljana University in Ljubljana, Slovenia. From 1990 to 1991, he served as deputy prime minister of the government of Slovenia and has been a consultant to the World Bank, the Planning Commission of Guyana, and the Inter-American Development Bank. He has been a visiting professor at the University of Pittsburgh.

IGOR MITROCZUK is assistant to the director general and executive specialist for development at the Polish Chamber of Commerce. He is an assistant on the faculty in the Economics Department at the Warsaw School of Economics.

KÁLMÁN MIZSEI is on the faculty of the World Economics Center of the Hungarian Academy of Sciences in Budapest. He has written extensively on economic and financial problems in Hungary and Poland. During 1992 and 1993 he served as Pew Economist-in-Residence at the Institute for East-West Studies in New York and analyzed the transition to market economies in Central Europe.

MARIA MÓRA is with the Department of Interbanking Relations of the National Commerce and Credit Bank in Budapest. Previously, she had worked for a decade at the Economic Research Institute where she dealt mainly with corporate behavior, long-term corporate strategy, and the relationships between state regulation and corporate management. Dr. Móra has done extensive research on privatization and corporate issues related to the transformation of the former centrally planned command economy into a market one.

MARK NILES is the assistant editor for *East European Production International*, a Glen Cove, New York–based magazine whose focus is to develop cooperation between industrial enterprises in Central and Eastern Europe and Western companies expanding into that region of the world.

ERZSÉBET POSZMIK is an associate professor at the Budapest University of Economics (BUE) where she has been teaching since 1971, first in the Department of Political Economics and later in the Department of Microeconomics. For many years, Dr. Poszmik did extensive research on personal incomes. Currently, she is working on corporate economics as well as the transformation of the Hungarian economy and its impacts on the organizational-institutional changes.

DENNIS A. RONDINELLI is professor of international business and director of the International Private Enterprise Development Research Center at the Kenan Institute of Private Enterprise, Kenan-Flagler Business School, University of North Carolina at Chapel Hill. Prior to joining the Kenan Institute, Rondinelli was principal research scientist and senior policy analyst in the Office of International Programs at the Research Triangle Institute and held faculty positions at Syracuse University's Maxwell Graduate School of Citizenship and Public Affairs and Vanderbilt University's Graduate School of Management. He has published 11 books and more than 140 articles in professional and scholarly journals on international economic development, privatization, and international development management. He has also served as an adviser to the U.S. Agency for International Development, the World Bank, the United Nations Development Program, and the Asian Development Bank.

MARKO SIMONETI is the director of the Agency for Privatization of Slovenia. Previously he was an undersecretary in the federal government of Yugoslavia and a senior research fellow at the Institute for Economic Research at the University of Ljubljana. Dr. Simoneti serves as chairman of the steering committee of the Central and Eastern European Privatization Network.

JERZY SUCHNICKI is vice president of Ost-West Consult Polska, an Austro-Polish consulting firm, and formerly was an expert in the corporate finance department of the BIG Bank, the first and largest privatized bank in Poland.

KAZIMIERZ ZIELINSKI teaches forecasting and programming of socio-economic development in the Department of Economic Policy and Regional Economics at the Cracow Academy of Economics. He has served as an expert on international comparative analysis of agricultural development and has published more than 50 scientific articles in the areas of his expertise.